Margaret Aylward, 1810–1889

Margaret Aylward
1810–1889

Lady of Charity, Sister of Faith

Jacinta Prunty

For Michael Downey,
may this woman of
spirit be an inspiration
to you on your own
journey of faith.
Jacinta Prunty

FOUR COURTS PRESS

Set in 10.5 on 12.5 Ehrhardt by
Carrigboy Typesetting Services for
FOUR COURTS PRESS
7 Malpas Street, Dublin 8, Ireland
www.fourcourtspress.ie
and in North America for
FOUR COURTS PRESS LTD
c/o ISBS, 920 N.E. 58th Avenue, Suite 300, Portland, OR 97213.

A catalogue record for this title is available from the British Library.

ISBN 978-1-85182-438-0

Printed in England by
CPI Antony Rowe, Chippenham, Wilts.

Foreword

It is common nowadays, especially among educationists and psychologists, to recognize the importance of building up people's sense of their own dignity and self-worth. Parenting programmes are seen to be needed and are much in demand, as well as training in budgeting, cooking and general household management. Systemic injustice is acknowledged as the root of many social evils. Awareness of the value of really attentive listening to each individual is the basis of much of today's flourishing counselling and psychotherapy services. All of these things have a very modern ring but in fact they were among the convictions and practices of one of Ireland's outstanding women, Margaret Aylward, affectionately known to Dublin slum dwellers over a hundred years ago as 'the Lady Aylward'.

This very able and fearless woman campaigner made a major impact on the Ireland of her day in the areas of child-care, education of the poor, religious life and church-state relationships. A woman of 'great and noble mind' (John Joseph Steiner), she had a clear grasp of the causes of destitution as well as its dire effects among the hovels and tenements of Dublin's streets and alleys. Her first-hand research and astute analysis is made public in the annual reports of the Ladies' Association of Charity, a powerful organization of socially committed women which she introduced to the city, and in the work of St Brigid's Orphanage, a boarded-out or family system of foster care which she founded. Not content merely to expose the poverty she witnessed, Margaret Aylward put her immense courage, creativity and business skills as well as her personal warmth and ability to inspire others to good use in combating the many injustices she encountered in her charitable work. Quality schooling for the very poorest was but one of several initiatives. She set herself the immense task of combating the proselytizing efforts of well-funded, well-organized Protestant evangelical missionary societies. This controversial work led to her being imprisoned for six months after one of the most sensational and public criminal trials of her day. It also led to her founding, in middle age, a new religious congregation, the Sisters of the Holy Faith.

Jacinta Prunty writes this account of the life of Margaret Aylward as a member of the congregation which Margaret founded, and as an historical geographer with a good grasp of place and sensitivity to the human story. This book originated as a PhD thesis on the social mission of Margaret Aylward, set within the context of the slum geography of nineteenth-century

Dublin. The ordering and cataloguing of extensive archival materials in the Holy Faith Archive, Glasnevin, and in the Dublin Diocesan Archive, Clonliffe, as well as the emergence of other new materials, have made this original research possible. Closely referenced throughout, this book will serve as an important foundation for future work, as individual threads in the story can be followed through to other new discoveries. As such it will appeal to students and professionals in the fields of women's history, the history of church-state relations and of education and social policy development in Ireland. In spite of the scholarly approach of its author, this book will also appeal to a more general reader. It tells the story of a woman who had the courage and the vision to go against the flow of practically every contemporary movement and to argue her case with the authorities of both church and state. Such a woman, such a person of moral courage and single-minded commitment to justice, has a universal appeal.

ROSEMARY DUFFY
Congregational leader, Holy Faith Sisters

Contents

FOREWORD by Rosemary Duffy, congregational leader,
    Holy Faith Sisters   5

LIST OF ILLUSTRATIONS   9

ABBREVIATIONS   10

PREFACE   11

  1   Waterford Roots   13

  2   Lady of Charity   20

  3   Mission Fervour All Round   40

  4   Shoulders to the Wheel   56

  5   Troubling Paris   79

  6   Prison Trials   91

  7   Schools of St Brigid   101

  8   Sisters of the Holy Faith   121

  9   Sources of Strength   138

10   Keeping Faith   154

BIBLIOGRAPHY   185

INDEX   189

Illustrations

FIGURES

1 Gardiner Street Lower, 1960s (IAA 7/24v4), photograph by
  T. Affleck Greaves, Irish Architectural Archive Collection   20

2 Henrietta Place, 1913 (RSAI 62)   21

3 Lady of Charity appeal, Dublin 1924   25

4 John Gowan CM, 1817–1897 (Glasnevin)   33

5 Irish Church Missions, Ireland 1860   45

6 The Night School, Alexander Dallas, *A Mission Tourbook
  in Ireland*, 1862   49

7 The Scripture Reader, Alexander Dallas, *A Mission Tourbook
  in Ireland*, 1862   51

8 *St Brigid's Orphanage, Fiftieth Annual Report*, 1907, frontispiece   57

9 St Brigid's Nurses, 1868–1874   69

10 John Joseph Steiner, 1832–1916, (GA: JS/BC/09 no. 1)   76

11 Raffle Ticket 1892 (GA: O/CD/18 no. 1)   78

12 Daughters of Charity (*Catholic Home Almanac*, 1885)   82

13 Copybook cover *c*.1906 (GA: GF/H/28 no. 8)   108

14 Copybook cover *c*.1906 (GA: GF/H/28 no. 8)   110

15 Glasnevin 1885 (*City of Dublin and its Environs, Thom's
   Directory*, six-inch OS sheet)   133

16 Ursuline manual, 1831 (Glasnevin)   140

TABLES

1 Irish Church Missions schools and homes, Dublin 1849–1900   43

2 St Brigid's Orphanage, 1857–1900   61

3 Entrants to Holy Faith Congregation 1859–1900   123

4 Holy Faith entrants 1859–1900, dowers and other income   128

Abbreviations

ARDP	Association for the Relief of Distressed Protestants
CB	Christian Brothers
CHF	Congregation of the Holy Faith
CM	Congregation of the Missions (Vincentians)
DC	Daughters of Charity (Vincentian)
DDA	Dublin Diocesan Archive, Clonliffe
GA	Holy Faith congregational archive, Glasnevin
IAA	Irish Architectural Archive
ICM	Irish Church Missions
NDU	North Dublin Union
ODC	Order of Discalced Carmelites
OS	Ordnance Survey
RSAI	Royal Society of Antiquaries of Ireland
SBO	St Brigid's Orphanage
SDU	South Dublin Union
SJ	Society of Jesus (Jesuits)
UCD	University College Dublin

Preface

My thanks to Professor Anngret Simms, Department of Geography, UCD, who directed the PhD research upon which this book is based, and who has supported its publication through her continuing generous support and wise advice.

This study was first undertaken at the request of Sr Rosemary Duffy, congregational leader of the Holy Faith Sisters, and the general leadership teams, Srs Constance Loughran, Miriam Anne Lucas, Mairéad Holton, Mary Glennon, Rosaleen Cunniffe and Carmel Campbell. Sr Rosemary and her team gave every support and encouragement throughout, as did Srs Laurentina Kennedy, Martina Traynor and Josephine Dowling. Their support was backed up at regional level by Srs Frances Barrett, Barbara Perry, Irene Dunne and the regional teams. A subvention from the congregation towards the cost of this publication is gratefully acknowledged.

My thanks to colleagues and postgraduate friends in the Department of Geography, UCD. Special mention must be made of Professor Anne Buttimer, head of department, and Drs Joe Brady, William Nolan and Arnold Horner, who each supported this production in very practical ways. Mr Stephen Hannon, cartographer, was unfailingly generous with his expertise in the field of cartography and graphics, while departmental secretaries Jean Molloy and Frances Scally provided essential moral support and back-up.

Colleagues in other UCD departments have also supported this production, most notably Dr Margaret MacCurtain OP, Professor Mary Daly and Dr T.P. O'Neill (History), and Professor Helen Burke (Sociology). I am grateful to Professor Vincent Comerford, Dr Raymond Gillespie, Monsignor Patrick Corish and Ms Mary Cullen (History, Maynooth), to the Irish Association for Research into Women's History, to Dr Phil Kilroy RSCJ (Armagh), and to Professor Patrick Duffy (Geography, Maynooth). Dr Maria Luddy (Education, Warwick) Dr Kevin Whelan (Notre Dame), and Professor Donal Kerr (Maynooth) made many very helpful suggestions while active encouragement to move from thesis into publication form was provided by Professor Emmet Larkin (History, Chicago) and Professor Richard Lawton (Geography, Liverpool). Special thanks to Mr Michael Adams, Mr Martin Fanning and Mr Martin Healy of Four Courts Press, whose support and professionalism made this possible.

Over the course of this research I have lived in the Coombe, New Ross, Tallaght and St Mary's Road, Ballsbridge, and I extend my thanks to each of the sisters with whom I have lived who have supported me in innumerable ways. The thesis and final book were both submitted from the Coombe, and a special word of appreciation to all who shared very practically in the final production stages. Sr Benignus McDonagh made available the records of St

Brigid's Orphanage, provided photocopying facilities, and helped in numerous other ways; Srs Pauline Clarke and Bernadette Grace assisted in the slow task of extracting information from the orphan registers. Sr Raymond Ledwidge helped with translation of documents in French. The Glasnevin community was always most welcoming on my many visits; special thanks to Sr Assisi Tattan (archivist 1981–91) and Sr Theodore Bugler (present archivist). Siobhán Fitzpatrick SRN helped with medical details. Original research by Br Romuald Gibson FMS and Dr Jim McCormack CM on the Aylward/ Gowan story was important to this work. Srs Euphrasia Bergin and Barbara Perry gave me the initial encouragement to undertake academic research, and their continued interest and support are much appreciated. Many, many other Holy Faith sisters and associates from Ireland and overseas have also encouraged this research through their active interest and warm encouragement, and to each I extend my appreciation.

For access to Irish Church Missions material I am indebted to Mr B.E. Sloan, Croydon, and to the Revd Bridcott, Bachelors Walk, who made me most welcome. Mr David Sheehy, Dublin Diocesan Archive, Clonliffe, was unfailingly helpful in locating material, as were Mr Raymond Refaussé (Church Representative Body Library) Ms Norma Jessop, (Special Collections) and Mr Tony Eklof (Official Publications) of the Main Library, UCD, Ms Mary Clark of the Dublin Corporation Archive, and the staff of the National Library. Sr Margaret Mary, Dunardagh, Blackrock, introduced me to the Daughters of Charity Archive, while Frs Séamus Enright and Brendan McConvery, CSsR, and Mr Julian Walton (Waterford) also provided me with essential reference material. The support of the newly-established Irish Religious Houses Heritage Association, under Professor Vincent Comerford and Fr Enright (Maynooth) is also appreciated. Permission to reproduce material from the Irish Architectural Archive (Figure 1), the RSAI (Figure 2), the Ordnance Survey (Figure 15) and the Holy Faith archive, Glasnevin is acknowledged.

Postgraduate friends have helped throughout with their interest, companionship and practical help. Dr Martina O'Donnell, Yvonne Whelan, Niamh Moore and Drs Edel Sheridan (Göttingen), Hélène Bradley (Chichester), Ruth McManus (Maynooth), and Ríonach Ní Néill all provided essential support in UCD. Margaret Preston (History, Boston) generously placed source material, including charity materials, at my disposal, and Dr Mary Ann Lyons (History, Limerick), was as always most supportive. Sr Anna Byrne DC (Belfast) has over the years taught me much about the spirit of St Vincent, while special encouragement also came from Monica Delaney CHF, Jane Forde CHF, and Mary O'Byrne (Enniscorthy).

Family members have been most understanding and encouraging throughout. Michael and Catherine Prunty located useful source material, Kieran Prunty has done many deliveries in connection with this study, Paul Prunty has helped with computer advice, while Edel Fitzgerald looked after me very well during my stay in London. To my parents, Agnes and Joe Prunty, and to each of my brothers and sisters and their families I again extend my thanks.

Waterford Roots

The Catholic merchant community in Waterford in the late eighteenth and early nineteenth centuries has been described as 'confident in themselves, a people of some wealth, therefore of some education' with a tradition of Catholic lay action and organized and generous charity.[1] Margaret Louisa Aylward was born into one of the most prominent of these families on 23 November 1810, the fifth child of William Aylward and Ellen *née* Murphy. There were ten children in all, and a half brother, Maurice Mullowney, from her mother's first marriage. One sister and two brothers died young. Mary, John, William and Catherine were older than Margaret; Ellen and Jane followed.[2]

William Aylward was a bacon merchant, one of a number of Waterford entrepreneurs involved in the lucrative provisions trade with the Newfoundland colony.[3] Originally from near Mullinavat, Co. Kilkenny, where Kilbeacon was the family burial-place, he moved to Waterford in the late eighteenth century and through his own initiative and good fortune rose to prominence in the mercantile world.[4] The family business and property interests were substantial, as revealed in the terms of William Aylward's will (1840) which lists 'the properties real and freehold and personal, lands and tenements, ships, shares in ships, monies and security for money.'[5] Much of the family's considerable wealth originated on the mother's side, with two unmarried sisters, Mary and Margaret Murphy, selling to their brother-in-law 'all the property he possessed in King Street, Waterford and in Thomas Street and other places.'[6] These two ladies still possessed and managed considerable property portfolios until their deaths in 1858, when their wealth came to their sister Ellen, Margaret's mother.[7] In a family and business environment where both men and women were substantial, independent property holders and administrators, Margaret Aylward developed exceptional business skills, including a grasp of the complexities of investment options, legal terms, and property rights. These abilities, combined with meticulous book-keeping, an excellent command of language both spoken and written, and a driving zeal to bring her projects to fruition, were to make her a formidable business woman and entrepreneur.

In the Aylward household political issues were hotly debated, the family sympathies being with the emerging Home Rule movement. The false promises of benefits to Ireland, most notably in increased trade, had prompted

William Aylward in 1799 to join a number of other Waterford citizens in signing a declaration in favour of the Act of Union.[8] Proved bitterly wrong, he was not afraid to reply to a request in 1830 on behalf of the Westminster government, for information on 'the trade of Waterford, foreign and coastways, from 1800 to present day'[9] with a scathing and well-informed condemnation of British colonial policy. He detailed the bills that had been passed 'against the interest of Ireland', and denounced the legislative system where 'the general diligence of Parliament is such that most frequently the House is adjourned for want of a House [forty members], so that at any time half a dozen clever working men will take the opportunity and manage so as to carry against this country minor measures that may be very beneficial to her poor population.'[10] Political agitators including Thomas Francis Meagher (a native of Waterford) and Daniel O'Connell were frequent visitors to the family home. Following the Municipal Reform Act of 1840 which allowed propertied Catholics to stand in local elections, the eldest son John was elected a councillor for Waterford City, while his brother William was elected an alderman on the same occasion.[11] William Aylward passed on his extensive business concerns to these two sons in 1834, six years before his death.[12]

Prominent in the city's business and political life, the Aylwards were equally notable for their support of charitable undertakings. The clothing lists of the Christian Brothers reveal William Aylward as a donor from 1813,[13] and in his will he was generous once more to the Christian Brothers at Mount Sion and the Irish Sisters of Charity; through an investment of £600 he provided pensions for 'six poor and needy salters' whose 'habits of life' have been 'moral, sober and religious.'[14]

As befitted their status as citizens of substance, William and Ellen Aylward sent their children to the best Catholic schools available: Margaret to the Ursulines in Thurles, Jane to the Benedictines in Princethorpe,[15] and the sons to Stonyhurst and Clongowes Wood.[16] Margaret's early education was in a small local Quaker school, until at ten years of age she moved to Thurles. Here she became fluent in French, the language of the school, and developed her artistic talents, as two watercolours, now displayed in Glasnevin, show. On the Thurles teaching staff at this time was Sr Ursula Young who, as author of three history texts, introduced a knowledge of Irish heritage and culture to the Ursuline and Christian Brothers schools which was unprecedented at the time; her *Catechism of Irish History* (1815) was noted with great hostility by establishment figures including the Commissioners of National Education and had the distinction of being forcibly withdrawn for a while.[17] Despite the scantiness of the surviving school records, it seems fair to deduce that Margaret's education in Thurles deepened her interest in Irish history, reinforcing the nationalism she had already imbibed at home. Following on her second-level schooling she continued for an extra three years studying Sacred Scripture, Latin, classics, art and embroidery.[18]

A vital element in Margaret's Waterford childhood was the family connection with the Christian Brothers congregation. Margaret's mother, Ellen, was a sister of Brother Patrick Joseph Murphy, one of Edmund Rice's earliest recruits, and the first superior of Mount Sion, Waterford (1831-51). A lifelong regard for the Christian Brothers and their mission was to ensue, Margaret having seen for herself how the Brothers combined family relief and tuition of poor Waterford boys, stayed outside the state system, and pioneered Irish textbooks for Irish children.[19]

Margaret also had direct family links with the Presentation sisters. Ellen Aylward, Margaret's mother, had first married John Mullowney, brother of Teresa Mullowney, a young Waterford woman who was to do her novitiate in the Presentation convent in Cork and return to establish the first community and associated Presentation poor school for girls in her native city.[20] Edmund Rice had supported the construction of their first premises but his involvement went well beyond being a mere benefactor. 'He saw in the religious life and rule of the Presentation Sisters a pathway to perfection through the Catholic training of childhood' and undertook to do for the boys of the city what Teresa was directing for the girls.[21] It was in the chapel of the Presentation sisters in Waterford that Rice and his first associates, on 15 August 1808, took religious vows.[22] On leaving the Ursuline school in Thurles, Margaret, then aged twenty years, went to work as a volunteer lay teacher in these poor schools for girls; although the Presentation annals themselves only make reference to two unnamed lay volunteer teachers, letters to Margaret including kind regards to named Presentation sisters make it clear that she was very much integrated into their Waterford mission.[23]

One of the most important aspects of Margaret's early life was the many personal friendships she established with leading clergymen who were also natives of Waterford: Tobias Kirby, a native of Tallow and perhaps the most influential of Irish churchmen of the nineteenth century, rector of the Irish College in Rome and agent of the Irish bishops, who died as titular archbishop of Ephesus in 1903; Philip Dowley, first provincial of the Vincentian Fathers in Ireland; Nicholas Foran, executor of her father's will and later bishop of Waterford and unique supporter of Daniel O'Connell; and as already mentioned, Edmund Ignatius Rice, founder of the Presentation and Christian Brothers, and her uncle Brother Patrick Joseph Murphy.[24] John St Leger of the Jesuits, Clongowes Wood, was another member of this close knit Waterford circle.[25] These early ecclesiastical connections were to be developed and used to advantage in pursuit of charitable schemes in Dublin, although familiarity alone did not always ensure co-operation.

After leaving school Margaret spent about four years at home. Alongside her commitment to the Presentation poor schools she worked in the *mont-de-piété*, a charitable pawnshop designed to protect the poor from the exorbitant rates of interest charged by regular pawnshops.[26] The Aylward sisters were much occupied in the charitable life of Waterford, as Margaret's sister Ellen wrote to her in Dublin in 1858, keeping her up to date on the local philanthropic scene, which on this occasion was fundraising for Margaret's Dublin charity: 'Our grand ladies and gentlemen in Waterford are daily busy and anxious about the bazaar for St Vincent's Society which commences today. Your friend Miss Howard has walked miles for sale of tickets and has succeeded admirably. There are great fears entertained that the whole proceeds will be much less than last year, but I hope better things for your charity.'[27] In a later letter Margaret reported in a similar vein on 'the great Catholic bazaar' in London, 'ladies at their stalls in *their hair*. Nobles and titles to no end – the Auctioneer "Lord Edward Steward"' (*sic*).[28] Other references point to her first-hand experience of the city's slums and the difficulties facing women and children especially in a port city in recession, while she was also familiar with the harsh regime of the local workhouse, where the inmates spent long hours on the treadmill.[29] It is clear that she belonged to a well-developed network of charitable middle–class Catholic women, who under able organization were ready to assist every good cause.[30]

Records are more complete from 1834, when Margaret followed her sister Catherine (Sr Mary Vincent) into the Irish Sisters of Charity in Stanhope Street, Dublin. Both had the full backing of their father, who wrote affectionately on Margaret's entrance that 'You know not the feelings of a fond parent on an occasion of this kind. But if you feel it is for your happiness most cheerfully will I bear it.'[31] Margaret received the name Sr Mary Alphonsus Ligouri, and taught in King's Inns Street as a novice. According to one source she suffered from 'weakness of the spine which obliged her to keep in a lying posture', and left under the advice of Fr Collier, her confessor.[32]

There was another, more sinister, angle to the time with the Sisters of Charity, recorded in their annals as 'Troubles from Within'. The novice mistress, Sr Ignatius (Ellen Augustine Bodenham) was dismissed from the congregation for allegedly creating 'mischief':

> The Novices were induced to think that in devoting their lives to the poor, they were squandering intellectual gifts which might be used to far greater advantage for the glory of God. The precise meaning of 'piety' and 'culture' became sadly confused in their minds. The old specious cry of Judas – why this waste? – was insidiously employed to influence their impressionable young hearts.[33]

There was havoc in the community; some considered that the founder and first superior, Mary Aikenhead, handled the situation unjustly, their sympathies lying with the undoubtedly accomplished and attractive mistress of novices. On her dismissal 13 of the 22 novices left, and two young professed sisters. This exodus included Margaret, with whom Miss Bodenham continued to correspond from 1839 to 1842.[34] Margaret herself has left no account of this period, but from the Bodenham letters it is clear that the former novice mistress lavished her with effusive praise and put her under considerable pressure to join with her in founding a new congregation in Hastings, England. Although Margaret herself had not yet abandoned all thoughts of religious life, she was more immediately interested in assisting the establishment of religious orders in Waterford, notably the Jesuit fathers and the Irish Sisters of Charity, than in Miss Bodenham's complex schemes.[35]

While Catherine was the only one to persevere in religious life, each of the Aylward sisters gave it serious consideration: both Mary and Ellen gave the convent a short trial, while Jane had one early unsuccessful attempt followed by an unhappy marriage, and on the desertion of her husband joined Margaret's embryonic community. Margaret twice entered religious congregations, and eventually began her own. The convent was seen as a realistic option by several of their peers: Ellen Aylward wrote to Margaret of her close school-friend Emily Fellowes, who had just visited: 'I believe her mind is made up not again to attempt the religious state'; another school friend became Sr Mary Josephine in a Waterford convent.[36]

In Margaret's case the decision to try her vocation again at the mature age of thirty-five years and enter the Ursuline convent in Waterford was the result of much agonizing, as evidenced in a series of letters from Fr John Curtis SJ, to whom she turned for direction.[37] In May 1845 he advised her to 'continue her fervent petitions to Heaven and your deliberations for *this* month', and 'Be fervent – very fervent – in prayer; ask the prayers of others; deliberate, compare and weigh all things as I have directed you; and form your decision wisely.' Margaret entered but almost immediately found it unbearable. In an effort to dissuade her from leaving too hastily, Fr Curtis tried to explain 'the state of trial under which you labour':

> Before your entrance into religion you possessed your full liberty – you had little labour, little annoyance of any kind; in religion, no liberty, no leisure – all occupation and labour. Thence your suffering. But if you can hold your ground, your fervour will increase, Divine Grace will strengthen its dominion over you, and the opposition and consequent suffering will cease. Were this not the case – were your trials to continue in their severity, I should say it were not for human nature to bear them.[38]

However, she was very soon to find the loss of liberty and innumerable 'annoyances' too great a strain.[39] In January 1846, after no more than two months, she left. She had to carry the disapproval of some family members and friends, but Curtis assured her: 'Do not be fretted at what people say of your late trial; you showed more sense in undertaking it than they do in reproaching you.'[40] She moved to Dublin, most probably to avoid the local gossip which inevitably followed on her second failure in religious life, and also to consult with doctors. In an undated letter which appears to refer to this time Curtis warned her against harbouring any further aspirations to religious life: 'Consider well with yourself whether you can now live in convent and work on your way towards heaven without being disturbed at the imperfections of others – form no judgment regarding my motive for suggesting this, but consider it well.'[41]

Margaret's intense and affectionate involvement throughout her life with her brothers and sisters reveal much about her character. Although the fifth child she was to prove the mainstay of her family, as numerous letters directed to her, on matters of great and small import, testify. It was Margaret who had the worry of Ellen, unmarried, and Jane, deserted, in Dublin in 1854, who 'not being satisfied to remain in their new lodgings want to reside at the Loreto Convent where they take in Ladies as Boarders, 43 North Great George's Street.'[42] Ellen, who suffered from a 'very excited state' and was 'difficult to manage', quarrelsome and short-tempered, later isolated herself in a rented house 'much too large' in Tramore, and became estranged from friends and relatives, always excepting Margaret.[43] Concerned family friends such as Fr Richard Fitzgerald in Carrick-on-Suir expressed the wish that Ellen 'could be induced to place entire confidence in you', which would be to Ellen 'a blessing' and 'a source of consolation to all who are interested in her welfare'.[44]

Her young sister Jane Fagan was another worry. She had married, but to a wasteful, self-absorbed young man who in 1854 (on incurring debts he could not meet) fled the country and escaped to Australia, leaving her to face the debtors.[45] From here relations between the couple deteriorated further, with John Fagan requesting his wife to 'leave that gloomy convent', where she had found refuge with her sister, and to spare him allusions to their recent dead child.[46] Finally he declares that 'tried by such a test' she has been 'weighed and found wanting' and it only remains for him now 'to echo your own frigid farewell and there an end'.[47]

Margaret also had the anxiety of her brother William and his wife Maria Clara *née* White, whose disastrous marriage was to disintegrate after only four years. In November 1845 matters came to a bitter head when William removed the two infants to his mother's house and prevented his wife from entering. Maria Clara initiated legal proceedings to sue her husband for the care and custody of the children, and also petitioned for divorce, citing beatings, drunkenness, adultery, attempted stabbing, hypnotizing their daughter, exposing this child to the cold, and starving his family.[48] In court he denied all charges, and accused his wife in turn of 'vituperative language', abusing the children, violence, purposely incurring debts, and cursing.[49] The court found in favour of William, and he maintained custody of the children, but that did not in any sense mark the end of his troubles, for on 30 November

1858 he was committed to Waterford Gaol by the Court for the Relief of Insolvent Debtors, and in 1860 buried his only son.[50] Margaret carried the pain of this family scandal, taking a special interest in her niece, who in time entered the Irish Sisters of Charity.[51]

Margaret's role as counsellor, mediator, financial and property manager in her family circle was maintained and indeed intensified despite what were to be exceptionally demanding undertakings in Dublin. Although the busy metropolis was to dominate her life from the 1840s onwards, her Waterford roots and family experiences laid the foundations upon which she would build.

2

Lady of Charity

The circumstances which brought Margaret Aylward to Dublin in the late 1840s were a confused mixture of ill health and an anxiety for a break from her Waterford circle. Dublin brought the opportunity of consulting expert doctors concerning her severe erysipelas. Equally if not more importantly, it provided her with some independence and anonymity following on her second failure in religious life, a break from the local gossips who had followed her entries and exits with unwanted interest, and a healthy distance from her close family and the weight of their problems. Uncertain of what the future might hold, of how and where God might be leading, she found immediate refuge in the Manor House, Clontarf, with her brother John, who was similarly placing some distance between himself and Waterford, and also endeavouring to recover his health. After a short stay with John, Margaret

Figure 1:²Gardiner Street Lower, 1960s, photograph by T. Affleck Greaves, Irish Architectural Archive Collection

Figure 2: Henrietta Place, 1913

took lodgings in the Gardiner Street district, and thus began her life-long involvement in the Dublin slums. Her conscious decision to settle in Dublin was not welcomed by her mother in Waterford, 'who said she would prefer to have you by her side', but consoled herself with pride in her daughter's achievements, 'and the poor mother's heart broke out upon her and she said you were a good girl and very willing to do all the good you could.'[1]

Dublin in 1848 was a city of vivid contrasts: terraces of stately town houses set along gracious squares and elegant malls (Figure 1), contrasted starkly with the rows of decayed tenement houses, and the warren of mud hovels and barely-converted coach-houses and sheds which packed the stable lanes and back yards of the city (Figure 2). In the medieval core and adjoining Liberties of the south side, and the early north side suburbs of Church Street, dilapidation, congestion and filth were particularly evident. Appalling housing conditions and exorbitant rents were only an indication of the social problems of the city centre, which was steadily losing status as the wealthy migrated to the attractive self-governing suburban townships on the city's margins.[2]

Margaret arrived in Dublin directly following on the great famine of 1845–7, which had decimated especially the western counties; the city acted as a refuge for the dispossessed and most destitute, some *en route* to what they hoped would be a new life in Britain, and via Liverpool, in America and Australia. There was chronic under- and un-employment, with an over reliance among men on casual labour at the docks, and a frightening dearth of job opportunities for women outside domestic service and dealing. The influx of unskilled and desperate persons did nothing to improve the situation of those already there.[3]

The city was packed especially with destitute women and children, widowed, orphaned, abandoned, or left behind as the menfolk sought work in England. The large number of soldiers barracked in Dublin, and the high proportion of Irish soldiers in the British Army brought its own problems: numbers of women, both married and unmarried, and their children, were left to fend for themselves when the soldiers were moved on, or returned to Dublin on the death or desertion of their soldier husbands. And with selective outmigration and suburbanization, there was increasing social and physical distance between the poorest and wealthiest, a situation which looked hopeless as the townships refused every effort to be drawn into the city's administrative and thereby financial circle.[4]

LADIES' ASSOCIATION OF CHARITY OF ST VINCENT DE PAUL

Margaret Aylward's first structured work among the poor of what soon became her adopted city was through the Ladies' Association of Charity of St Vincent de Paul for the Spiritual and Temporal Relief of the Sick Poor. Founded in 1617 by St Vincent de Paul, this lay charity opened its first Irish branch in Kingstown in 1843, on the occasion of a mission by the Vincentian fathers, with the support of Dr Murray, Roman Catholic archbishop of Dublin. Although Margaret had at least some contact with a Waterford branch opened in 1847, her first recorded active involvement was with the Kingstown group which was headed by a Miss Margaret Kelly. By May 1851 Margaret Aylward had founded her own branch in the metropolitan parish of St Mary's, Marlborough Street, but would continue to collaborate on many fronts with the Kingstown ladies.[5] This first major Dublin project was to propel her very soon into larger and more complex ventures.

The Vincentian origins of the association determined its spirit and approach, and guided its policy decisions. There were two classes of membership, active and honorary. 'The first apply themselves, as directed by rule, to the active functions of the Institute; the latter aid it by contributing to its funds.' Active membership was open to all women, married, unmarried or widowed; honorary membership widened the circle to include other women who subscribed to or otherwise contributed to its resources, and a large number of men, including husbands, fathers and other supportive relatives of individual lady members, along with local clergy, working men and business men, and any other men whom Margaret could prevail upon to become part of this Ladies movement. The association was attached to the local parish and under the guidance of the diocesan clergy, from whom requests to make 'sick calls' generally came. The committee of management was made up of women: a superior, two assistants, one of whom acted as treasurer, and a secretary. A clergyman acted as honorary president; his main function was to chair the annual general meetings. The 'sick poor' were the special object of relief, and the family was the unit dealt with.

St Vincent de Paul's teaching on charity was the guiding vision. 'Far from regarding charity in the light of philanthropy only, or mere human benevolence' Vincent de Paul 'considered it, and practised it, as a Christian virtue'. The gospel basis was very simply stated: the members were to consider 'that in ministering consolation and relief to the sick poor, they are doing so not to them, but to Jesus Christ in them'. 'Whatsoever you do unto these the least of my children you do unto me.'[6]

The mission of the Ladies of Charity was intended to be all-encompassing, with a special concern for the 'spiritual wants of the poor in their sickness'. The approach therefore involved combining the relief of distress with catechesis, instruction in parenting and household management. The lady visitors 'besides bringing to each family the relief-order allotted to them for that day' were instructed 'to read for the Sick, to instruct them, to pray with them, to induce all to frequent the sacraments', and while encouraging the parents to send their children to Catholic schools and to catechism class, were 'to insist, as far as they can, upon cleanliness, order, industry and regularity being perceptible in their homes.'[7]

In addresses to her co-workers, and in an effort to attract new members and material support, Margaret repeatedly elaborated on her understanding of the role of the Lady of Charity. The 'pecuniary relief' afforded by the ladies was only secondary to the gift of 'their counsel, their care', the principal end of their ministry to cherish the Christ in their neighbour, each of whom shares in 'the dignity of children of God'. Fostering self-respect and confidence among the poor in themselves and in an all-provident and loving God was therefore fundamental to the ladies' mission. Margaret's passion for intelligent and generous action was combined with an appreciation that these things take time, that 'patient, earnest, gentle perseverance' is necessary on the part of those who would claim to truly befriend the poor.[8]

Geographically, Margaret's metropolitan branch attempted to serve the two Catholic parishes of St Mary's, Marlborough Street, and St Michan's, Anne Street, and extending beyond the Royal Canal into St Peter's parish, an extensive area covering most of the urban district north of the River Liffey. From 1851–54 its headquarters were at 20 Lower Dorset Street; in 1855 the offices were moved to 6 Middle Gardiner Street, at which period Margaret had lodgings at 14 Middle Gardiner Street. Later moves were within immediate reach: to 6 Berkeley Street (1857) and finally, in 1858 to 42 Eccles Street (renumbered 46 in 1869), the 'home resting place' of a small number of companions who were to devote themselves full-time to the charities, and a settled address for committee meetings and administrative purposes. The two parishes in which the association operated included both the formal Georgian squares and wide streets of the Gardiner estate, much of which was steadily being reduced to tenements, and a warren of back lanes, enclosed courts and alley ways, with some of Europe's worst slum housing. The parish of St Mary's also included the notorious red light district known as the 'Monto', famed in Joyce's *Ulysses* as 'Nightown', and as early as the 1830s well established as the home of 'huxters, a great number of destitute Poor, dissolute and depraved characters in both sex, labourers.'9

State provision for the poor in Ireland at this time was in practice largely limited to indoor relief, under the Poor Law (Ireland) act 1838. Those requiring assistance had to submit to workhouse incarceration, which included family break-up as well as the surrender of all holdings greater than half an acre. The widespread abhorrence among many of the poor for the relief thus provided made the visitation of the 'sick poor', the particular focus of the Ladies of Charity, a very evident area of need.10 The scale of the problem in the densely populated north city parishes was huge: Margaret claimed that at least '3,000 persons arise every morning in this parish without the means of breaking their fast' and the 'number of poor who occasionally require relief is calculated at 7,000 or 8,000'.11

The first task facing Margaret was to persuade others to join her, convinced that 'individuals, each one of whom singly is weak as the reed which bends before the breeze', becomes by association 'like to a "strong castle"'. She called a preliminary public meeting in the Jesuit Church of St Francis Xavier, Gardiner Street, 6 June 1851, to introduce the association and outline the rules, after which 'the Ladies volunteering to be Active Members gave in their names and an adjourned meeting was fixed for June 24th to elect office-bearers.'12

In the published annual reports Margaret expanded at length on the philosophy and practical aims of this work of St Vincent. The involvement of 'ladies' of some social standing was an aspect of the charity that was constantly advertised. These ladies

> assiduous in their domestic duties in the morning and perhaps mingling in the course of the day in innocent amusement and recreation, and in society more congenial to their rank, will be seen going into these obscure alleys without a witness but God, and there finding their way into the abodes of the Sick, the unhappy, and the miserable, and silently relieving them.13

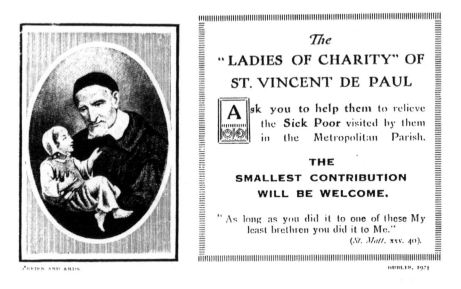

Figure 3: Lady of Charity appeal

The appeal was directed to women in their traditional role as home-makers, coming from happy homes to bring relief to the poor and bringing the blessings of the poor back to their own families, who were in turn drawn into the circle of service: 'the mother who is a Lady of Charity, tells her children the scenes she has passed through in visiting the sick, the sister tells her younger sisters, and all become attached to the interests of the Poor, and the Poor look up to them and bless them.' The 'advantages arising both to rich and poor from constant mutual intercourse' were also stressed, Margaret claiming that at the heart of many of Dublin's problems was class segregation.[14]

Unceasing public appeals for volunteers and funds were necessary (Figure 3), particularly as the north city lost better-off residents to the suburbs and the downgrading of good houses to single-room tenements continued apace. Although the association could rejoice that they had not actually *lost* a single member 'Some have left town, and reside now in France, England, and in the country parts of Ireland, and they have brought with them an undying love of the Poor and an ardent desire to benefit them.'[15] It was necessary for others to fill their places locally, leading to impassioned pleas to 'every Catholic lady in this city', who were promised 'tales of unheeded suffering, that would not let them rest by day nor sleep by night, till they found themselves contributing out of their affluence and their leisure to its alleviation.' Each respondent was assured that 'sweeter to the ear than sweetest melody is the blessing of the afflicted wife or widow, as she follows the retiring steps of the "Lady of Charity", with "May the heavens bless you, dear Lady. May God and his Holy Mother protect you!"'[16]

In their ministry to the very sick the Ladies were to make every possible preparation in advance of death: exhorting the person to receive the last sacraments, and arranging for a priest to visit; providing rosary beads and crucifixes, and putting the room in order, so that the it could be noted that 'everything was neat and clean around. The zeal of the Visitor had provided for all.'[17] Between twenty and thirty persons on the 'sick roll' died each year (1851–62), so that aspect of the visitation was important.

The relief activities of the Association were not limited to those mentioned in the official records of the association, but included countless 'kind acts done in secret'. Each lady was urged not alone to 'visit and help the sick poor in the best manner' but 'to endeavour to provide substantial comfort for them', making herself 'their purveyor in her family and in her circle of acquaintance', collecting small sums, and altering clothes, so that, emulating the charities of France, 'Everybody gives a little, and a great many collect a little, and as they would say themselves, "*Voilà tout*".'[18] The records of the association make it clear that it was in fact the multiplication of many such small efforts that was the mainstay of the charity.

Margaret, with her 'very imposing appearance and attractive and engaging manner'[19] personally took the platform at the public meetings which she convened to launch the published reports, an unusual role for any woman in Dublin at the time. To engender support an on-going requirement was to publicize the position of the poor, and the efforts of the society; this was achieved by including in the annual reports not the 'isolated or extraordinary facts, however, interesting in themselves', which might make for sensational media coverage, but a selection of 'such cases as seem best to illustrate the every-day nature of our charity.'[20] Factual accuracy and attention to detail were important, so that addresses were included, though the identity of the families was protected by using initials in place of names. By using direct quotation Margaret tried to be faithful to the poor men and women's own stories and their requests for work or for the means to be set up in dealing. Typical was that recorded during the exceptionally harsh winter of 1854–5 when one woman cried out 'The starvation of the winter,' she said, bursting into tears, 'it was that came against him, he wasn't used to it.'[21]

The stories were invariably told in the popular journalistic style of the period, the drama of penetrating the upper floors of dank tenement houses, or stinking cellars, played out to full effect. In one wretched cellar a consumptive man lay dying on the bare ground, 'his only covering a worn-out quilt, no fire, and not an article of furniture in his damp and dreary abode.' Only when the lady visitors became accustomed to the darkness could they distinguish his features; his weak voice 'gained strength when he raised it to bless God, and resign himself without reserve into his hands.'[22] In another 'large waste room', reached by clambering up a staircase in total darkness ('a little boy charitably preceded us to show the way'), the ladies interviewed the sick woman: 'We asked where she slept; she pointed to a handful of straw. "Where is the bed covering?" we inquired, – the coat which her husband wore, (a small one), this was the covering':

> A spark of fire she had not; cold, keen and bitter was the wind that day, and as night approached, and the blast howled around, and sent its withering influence into that dilapidated abode, great was the comfort experienced by the Visitors in thinking that Divine Providence had graciously vouchsafed to use them as instruments in bringing fire, and light, and food to that dark, damp and drearisome abode.[23]

In 'one of the narrow lanes of St Michan's parish' a poor woman lay 'on a damp, earthen floor' a few particles of straw serving as a bed, reliant on the meagre earnings of her child, a situation repeated innumerable times throughout this district.[24] A particularly poignant scene was that of two elderly sisters who had lived and worked together all their lives but now one was sick:

> You enter the little room; it is almost dark, for four of the six panes of glass are patched with paper to keep out the cold. There is no fire, very little bedcovering; one-and-threepence must be paid weekly for the rent, and the income is now six-pence a day, with one or two idle days in the week. The poor creature lies upon her sick bed all day and suffers in silence. Her sister comes home in the evening and tries to light a little fire and to prepare a little food. A cup of miserable tea and a little dry bread, the whole costing about two-pence, form the chief, and almost only meal, of the two sisters. This is how the poor live, and how the Sick Poor suffer; and yet when we entered, that poor sick one was saying her beads for the conversion of sinners; yes, for the cold world that surrounded her.[25]

Margaret was not satisfied with merely recording the nature and extent of destitution in the city, but sought to expose its root causes. The want of employment, especially among women, was the over-riding cause of destitution repeatedly noted in the charity records. Sickness and the consequent inability to labour was often disastrous for a poor family, in the absence of acceptable state or other assistance. A long and detailed report on poverty in this parish was prepared by a curate, Fr O'Neill, with whom Margaret worked closely,[26] and focused especially on the low wages and the dependency of women on 'the proceeds of the *father's* labour and exertions' to such an alarming extent that desperate for work, 'while men have been paid from nine to twelve shillings per week wages, I have frequently known able-bodied women to be most happy to be engaged at *manual labour* at *three pence* per day!'[27] In time of illness these families hovered on the brink of utter ruin, bringing '*immediate* and *absolute* want' to all the family members, and as illness 'always must bring additional expenses' it invariably has the effect 'of inflicting great privations on those whose scanty means were already overtaxed.'[28] It was in such situations that the Ladies of Charity, with their timely and flexible approach to needs, could literally save lives.

The division between the utterly destitute and the labouring poor was wafer thin. The availability of employment, generally unskilled, manual work, and the health and strength of the men, and indeed women, that they might procure such employment, was the major factor in determining which side of the line one fell. Important too was the sense of responsibility, when earning, in providing for dependents. Reporting on the twenty-six families on the 'Sick Poor Roll' in 1861 the association simply stated: 'They are poor now for they are sick and they cannot work.' There were also recipients who were formerly of better positions, whose distress is 'screened from the public eye'; in these cases help was provided 'as secretly as possible' so that they might be spared further anguish, 'and that they may see and feel that their poverty, which they would fain hide from those nearest and dearest to them, is sacred with us'.[29] The most prevalent kind of sickness among those visited was pulmonary complaints: consumption, cold, bronchitis and 'chest disease', while the general terms 'weakness', 'decline', 'debility' and 'delicacy' were also apparently related to the prevalence of tuberculosis; damp, overcrowded and insanitary housing, along with malnutrition, ensured that such diseases took the firmest hold.

The failure of persons who had migrated to Dublin in search of work to realize their hopes was highlighted by Margaret, as thrown among strangers, they were particularly vulnerable. One aged widow in Greek Street 'was not so fluent in English as in her native Irish'; this family 'came from the country; they were one among the many who have been swept away out of their little holdings into the back lanes of the city.' On the death of that woman her distraught daughter 'in the howl peculiar to the country, was giving immoderate vent to her grief'. Her keening was hushed by the visitor, 'and the afflicted woman knelt, her own babe beside her, by the corpse, and united with the Ladies in the prayers they offered for the repose of the departed soul.'[30]

A recurring theme in Margaret's reports was the care of the poor for one another, particularly of women taking care of children alongside their own. The first refuge of the poorest in times of crisis was among their own relations and neighbours. One dying widow lay on 'a hard palliass' with the ticken removed to serve as a cover; this wretched straw bed was obliged to accommodate, 'beside the dying woman, her two children and her sister's two children'. In another instance one poor, starved widow and her children, enjoying the rare treat of sheep's head broth, were sharing with 'a decent tradesman's family' in the same house who would have died if it was not for the charity of their neighbours.[31]

The relief books tell exactly what was given by the Ladies to each family, while the annual reports provide the context in which the particular type of relief was decided upon.

> The relief in kind comprises almost everything that could recover, sustain, or console the poor sufferers; indeed not less than twenty-four different species of relief will be found in the table of expenditure. All this shows a painstaking charity on the part of our Associates, a tender feeling, and a nice discrimination in trying to suit the relief to the case.[32]

The two largest items of expenditure were 'just those most wanted – bread and fuel'. The greatest care was taken to 'unite economy with real relief, and discrimination with kindliness'. Some were visited and relieved almost daily; others, 'two, three, or five times a week, according to their wants and necessities.'[33] The emphasis was on the intervention of 'timely aid and encouragement', to try and prevent utter destitution, though it appears that many of those relieved were already in a state of great want. Help towards securing employment was high on the agenda. Typical entries record the release of clothes from pawn to enable a daughter who had been in service, 'with good discharges, but no clothes now to make "an appearance"', 'towards procuring a mangle for a poor family', 'to a widow to assist her in business', to recover tools, 'purchase working implements for labourers', or apprentice a 'poor lame girl to the boot-closing trade'.[34] Members often took on individual 'cases' and secured employment among their contacts, 'and thus kind acts have been done in secret, and bonds of Christian friendship cemented between individual Members and the Poor, delightful to both.'[35] Where the breadwinner had employment to return to, or where some work could be procured for him/her, there was a real possibility of effecting a lasting improvement in family circumstances; one man was enabled to recover his tools, and 'put a little clothes upon himself,' 'so, he is at his work again, and thus the whole family are raised up. They are not yet, indeed, out of poverty, but they are content.' The 'sick poor' funds could only be used for such needy persons; however the council 'as well as many individual members, had recourse to other charitable persons, in favour of the more distressed' and also operated a small 'destitute poor fund', amounting to £13 4s. 6d. in 1855.[36]

'Donations of old clothing, carpeting, sheets, rugs, blankets, shoes etc,' were repeatedly invited. The items of clothing most often distributed may be listed as follows: bedgowns, flannel petticoats, calico chemises, shawls, vests, night shifts, drawers, stockings, night wrappers, bonnets, frocks, gowns, shirts, coats, jackets, trousers and, less often, shoes and boots. The provision of warm underclothing was the most important area of clothing relief, along with bedding: sheets, carpet for covering, or simply 'bedcovering', or 'bedstuff', blankets, quilts, bedticker, pillow, were all distributed between 1851 and 1856.

'The poor man's bed (straw), which alas! is often a great boon, has been given to every one that asked it.'[37] Sheets were 'lent'; presumably the Ladies of Charity took the same precaution against the pawning of bedclothes as did the Association for the Relief of Distressed Protestants, which had its blankets branded and all pawnbrokers warned against accepting them in trust, as they were the property of the ARDP.[38] In 1854 the association publicly thanked the anonymous friend who sent 'during the past winter, forty-five new, heavily-lined quilts, for the Sick Poor. These are perfect specimens of practical, laborious industry and true charity, made of pieces of drugget, velvet, and moreen, sewed together and well bound. We say this much, hoping that others may be induced to imitate such good example.' And again 'it is good to remind those who may be able to make gifts of old clothing and covering, that there is scarcely anything more useful to the Poor.'[39] Money relief, recorded from 1877, but in operation previous to that, was given in association with 'tea, sugar, bread.' The sums were small but not insignificant: 2s. 6d., which would be just above the rent demanded for a one-room tenement.[40]

While the Ladies' Association was a model of efficient organisation, judging from the surviving manuscript records of those who contributed to and those who were helped by the charity, along with lists of subscribers and financial accounts, its role as a relief agency was not to be detached from its primary purpose as an example of Christian charity in action. The ladies are to remember that 'to the warm Irish heart', it is, perhaps, 'the compassionate look, the soothing word, the kind inquiry, the hushed voice, the gentle step, the reverential bearing (for to our Lady of Charity her poor sick sister or brother holds the place of Him who redeemed her)' that will make the most impact.[41] The quality of listening is to take primary place, with the ladies repeatedly urged to use the 'kind inquiry' as a means of allowing the sick or troubled person to be the focus of the visit:

> It is a sweet and consoling task to visit the poor, to sit by the humble pallet or straw bed, whispering relief to the bosom of pain, to make the kind inquiry and allow the pining invalid or the half heart-broken wife or mother to pour her pent-up anguish into a friendly ear; to behold the dim eye sparkle, and the care-contracted brow expand at the voice of sympathy or prospect of relief; and better still, to vindicate practically, as it were, the Providence of God in the eyes of the Poor by showing them, that He does care for them, and raises up friends to them.[42]

Such a large-scale and complex relief system was possible only because of the quality of commitment which Margaret attracted. Providing leadership to such a disparate group of volunteers was not always easy, Margaret complaining privately, ''tis such a misery to be eternally humouring everyone'.[43] However, within five years she had built up her numbers to 148 active visitors. Most were recruited by the well-tried if tedious method of calling on individual ladies and extending the invitation personally, following on advertisements from the pulpits of local Catholic churches. Support came from some unexpected quarters. From the Dominican convent in Eccles Street, a number of young 'lady boarders' feature among Margaret's earliest volunteers. Outstanding individuals included Mrs Frances Murray, first treasurer and a native of France who 'had long ago taken Ireland for better for worse, and she was faithful to her plighted troth to the end', giving considerably of her own means, 'besides, her interest, her time and her information were at the service of those who had recovered from sickness, to procure situations for them.'[44] Agnes Mary Scully of 9 Fitzgibbon Street was responsible single-handedly for securing huge amounts of clothing for the poor, exploiting her contacts throughout the city and suburbs, and is credited in later records for her role in developing the Ladies' Association offshoot, St Brigid's out-door orphanage (chapter 4). Analysis of the home addresses of both subscribers and donors of clothing and other items between 1851 and 1853 reveals that the active membership was drawn largely from three social groups: the wives and daughters of solicitors, barristers, and doctors; the wives and daughters of wine merchants; and women from manufacturing and business families, particularly from families engaged in the provisions trade, but also in drapery, baking, candle-making, and pawnbroking. And well aware that recruitment was but the first step in ensuring the long-term good of the association, Margaret invested considerable efforts in the continued formation of the members, urging that each member 'might strive to become better every year, and do more for the Poor – better, by striving to be more holy', each to work towards becoming 'more humble, patient, unselfish, gentle and loving'.[45] Practical supports towards such noble ends were provided by arranging for a priest to give regular 'conferences upon our duties', organizing annual retreat days, and composing her own *Manual* 'expressly designed and composed for the use of the Members, which, we trust, with the Divine blessing, will greatly aid them in instructing and consoling the sick poor.'[46]

In the areas of fundraising and accounts Margaret's business acumen and ingenuity come to the fore. The annual subscription was set at 4*s.* 4*d.* but by urging half-yearly and quarterly payments the net was thrown quite widely. Private collections of money and articles were from the outset supplemented by raffles and charity sermons. In 1853 'a valuable gold bracelet set with turquoise' was raffled and raised £34; other welcome lottery prizes were a gold chain, a beautiful crucifix, wax models of the Madonna and of the scourging of Our Lord at the pillar, and under a glass shade, a 'splendid eastern figure', also modelled in wax. This developed into the very successful annual bazaar, widely employed by women in the nineteenth-century to generate funds for every possible charitable cause; 'most of the beautiful things exhibited [at the Annual Lottery and Sale of Fancy Articles] were the work of the ladies who presented them', and many of these 'displayed great taste in their conception and exquisite delicacy in their execution'.[47]

A further reason for Margaret's success was her good fortune in securing very useful clerical support from the outset, with John Curtis SJ, the first honorary president, and Edward McCabe (archbishop 1879), vice president. The 'auspicious advent' of Dr Cullen to the Dublin diocese led Margaret and her Kingstown mentor, Margaret Kelly, to request an audience, 'in order to commit their institute to his protecting care, and to obtain his episcopal benediction upon its works.'[48] His support for the charity was evident from the outset, and he directed large sums of money through the Ladies for the relief of cases which came to his notice, Margaret reporting on 'those who applied to Your Grace whom you wished me to visit and for whose relief your charity gave me money.'[49] In the 1856 report it was reported that their generous friend Cullen 'has even take us immediately under his paternal care, in becoming our president', chairing the annual meeting now held in the 'New Chapel attached to the Church of the Immaculate Conception, Marlborough Street.'[50] The relationship between Cullen and Margaret was to deepen over the years, and he undoubtedly valued her personally as well as for her work. Rose Gaughren, who worked with Margaret from 1861, put it very simply: 'Margaret Aylward could go to him at any time she wished and was always received with the greatest kindness.'[51]

In terms of personal support the appointment of a former diocesan priest, Fr John Gowan CM (1817–97), to the Vincentian mission house in Phibsboro in the early summer of 1851, was to be of enormous consequence (Figure 4). He became Margaret's spiritual director in 1852, in the critical founding days of her branch of the Ladies of Charity.[52] While he was to play a more public role in the charities and sisterhood which developed from this first venture, surviving letters reveal the depth of his early support for the newcomer from Waterford. He encourages her to use her 'great gift of humouring others' and promote the full participation of the other women volunteers.[53] Her misgivings he is familiar with, and tries to dispel, urging 'You must try and do your work cheerfully now that it is put upon you. You know that you are doing God's work – at all events not your own whims, no murmuring any more.'[54] The correspondence also reveals how heavily the challenge of directing the metropolitan branch of the association weighed on Margaret at times; John Gowan offers practical and spiritual advice in response to the difficulties she has expressed:

> Some of the officers will make mistakes, you will watch over all, you will use your judgement and experience to correct mistakes in the beginning, other mistakes will try your patience for you will have to allow them to accumulate till they cure themselves. In all this you will have need of great patience and great charity; you will have to accommodate yourself (as you remark) to other peoples' manners and

Figure 4: John Gowan CM, 1817–1897

whims, perhaps against your own feelings. However, you have a great gift in that way, and that gift will be of great service to yourself and to others if you only exercise it quietly and good humouredly. But you say 'tis such a misery to be eternally humouring every one? Things are so: God Almighty allows it, that we may have every day opportunities of practising virtue.[55]

John Gowan had unbounded confidence in Margaret's abilities, considerably more than she had herself:

You have a great future before you for God and for his Church, Be firm in your vocation. Be cheerful. Be patient in your troubles. Wait for God and he will not fail to console you. Firm in matter and agreeable in manner, this is your course.[56]

While Margaret won the respect and support of many of the city clergy for her Ladies' Association, such was her commitment that she could not tolerate half-heartedness on their part, for whom the poor, she believed, should be a special care. Eloquent in her public thanks of named clergymen who assisted the association, she was not afraid, privately, to berate those whom she considered negligent, and even to bring significant incidents to the attention of the archbishop. One such scandal involved a poor man who could not get a priest to attend him on his death bed, the details of which Cullen requested Margaret to write out. Despite repeated messages to the vestry in Anne Street it was 'not till two Ladies called at the Chapel House and saw one' that a priest could be got, but evidently he came in very bad grace. Miss Campbell, one of the visiting Ladies involved said 'she *dreaded* yesterday the curate going in *there*, she expected he would be so annoyed for her note or call going to him' and Margaret adds: 'It will be hard for a poor Sinner to be very candid or confidential with a person if they enter as before "in a passion".' The clerk 'was as usual inclined to be *uncivil*' and 'he of course takes his tone from those over him.'[57]

The visiting of the sick was regulated by rota, 'and the duties are so distributed, that each Member's turn for visiting reverts but once in the month'. The visitation, undertaken with a companion (who need not be a member) was the core duty, the only one to which the members bound themselves, for 'if the Institute were open to have every good work which might spring up from time to time, imposed upon the members, many would be deterred from joining a body, the engagements of which should be so undefined, and the management of which, also, should be liable to so much embarrassment and complication.'[58] In practice individual members gave 'volunteer services' in a wide variety of allied works: 'teaching the ignorant, rescuing the poor from the proselytisers, protecting widows, sending children to school, procuring employment and places for the destitute, bringing absentees to their duty.'[59]

ST MARY'S INDUSTRIAL INSTITUTE, 1853–1855

The visitation of the 'sick poor' in their homes and the distribution of relief orders were certainly of some significance locally, for although Margaret was the first to admit to their smallness she upheld that 'where there is one sick, and one or two earning, it is a little thing that keeps them from the pawn-office.'[60] The launching of St Mary's Industrial Institute in 1853 under the auspices of the Ladies' Association of Charity was a more ambitious effort to tackle the root cause of much local distress. In response to 'the pressing necessities of the Poor' and 'their earnest and oft-repeated entreaties for work, in our constant intercourse with them' Margaret branched into what she termed an 'accessary work of the institute':

> We have taken, for this purpose, the concerns, 5 Upper Dorset-street (late Commins' Coach Factory); the work-rooms are spacious, and capable of accommodating hundreds of workers. At present a large number of persons are employed therein. A Mistress from the north of Ireland has been engaged, who understands the sewed-muslin-work or embroidery in all its branches, to teach the same gratuitously to all who may wish to learn.[61]

This relief project aimed to provide poor women with training and employment. It was an ambitious effort to overcome the huge difficulties faced by these women in securing an adequate wage in an over-supplied, semi-skilled market. These women had 'a decided objection to any eleemosynary relief, if they only had the most scanty earnings for their support'. Domestic service, often residential, was the most usual option, with charring, washing and dealing of various sorts the other principal areas. One young woman left widowed was distraught: 'the Poor-house stared her in the face; few saw any prospect of support for her, for she knew not how to sew or wash'. Home needlework or piecework was a traditional area of employment, but Margaret and her lady visitors knew from their rounds the difficulties that could arise. In one case the daughter 'used to get plain-work from a shop, her landlord having gone security for her; she got a girl to help her with some shirts; in her absence the girl pawned them; some she succeeded in finding, others she had to replace. To do so, she had to sell all their little covering, even the blanket off the old woman's bed.'[62]

The Council of Ireland of St Vincent de Paul contributed the substantial sum of £75 from 1853 to 1854, and various other small sums were solicited to cover the heavy expenses of establishing the institution. As with the sick poor fund, raffles (for pearl earrings, rare Turkish cushions and a silver snuff-box) brought in significant sums.[63]

Skilled needlework was selected, after some research, as the most hopeful area. The initial advertising was most optimistic:

> The *Public* are, doubtless, aware of the extensive earnings afforded in several parts of the country to females of the humbler class, by sewed muslin and other kinds of ornamental needle-work. The demand for work of this kind is unlimited; the employment it affords is capable, consequently, of being indefinitely extended, and the wages it yields to the workers are highly encouraging in all places where it has succeeded.[64]

The greatest obstacle to success was considered to be the attempt 'to combine the work with general education in schools, or to an improper selection of persons, who could not afford time to occupy themselves sufficiently at it.' To ensure success St Mary's will only admit 'such persons as will be free to devote to it *their whole time, and to follow it up as a regular pursuit of industry*.' After three or four months application it was expected that a woman would earn from 2*s*. 6*d*. to 4*s*. per week, 'which of course will increase according to the quality and quantity of work they will be capable of executing by continued practice'. It was also proposed that a pre-school be established in that 'populous neighbourhood' so that mothers 'who are good needle-women' would be free to avail themselves of the work available in the Institute. St Mary's further proposed 'to avail itself, according to opportunity, of every prudent speculation that shall present itself for the advantage of the workers in every kind of employment suitable to females.'[65]

It was hoped that orders 'for work of all kinds, for plain-work, muslin-embroidery, dress-making, knitting, netting, crochet, and quilting' would be sufficiently valuable to allow the Institute to be self-supporting in time. While the wages offered would of necessity be small, the boost to morale was considered as important, increasing self-worth and confidence, and, in tune with current theories of political economy, there was also the attraction of diminishing the demands made on charities:

> The friends of charity may easily calculate what a source of benefit such employment would open up to the Poor. It is not too much to say, that in a population of one thousand poor families, there is one female in each, on average, whose services could be entirely spared from the works and wants of the family. Such a population would therefore, furnish one thousand workers, who, at the rate for instance, of 3*s*. per week each, would earn a total of £150 each week or £7,500 a year! What a sum to distribute amongst the poor of a district; and how much more serviceable to the recipients than if it were given in the way of gratuitous charity![66]

The initial optimism was almost extinguished in the first year, and by 1856 the institute folded up. The reasons it failed are a good indicator of the insurmountable difficulties facing local women who attempted to secure an adequate livelihood by needlework alone. It was a bitter disappointment for Margaret. She enumerated the reasons for the benefit of those who had so generously supported the undertaking: the women who applied to the institute were not experienced, 'consequently the work which could be put into their hands being only improver's work and low priced, we found their attendance irregular and unsatisfactory'. The biggest difficulty, however, was structural:

> The only work to which we could look, was shop-work, and the prices paid for work of all kinds being now so low, we never could hope that the Institute would be self-supporting; on the contrary, it would always require rather a heavy outlay. Add to this, the demand for this kind of made-up goods with the merchants and shopkeepers varying according to the season, caused the supply to be oftentimes uncertain, and insufficient to give full work to all in attendance. The foreign markets, Australia for instance, had an influence on the Institute. If the markets

were dull or overstocked, the work was either withheld altogether, or given in very small quantities.[67]

In an effort to improve the situation the institute confined itself for a while to sewed-muslin embroidery, which was a little more reliable, 'but here, also, we regret, the prices paid by the merchants are too low'. The training or retraining of women, apparently a wise response to the unskilled female labour surplus in Dublin in the 1850s, was here unworkable:

> Whilst children are at school, they should be taught the industrial works, for it is expecting too much to think, that they will sit down patiently to learn, or to improve themselves, with scarcely any remuneration whilst so doing, and no other means of support.[68]

The large gap between the Institute's income and expenses could not continue to be bridged by fundraising, and the venture was wound up.

'INSTRUCTION OF THE IGNORANT'

A further 'accessary work' of the Ladies' Association was the involvement of members in adult catechesis, holding twice-weekly classes in the Church of St Francis Xavier, Upper Gardiner Street, for persons of any parish who cared to attend, mostly preparing adults for the sacraments. The neglect of religious practice among the poor Margaret presented as 'the very cancer of society, the feeder of the poor-house, the prison, and the hospital' yet they are 'good material', there is an 'abiding faith and goodness in the Irish heart which never fails to spring up under the pressure of want of want and sickness'. The adult classes were never well attended, and it was stressed that for adults who had never before learned their prayers or the mysteries of faith it would be necessary to adopt a different approach: 'to go to these poor people, to meet them after their work, and on Sunday evenings and in their courts and alleys, and waste houses, and teach them in threes and fives, then bring them to the church in batches, and set them down beside the priest in the confessional.' Likewise some members undertook the instruction of the First Communion children in the parish schools of St Michan's, with more apparent success.[69]

CAPE CLEAR FUND

While Margaret worked within a well-defined geographical area in Dublin, she did not isolate the association from even more desperate needs elsewhere, 'believing that, according to the spirit of its holy Founder, St Vincent, its services should not be confined to one place or one people, but that they should gladly be rendered in any place where the Poor of Christ are to be served.' In 1853 Fr Henry Leader, parish priest of Rath and the islands of Cape Clear and Sherkin, Co. Cork, made an impassioned appeal for relief for his poor parishioners devastated by successive years of famine, disease and emigration; 'in want of clothing, whole families were unable to leave their wretched homes: the chapel and the schoolhouse were alike neglected.' Fr J. McNamara CM, Phibsboro, brought the case before the Ladies of Charity who undertook the collection of clothing and money, he himself collecting £39 of the £62 in cash which was the final sum contributed. '159 articles of old clothing were received from charitable individuals for this truly meritorious purpose; which, together with 473 articles of new clothing (making a total of 632 articles), were forwarded to the Revd Henry Leader for the poor of that district.' The largest single items in the several bales dispatched to the islands were 150 great coats, 50 capes, and over £20 worth of materials for clothing, all new, and no doubt a considerable addition to the comfort of the parishioners that winter.[70]

CONCLUSION

Margaret Aylward's establishment and leadership of the metropolitan branch of the Ladies of Charity reveal many aspects of her personality. Convinced that Christ is to be served in the poorest and most vulnerable of his brothers and sisters, and frustrated with the lethargy which seemed to paralyse much of the Catholic middle class, she undertook to organise and direct the energies for good which she was convinced existed, despite her own personal 'anxiety of mind and fatigue'.[71] And all this from a newcomer, with only the scantiest knowledge of the metropolis, and few useful contacts to date. The spiritual basis and organisational design of the Ladies of Charity provided her with a solid structure on which to build, entwining both religious and humanitarian values. Her own personal warmth, and considerable ability to inspire and co-ordinate action, were matched by the generosity of those who joined with her, and ventured into the garrets and hovels of their poor neighbours, risking infectious disease and – possibly – misunderstanding and hostility from those they wished to help.

While Margaret's active management of this branch of the Ladies of Charity was to span only ten years, she had founded a local association which continued its work for almost 130 years. It was also important in fostering daughter branches elsewhere. The Kingstown branch which led to the founding by Margaret Aylward (1851) of this metropolitan branch, in its turn led to a new branch (1853) in the parish of St Paul's, Arran Quay, under the superintendence of Dr Yore, PP, and in Cork, 'under the personal care of the Bishop of that diocese'.[72] In January 1857 at a spiritual retreat organised by the metropolitan branch to which 'the different associations of the city and suburbs were invited' more than three hundred ladies attended, from Rathmines, Clontarf, Kingstown, and of course the organizing branch.[73] Other Dublin branches such as Westland Row (1876) were opened in later years. In 1881 Margaret was in correspondence with the parish priest of Portadown, with reference to the establishment of a new branch of the association.[74] The Dublin metropolitan branch was able to look back with satisfaction 'to the help we gave to some of them in their infancy'.[75]

The first-hand contact Margaret experienced through the visitation of the 'sick poor' was the basis for her later works, and most significantly exposed her to the activities of the Protestant missionary societies in the city slums, a campaign with which Margaret was to be increasingly identified for the remainder of her life.

3

Mission Fervour All Round

The family visitation undertaken by Margaret Aylward and her Ladies of Charity alerted them to the extent of English Protestant missionary activity in the Dublin slums, and was accompanied by a systematic campaign of publicizing alleged abuses. An understanding of the role of the evangelical movement in nineteenth-century Ireland is vital to a study of Margaret's life, as religious and denominational considerations dominated public discussion of the state's role in education, childcare, health, and poor relief. It was also the context within which church-sponsored charities drew up their manifestos. The very first published report of the Ladies' Association includes an account of proselytizing schools in the parishes visited, and the report for 1859 contains the first of many 'blacklists' of Protestant charities accused of proselytism. These accounts were based on the evidence of the societies' own published reports as well as field evidence, and designed to 'expose' the nature of their operations, their real motivation, their financial situation, and the names of their major subscribers and active members. For the rest of her life Margaret was regarded as an authority, if not the authority, on this subject.

Among the principal characteristics of the evangelical missionary movement in Ireland are the extensive links with parent organizations in England, the significant role played by wealthy and middle-class women, and the colonial nature of its inspiration. Nineteenth century England, controlling an empire out of all proportion to its own small size and population, felt itself at the centre of the civilized world. Many Englishmen felt that the enormous political and economic power which benefited the mother country also carried with it the obligation of spreading the good news in darkened parts, putting into practice the gospel exhortation to 'go therefore and make disciples of all nations'.[1] The *Classified Guide to London*, 1851, reports that the annual voluntary contributions to all the London societies for the propagation of the Gospel at home and abroad is now nearly £500,000, and exclaims:

> It has been well said, and often quoted by the Christian advocate, that it is England's privilege to teach other nations the way of life.

This enthusiasm for missionary activity involved sending preachers to the most distant parts of Australia, Africa, India, and the West Indies. Some of

the societies undertook the challenge of bringing the good news of the reformation to Ireland with its huge Catholic population, which to date had proved
stubbornly resistant to joining the fold. Dublin with its large population
presented an undeniable challenge:

> Two hundred thousand Roman Catholics! What a mass of souls wandering on in
> ignorance of their danger, rushing on to destruction, and no cry raised to warn
> them of their danger, no hand stretched out to save! *Something* must be done.[2]

The great wave of missionary activity evident in the first decades of the
nineteenth century, and fuelled by Protestant anxiety in the face of Catholic
emancipation (1829), was characterized by the distribution of huge numbers
of bibles and tracts, and the holding of controversial meetings. By mid-century
there was a distinct change in the methods of the societies, reflecting both the
social conditions of the people and their stubborn and deep-rooted resistance
to the former approaches.[3] The increasing wretchedness of the rapidly expanding
and impoverished population culminating in the terrible climax of the great
famine encouraged the societies in a new approach. Combining material aid
with spiritual instruction was seen by many missionaries as eminently Christian,
putting into practice both the gospel command to spread the good news, and
the precepts to feed the hungry and clothe the naked. The term 'proselytize'
– to win over or to convert from one religious faith or sect to another – had
by now become associated in the Irish popular and Catholic press with
accusations of unfair practices, bribery, souperism and colonial exploitation.[4]

IRISH CHURCH MISSIONS TO THE ROMAN CATHOLICS OF IRELAND

The society which Margaret Aylward most vociferously denounced was the
Irish Church Missions (ICM), and associated network of Smyly schools. It
was clearly and openly a missionary society, its object:

> To communicate the Gospel to the Roman Catholics and converts of Ireland by
> any and every means which may be in accordance with the United Church of
> England and Ireland.[5]

Its principles make specific reference to the work of 'controversy', namely
the systematic exposure of the errors of the Catholic faith:

> An open, plain, faithful and affectionate declaration of the gospel of the Holy
> Scriptures, especially shown in contrast with the teachings of Rome.[6]

The society was founded by Alexander Dallas in 1847, with the very active
assistance of two Dublin ladies, Fanny Bellingham and Alicia Mason, who

were already engaged in their own projects 'for the spiritual good of the Irish'. Preliminary efforts to communicate directly with 'Romanists' country-wide without being hindered by 'the jealous watchfulness of their priests' were conducted through the newly established 'penny post'.[7] However, it was the famine holocaust of 1847 which precipitated its formal establishment, when it was claimed, 'the sympathy and succour which rolled over the Channel from Protestant England at this time melted the hearts of the starving Romanists' and made them more receptive to conversion. Among other inducements, a sum of £100,000 was expended in providing the children who attended the mission schools in the famine-stricken regions with food, the type of 'souperism' that was to render the society particularly vulnerable to attack.[8] The society claimed that its funds were 'devoted wholly to spiritual work, and are never expended in temporal relief', and that the view is 'exclusively religious and in no wise mixed with political matters of any kind',[9] yet in practice the society was unable to disengage itself from political controversy or substantial material aid. An appeal in the *Daily Express* to the Orangemen of Ireland just before 12 July 1857, placed by an ICM agent seeking funds for the conversion of the 'poor oppressed Romanists of Ireland', was hardly apolitical; Dr Whately himself complained to the London head-quarters that there was 'nothing more designed to embitter the minds of Roman Catholics against the reception of truth than a connexion with orangeism', but the damage was done.[10]

The question of material aid, which most outraged Catholic and nationalist opinion, and also caused offence among some Established Church adherents, was complicated. Dallas considered the establishment of poor schools and residential homes legitimate 'missionary' activity (*see* Table 1), and arranged, in the case of Dublin, that the Irish Church Missions should take charge of the education department of the work but the material side would be the care of his zealous and very able friend, Mrs Ellen Smyly, and her committee.[11] In the case of the Birds' Nest Home, Kingstown, for example, the teachers were paid by the society, but 'private charity' maintained the children.[12] The provision of schooling of any denomination for the very poorest inevitably necessitated material relief, as the ICM stated:

> The separate collections [for the schools] are devoted to supplying the bodily wants and raising into a state of civilization the poor wanderers. Without such means teaching and schools would be of little avail.[13]

The Irish Church Missions was a highly organized society, governed by a general committee which sat in London, with volunteer committee members and paid officers. More than 80 per cent of its funds were raised in Britain, with volunteer collectors in each region,[14] the total income for 1860 amount-ing to £26,212.17.6.[15] However in the case of Dublin, the schools and homes

1850	Inquiring Class, and Sunday School, St Michan's School Room, Bow Street (ends in 1855) (pre 1854, Mountjoy School, Inquiring Class)
1852	Mission House, 27 Townsend Street, Sunday Ragged Schools
	Mount Brown Sunday School
	Ragged Day School for Boys, 27/53 Townsend Street (then to 167 Townsend Street)
	Ragged Day School for Girls and infants, temporarily in stables rere of Mission House, Townsend Street
	Ragged Boys' School, Grand Canal Street (corner of Grattan Street); also (later) girls' and infants' day school, and sewing class for women, night school for boys
1853	Mission House licensed for Public Service
	Boys' Ragged Schools, firstly in Weavers' Hall, removes to Skinner's Alley, the Coombe 1857
	Ragged Schools, Lurgan Street (near the Barracks)
	Girls' and Infants' Ragged Schools, firstly in Weavers' Hall, in 1854 removed to temporary accommodation in New Row
	Girls' and Infants' Ragged School, 19 Luke Street
	Training School for Female Teachers, 18 Luke Street
1856	Oriel Street, St Thomas's parish
	Irishtown Sunday Schools (closed 1857)
1857	Coombe Schools – new school house
	Ragged Sunday School, Fishamble Street
1858	Boys' Dormitory, 52 Townsend Street
1859	Birds' Nest, 12 York Road, Kingstown (new building 1861); branch home called 'Nead le Farraige' at Spiddal
1861	Grand Canal Street Boys' Dormitory
1861	Luke Street Girls' Dormitory
1868	Boys' Home, Coombe
1870	second Girls' Home in Luke Street
1872	Elliott Home for Waifs and Strays, 167/168/169 Townsend Street (later to Bray, and then to Charlemont Street)
1883	Home for Big Lads, 168 Townsend Street
1888	'Helping Hand' Home, 18 Hawkins Street

Table 1: Irish Church Missions Schools and Homes, Dublin, 1849–1900

had their own separate fundraising networks, with associations throughout Britain, so that the income of the ICM proper does not at all represent the total invested in furthering the aims of the Society. Financial and moral support came from 'British Christians' as far away as India and New Zealand.[16] The society published its own magazines, such as *Erin's Hope*, and the *Banner of Truth* and distributed vast quantities of handbills and literature to both 'inquiring Roman Catholics' and supporters; Margaret Aylward made it her business to collect samples of such literature on an on-going basis.[17] In 1850 between eight and twelve thousand handbills, advertizing the text for the next sermon and controversial class, with study questions, were distributed weekly in Dublin alone, and printed in the daily newspapers, while placards and posters were put up throughout the city.[18]

The ICM attempted to cover the whole country (Figure 5). Its first missionary effort involved dividing the country into four routes, and sending a pair of agents, armed with maps, in each direction, their daily progress to be noted by the postmarks on their reports to headquarters.[19] A proposal in 1859 to reduce the number of mission stations resulted in Dallas's eloquent defence of all the existing stations on geographical grounds:

> A glance at the map will shew at once that the Missions of the Society are placed in a manner calculated to produce a general circulation of knowledge concerning the Reformation movement all over the Island but that the Stations are so far apart that the omission of any one of those now existing would seriously impede that general system of communication. The greatest publicity is given from the prominent post at Dublin, and the chain of communication is kept up to the North by steps from Louth with Kingscourt inland through Forkhill to Antrim. Thence the space is wide to Sligo, but not too wide for current knowledge from one to the other. From Sligo the communication is more immediate through Mayo, (where, though we have given up Balla, yet we continue Hollymount and Bunlahinch) to our great district of West Galway where our work blazes as a beacon on the highlands of that lovely land. Aughrim stands in midway to carry our reports through Kings and Queens Counties by the Portarlington mission to Cork, where from Bandon and Fermoy the intelligence of our operations reaches to Kilkenny, and onward through Borris, to complete the circle of the country in Dublin. It would be a very serious detriment to widen any of these distances by retiring from any of the stations now left to us.[20]

Alexander R.C. Dallas,
Honorary Secretary for Missions, 9 June 1859

In a *Mission Tour Book for Ireland* 1862 Dallas directs the English visitor to the ICM stations to see for himself the fruits of his investment, and to discount criticisms that the missions are failing to make and keep converts. The missions in Borris, Kilkenny, and Portarlington to the south, and Drogheda, Kingscourt, Forkhill and Glens of Antrim to the north, are passed over with the statement that 'in none of them has there yet been matured

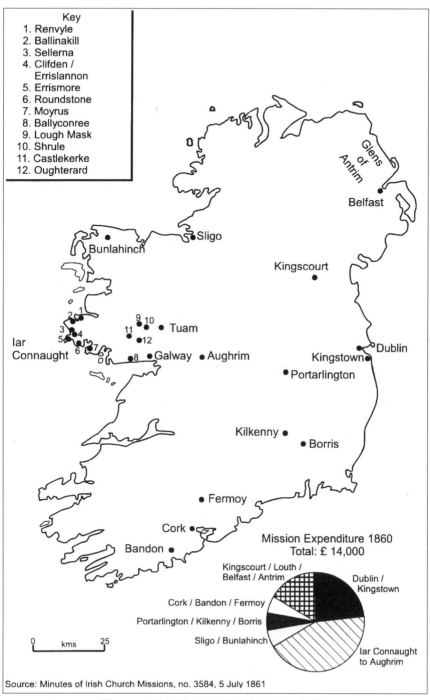

Figure 5: Irish Church Missions, Ireland 1860

such a body of converts as to constitute a separate congregation.'[21] However, in the Galway area 46 centres of activity are listed,[22] while in Dublin the visitor is directed to eight stations.[23] The relative importance of each station to the Society's overall efforts can be mapped for 1860 (*see* Figure 5), based on the proportion of the society's total income that was spent in each area. Funds were expended on the salaries of missionaries, bible readers, school teachers, and the costs of publishing tracts and bible extracts; although this was supplemented by volunteer activity, the total local expenditure is still a fair indicator of the energies devoted to each area. Galway and Dublin emerge as the most important areas of activity.

The minutes of the Irish Church Missions clearly state the importance attached to the Dublin mission:

> The most important missionary station of the Society is Dublin. Here are our Training establishments, our model schools, our largest material to work upon, and our most important machinery. I need say nothing to convince the committee that the Dublin mission with all its accompaniments must beyond doubt be maintained.[24]

Dublin was a locality 'most likely to attract and sustain the interest of all parties', 'offering such promise to missionary labours'[25] and 'may be considered the depôt and arsenal from which our weapons are drawn and where our recruits are trained'.[26] A large house in one of the worst streets of Dublin was purposely sought for the instruction of the poor, to act as headquarters, and as training school for the agents. Significantly, Townsend Street, in the south dock area, met the requirements, and no. 27, one of many tenement houses, was refurbished. The text 'Search the Scriptures' was boldly stretched across the facade. The plan of the new mission church (1853) is indicative of the climate of hostility which the ICM expected, and of their express mission to the poorest: it had two entrances, the main entrance through the Mission House, and another at the back, through Rath Row, for 'the Nicodemuses who came in secret, the poor persecuted ones who wished to be hidden, and the shivering naked poor ones, who clustered round the stove warming their poor bodies, and perchance catching the good news of a home prepared in heaven even for them.'[27]

Within the Dublin diocese most valuable backing came from Archbishop Whately, the Protestant archbishop, who supported the ICM in the face of public attacks, and whose wife and family were very fully involved in the society.[28] Miss Whately, 'the youngest member of a family whose wealth, talents and influence were all consecrated to the service of the church' agreed to sponsor a daily Ragged Mission School in Townsend Street in 1852; her mother undertook to raise the funds to establish the new Mission Church in 1853.[29] The death of Mrs Whately and another daughter Mrs Wale within months of each other in 1860 was regarded as an immense loss, but the youngest daughter continued as one of the ICM's most indefatigable missionaries.[30] The other staunch supporter of the ICM in Dublin was Mrs Ellen Smyly, whose daughters Ellen, Annie and Harriet taught in the schools, while her husband Josiah 'embraced the cause [of the ICM] with his whole heart. He ever stood its firm friend and unwavering supporter.'[31] In 1859 the ICM committee record their thanks to the 'two kind ladies, Mrs J. Smyly and Miss Whately, who have collected £490 to fund the repair and restoration of Townsend Street' headquarters and training establishment.[32] The involvement of very able and fearless women campaigners, each with her own deeply committed co-workers, on either side of a very deep denominational divide, ensured that head-on collision was inevitable; the intransigent Ellen Smyly was to meet with the immovable Margaret Aylward.

The ICM mission schools and homes in Dublin targeted the very poorest Catholics, and were strategically located in the heart of populous districts. The Coombe was considered 'the stronghold of Papal darkness and intolerance', a place of 'squalor and wretchedness', where physical poverty and spiritual destitution went hand in hand.[33] In Townsend Street 'the wildest, and the lowest and the poorest were invited to come in'.[34] Protestations by the society that it never provided food and clothing for the children attending the mission schools, but that 'these charitable adjuncts have always been supplied from private and independent sources'[35] were dismissed out of hand by its critics, and is unlikely to have concerned the persons most concerned, namely the parents who sent their children there. The expansion of the ICM/Smyly network including the take-over of existing mission schools, was another cause for concern; in 1870 the full care of Lurgan Street Ragged Schools was handed over to the ICM, and two years later it assumed responsibility for the Birds' Nest institution (Table 1).[36] The Chancery Lane Dormitory, not an ICM school but also notoriously proselytizing, was granted permission in 1870 to build a refuge for boys on property belonging to the ICM in the Coombe.[37] Although each school had its own committee and published its own report, the same members sat on several committees and only the slightest efforts were made to keep the material and spiritual sides of the enterprises separate.[38] This practice parallels that of all the Catholic charities, including Margaret Aylward's sick poor visitation, and later boarding-out orphanage and poor schools, where 'temporal and spiritual welfare' were intertwined, while the care and education of children was viewed by all the churches as essentially a religious and moral task.

THE DUBLIN VISITING BRANCH OF THE IRISH CHURCH MISSIONS

The Dublin Visiting Mission was established by Fanny Bellingham and Arthur Guinness in 1848, and so predates the ICM.[39] Its first mission district was in Bow Street, near Smithfield, and in the Established Church (Protestant) parish of St Michan's. By February 1850 it had allied itself with the ICM and became one with it, although its funds were administered separately and expended solely on providing visiting agents. Its agents were trained and superintended by Revd C.F. McCarthy, at the ICM mission headquarters at 27 Townsend Street. It described itself as

> an association for sending Town Missionaries into the back streets and lanes of the city – visiting from room to room – not passing by Protestants, but especially seeking out Roman Catholics, teaching them, from their own Bible, the way of Salvation through Jesus Christ.[40]

It maintained 'a band of the best scripture readers' whose function was to 'to go in and out amongst the people, inviting them to schools, classes and services', organized by the ICM, and as 'the connecting link between the teachers and the taught' were considered vital to missionary endeavours.[41] Systematic and frequent visitation was regarded as essential, for 'Ignorant Roman Catholics will not go to the well of life for themselves; we must bring them little tastes of its refreshing waters, and then they will go to the sermons and classes to get more.'[42]

The instruction to 'avoid the giving of temporal relief as not your department of Christian effort, and as interfering with the integrity of your special work' was understandably difficult to observe, the visiting agents reporting how hard it was 'to speak to those in my ward about their souls, whilst their poor bodies are in want of the common necessaries of life'.[43]

The results of such well-ordered visitation were measured in attendance at mission activities, at 'Ragged Schools, Sunday Schools, interesting Discussion Classes and other meetings of different kinds'; general tolerance ('I might almost say their decided appreciation') of the work was also a good sign, but most heartening of all was the 'spasmodic efforts at opposition made by the priests – very earnest for the time, but dying out like a lamp without a supply of oil'.[44]

The Dublin Visiting Branch boasted very publicly of its successes in 'freeing those bound by so many Romish ties' counting among its achievements the number who 'safely passed without the priest's anointing, leaning only on Jesus,' the 'rescue' of Catholic children from Catholic orphanages, and the conversion of little children, who prove to be their best agents, 'they carry their hymns and texts into dark places where there is no other light, and to their playmates they tell the things of which their hearts are full'.[45] The conversion of adults was repeatedly ascribed to the success the ICM had with their children. There can be no doubting the zeal with which this visiting branch followed up possible converts or 'inquiring Romanists', counting up the number of visits which were required before securing entry, so that one agent reports proudly that on his fourteenth attempt to gain admittance to one particular tenement he was met with the greeting, 'There is no standing your boldness; come in and let us hear what you have to say.'[46]

The 'controversial classes' conducted by the Irish Church Missions were attractive for all sorts of reasons: the ICM claimed they were 'the delight of the people who found in them an arena for the display of their powers of argument and ready answers', and were noted for the 'perfect freedom of discussion and equal good humour among all who were present', with 'curious illustrations of Irish humour and glee'.[47] They certainly provided opportunities for repartee and camaraderie, around the comfort of a warm stove, and their prohibition by the Catholic clergy must have contributed to their appeal. Illustrations from 1862 (Figures 6, 7) represent the attraction of the evening classes to a very neglected city population, and the warm reception met by ICM home visitors.

The ICM revelled in open controversy, Alexander Dallas alerting the London committee to 'the importance of active missionary efforts of an aggressive character',[48] sending agents particularly skilled in 'controversial

Figure 6: The Night School, Irish Church Missions (Dallas, 1862)

debate' to follow Catholic missioners around the country, and provide 'counter missions'; the Jesuits, Dominicans and Vincentians all had to compete with ICM preachers from Londonderry to Limerick, from Waterford to Louth.[49] 'The intended visit of Romanist missioners calling themselves Redemptorist Fathers, whose coming was producing much expectation amongst all classes' in the parish of Tinahely, merited three extra experienced readers, 'and special instructions were given to them how to carry on the controversy under the peculiar circumstances'.[50] Cardinal Wiseman's visit to open a new church in Ballinasloe was regarded as deserving of a full week's effort, the ICM arranging to have their efforts covered in the *Record*, *Morning Herald*, and *Standard*.[51] Subscribers who might scruple that such heavy-handed tactics ill befit the gospel message were reminded 'that Rome knows no neutrality. If we are not aggressive towards her, she is aggressive towards us.'[52] Several agents suffered violent attacks and houses were occasionally burned.[53] Publicity was essential, with the ICM constantly inviting persons to visit its centres, and afterwards publishing their reports, if complimentary; the bishop of Rochester and earl of Harrowby were among the dignitaries who thus promoted the ICM.[54]

ROMAN CATHOLIC OPPOSITION

The very publicly-reported successes of the evangelical missionaries alarmed Catholic clergy and charities who felt they were facing unfair competition. Among those Archbishop Cullen circulated seeking details of proselytizing practices were Margaret Aylward and her Ladies of Charity, requesting her to forward him reports of particular Protestant societies 'in which they boast of having Catholic children in their hands',[55] and 'beg [of the Ladies] to keep a watchful eye on the movements of the proselytisers, so anxious to pervert the poor children'.[56] Though loath to claim credit for her own good detective work, she does admit that 'their startling contents failed not to excite his Grace's alarm' and contributed to measures to check its progress.[57]

Cullen responded to the proselytism of the ICM and the Smyly schools, and other such institutions, with great vehemence, declaiming them from the pulpit and in pastorals, and warning Catholics to have nothing to do with them. His personal attacks on these mission agents were vicious:

> Men taken from the dregs of society, colliers, drunkards, profligates, and who to add to their other qualifications, sometimes add that of apostacy from the ancient faith, are not unwilling to have the management of those funds placed in their own hands; and to increase their resources, they boast at every hour of success. Ladies whose age, infirmity, or deformity leaves them little hope of happiness in this world, turning their thoughts to the study of the Bible, pretending to penetrate and

propound its mysteries, as if the interpretation of the most difficult book of all books were a work suited for those who had neither mission nor capacity for so serious a task, such ladies make themselves active emissaries in the work of proselytism.[58]

Others argued in a less offensive but still strenuous way, such as Fanny Taylor, an English Catholic, who claimed that English backing of this movement could only serve to further alienate the Irish:

> Here they see £26,000 sent from England annually, for no other purpose than to try to undo or to mar the efforts of their whole lives. They see ladies and gentlemen, when they find themselves unable to turn the poor man from his faith, bribing him to give up his children to be brought up in one which they must know that in his secret heart he disbelieves, and they see this work wrought by English gold and too often by English hands, supported by noble names, patronized sometimes by the very rulers whom they are bound to respect; and then at the same instant they are told that in England truth and honour are valued beyond all other possessions. The latter assertion must seem to them a mockery, and the whole proceeding must tend, and does tend, to estrange them from a country from which they have a right to expect better treatment.[59]

The Catholic periodical *The Month* claimed that fraud and hypocrisy were its chief features:

Figure 7: The Scripture Reader, Irish Church Missions (Dallas, 1862)

In Ireland many can tell of the very prices given to starving relations to surrender their children, of Protestants paid to personate Catholics and be defeated in controversy, of Protestants being refused relief when they asked for it, as Protestants, and getting it at once, with a bundle of tracts, when they applied for it as 'enquiring' Romanists.[60]

The ICM was not in the least daunted by the viciousness of the attacks, quoting considerable extracts from Cullen's declamatory pastorals and various letters from the Catholic newspaper, the *Freeman's Journal*, to illustrate the extent of the opposition it faced, and how deserving it therefore was of Protestant support. It prided itself on having awoken the 'slumbering sentinels' of the Catholic church, and hailed the publication of a cheap Catholic edition of the Bible as a triumph for the Protestant faith.[61] Catholic efforts to keep their children from attending ICM schools were ridiculed:

> Dr Cullen's new organization is in full force. Priests, nuns, shopkeepers and even coal-men go through the streets and lanes inquiring of every person where they send their children, and where they go themselves.[62]

St Brigid's Orphanage (chapter 4) and the Society of St Vincent de Paul are singled out for special mention, as one of the reasons for their foundation was to counteract the work of the ICM.[63]

LADIES OF CHARITY ANTI-PROSELYTIZING DEPARTMENT

Margaret Aylward's first encounter with the well-organized Protestant missionary societies was undoubtedly during her apprenticeship as a Lady of Charity in Kingstown, one of the first ICM mission areas.[64] Her first documented experience was in the parish of St Mary's, where the Ladies of Charity became quite well informed of the energy the local bible-readers spent on visiting the very houses that they themselves visited. One ruined tenement was so full of holes that 'when the bible-readers were engaged with some of the miserable occupiers below stairs, they could be heard distinctly above; and when the ladies read or prayed with the sick woman, there were, unknown to them, attentive listeners on high.'[65] In the first year of operations the ladies of the 'anti-proselytizing department' organized a fact-finding mission throughout the city. At first Margaret 'divided into districts the portion of the city over which our concern extends'; later the ladies were to investigate the situation in Townsend Street and the Coombe.

> To each district we appointed two members, to find out the children therein going to proselytizing schools. We sought to induce the parents to remove them, and send them to Catholic schools. We moreover, kept a register of their names, with

notes of the schools to which they were sent. We occasionally visited these schools, in order to see the attendance of the children, and we sought to secure their permanent attendance, by promises of clothes, which we distributed at Christmas and Easter. Our endeavours in this department realized discoveries of a fearfully extended and active organization of the perversion of the children of the Catholic poor.[66]

Fragments of some of these lists survive.[67] The parents repeatedly claimed they had been assured that 'the children's religion was not meddled with' and protested that 'there is nothing else to keep them out of the poor-house'; both the published evidence and field research confirmed that whatever undertakings might have been given, the undermining of Catholicism was a central tenet.[68] The Association set up a small but separate 'anti-proselytizing fund' to cover children's clothing, school books and, in 1851, the publication of anti-proselytizing pamphlets.[69] Her analysis of the situation is characteristically forthright:

> It is the poor and the helpless and the innocent that are attacked by the enemies of their faith. It is base, it is cowardly. Why doesn't Dr Whately or Mr McCarthy go to some of our Catholic judges or to some of our Catholic nobility and ask them for their children? But they go or send their agents to the poor widow who has pawned her last article of dress and while the hunger cry of her infant is rending her heart they say 'we will take your children, and educate them and raise them in the world, and we will procure a situation for yourself and to prepare you for it we will send you to the Providence Home'.[70]

The early fact-finding excursions very rapidly became open warfare, with the zealous Ladies of Charity actively involved in removing Catholic children from Protestant institutions, and equally zealous Protestant missionaries determined to persevere in their evangelizing activity.

Margaret Aylward and her friends picketed the Sunday schools where 'crowds of unhappy Catholics, men, and women, were to be found, lured by the offer of a small cut of bread, and then obliged in return to listen to blasphemous language, and a sermon from a minister'.[71] The Ladies failed to gain admission to Lower Rutland Street, but 'witnessed, however, quite enough to establish the fact of the chief part of the school being baptized Catholics'.[72] Outside Lurgan Street Sunday School Miss O'Reilly and Margaret 'entered several names – they thought we wanted needlewomen &c. It was not a very pleasant office, we were surrounded by a wretched crowd in a short time.'[73] To ensure there were no inaccuracies in her list Margaret later visited several of the homes, and reports on the appalling conditions. She assigns starvation as the reason for attendance at this Sunday school. Outside another ICM school, the Coombe, several poor women came to give them their name, address and religion, 'in the hope that they could get them employment'.[74] There are reports of children being dragged away by the school mistresses to prevent them being interviewed by the Ladies of Charity, of the Catholic ladies distributing crucifixes among the children, to the 'ineffable contempt' of certain Protestant missionaries who accused them of handing out 'idols', of crowds of Dublin men, women, and children assembling to join in the excitement, urging on the disputing parties with cries of 'more power to you!'[75] Nothing daunted, the ladies persevered. 'The disagreeable labour of watching these schools, of pursuing the poor children through the windings of the wretched lanes and courts, of breaking through the excuses, equivocations, and lies of the infatuated parents, was cheerfully endured by them.'[76] On several occasions the police were called, and names taken. In the Coombe one police man was pressurized by the Protestant superintendent to 'make a clean job of it, man, and take them to the station-house', while crowds of bystanders gathered protesting 'shame on you, to speak so to ladies!' and calling out derisively 'who charges her and with what?' Ignoring the police request to await the arrival of their sergeant ('their business not being either with the sergeant or the force, they continued their way'), a critical point was reached:

> The crowd poured out benedictions, a body guard surrounded them, declaring they would protect them while the sky was over them. They expressed a wish for a car; a boy flew, apparently with winged feet, to get one for them, and still the poor Souper appeared not satisfied, and at the car, he stood waving his hand after those who entered it.[77]

This particular Coombe incident spurred the ladies on to greater efforts, even more members volunteering to watch the ICM school in Townsend Street the following Sunday; on this occasion the ladies stood aside, 'quietly entering the names' while the 'wretched hired apostles' rushed out in a frenzy, powerless to prevent the inspection in the face of another protective assembly.[78]

The acrimonious exchanges between the Ladies of Charity and the agents of the Irish Church Missions came to a very public head in March 1859, when both organizations held their annual fundraising bazaars on the same day in the Rotunda Rooms, Rutland Square. The 'ragged devices of the Townsend Street folk', whereby the ICM picketed the entrance to the Ladies of Charity bazaar, redirecting some of the Ladies' supporters into their own opposing camp and refusing to refund entrance money, caused uproar.[79]

Accounts of the 'battles' fought by the Ladies of Charity for the souls of the Catholic poor were included in the annual reports of the Ladies' Association by Margaret Aylward for the purposes of generating moral support and attracting recruits and finances to the branch. It was a commonplace tactic in mid-nineteenth-century Dublin to emphasize the exceptional efforts being made by the opposing denomination, and hence the necessity to counteract them by providing a similar or superior service; in the case of the ICM the flow of funds from English support groups could only be enhanced by exciting accounts of the challenge the mission faced.[80]

However, Margaret's writings must not be understood as solely or even principally for propaganda purposes. She held an unshakeable conviction of the value of faith, a priceless treasure 'compared with which, this whole world, nay a thousand worlds, would not weigh as a grain of sand'.[81] Following directly from that conviction, talk without action infuriated her, as she confided to a friend in Rome: 'Our good archbishop has written again and again about it, but *writing* alone will *not* do. To put it down an effective organization is necessary.'[82] She challenged her fellow Catholics at the annual meetings of the Ladies' Association to emulate the commitment and good organization of the ICM:

> Could not we have our own auxiliaries and agents and correspondents also? We say this not complainingly, but it is manifest that with half the amount of organized action and a thousandth part of their income, we could save all our children that are in danger of loss of faith.[83]

So too Margaret claimed some shame attached to Catholics 'for not voting Catholics into such places of trust as poor law guardianships' but leaving the control of, for example, the South Dublin Union in almost exclusively Protestant hands.[84] To Margaret the only solution was clear: the provision, by the Catholic community, of free schooling with associated food, clothing and family relief in the poorest areas, already targeted by the ICM, and the provision of substantially more residential or foster care places for the many children in need of such services, either temporarily or permanently. She had her agenda for action.

4

Shoulders to the Wheel

The evil Exists. <u>AND to a great extent</u>. Let us look at it boldly, but let us be prepared to put our shoulders to the wheel to remedy it.[1]

Residential child care for Catholic children was the most urgent requirement in mid nineteenth-century Dublin. Of this Margaret Aylward was convinced, having seen for herself both north and south of the Liffey the widespread destitution which left orphaned, abandoned and neglected children most vulnerable to manipulation by proselytizing missions. But the type of child care envisioned could not be the kind of enclosed, institutional regime which Margaret herself found so distasteful. Nothing could replace the warmth of the family circle, so that the system formulated was based on 'outdoor' or 'family rearing'. This was the founding principle of St Brigid's Orphanage, one which would require constant defence against the sceptics who claimed that it just could not be done.

But the decision to embark on such a radical project had not been made alone. Fr John Gowan as a young diocesan priest had spent the famine years working in the isolated parish of Glendalough, Co. Wicklow; on return visits in the 1860s he speaks movingly of the spectral landscape, roofless cabins where he had formerly christened the children and visited the sick and now, 'not a soul to be seen, scarcely a house standing, only one plough in six long Irish miles, no whistle, no laugh in the fields, all was silent as the grave.'[2] On joining the Vincentian community he had worked with parish mission teams throughout Ireland and among poor Irish immigrants in Britain; first-hand familiarity with the faith and family warmth of the poor cottager class, the well-funded country-wide Protestant proselytizing machine, and the heartbreak of emigration were to fuel his zeal for St Brigid's mission.[3]

The boarding-out orphanage was in essence a collaborative venture: while Margaret Aylward both founded and managed the institution, she was the first to credit John Gowan with guiding and directing her in this work, noting that its success 'is in a great degree attributable to him with God's blessing.'[4] The compilation of the annual published reports illustrates this point exactly: Margaret Aylward was presumed by close contemporaries, such as John Curtis SJ, to be the author and the work was certainly within her competence, as evidenced from the Ladies of Charity reports.[5] John Gowan CM however was responsible for formulating some of its philosophy and for certain lengthy nationalistic sections.[6] On at least one occasion he forwards draft sections to Margaret for her to edit, with requests that their loyal co-worker Ada Allingham send him on some of her register entries for inclusion as case studies.[7] The team-work aspect is what matters; the vision of the 'lady manager' cannot easily be detached from that of the institute's 'spiritual director', while there were other key individuals contributing to policy formulation and execution, such as the aforementioned Ada Allingham, who devoted herself to the charity from 1861. Mrs Marianne Scully, who signed formal documents as 'Agnes Mary Scully', was one of the founding committee of the Ladies of Charity and later titled 'first secretary'; in a letter accompanying subscriptions to the orphanage after her death, her daughter speaks of her as 'co-founder of St Brigid's' with Margaret Aylward.[8] Mrs Frances Murray, also of that founding group and treasurer until her untimely death in 1861, certainly merits similar recognition. But however good the crew, someone has to take the helm; in this case it was Miss Aylward who set the course, and took the consequences.

In the work of St Brigid's Margaret displays immense courage, creativity and organizational skill. She could see no advantage in tackling what was a drastic situation with 'a pennyworth of plaster', and from its foundation set

Figure 8: *St Brigid's Orphanage Report* 1907, frontispiece

an ambitious target: St Brigid's 'would not stop till five hundred children had been saved' for 'to grapple with the evil a small orphanage would be of little value.' Dr Cullen, despite his public denunciations of child proselytism, baulked at the scale of her project and refused permission, 'he saw what appeared a rash undertaking, an immense orphanage to be founded, depending almost entirely on an invalid who might at any moment be struck down by sickness, and in that case the whole responsibility falling upon him.'[9] Her stubborn attachment to the boarding-out system, which could not be as closely monitored as the traditional institution, did not help. Reading the church power structures very accurately, she knew that without the approbation of the diocesan clergy the project would collapse at the outset. The backing of the priests was vital for the assessment of suitable cases, the collection of funds and the creation of a climate of support. Through continued pressure Margaret received the necessary approbation, and on 1 January 1857 the first child was received. Two more children were accepted in May, and then an extraordinary demand was made upon the fledgling institution.

The law decreed that all children presented for admission to the work-house, the religion of whose parents was unknown, should be reared in the Established Church, a ruling which caused immense bitterness among the Catholic citizenry. It was obvious that the proportion of non-Catholic children among the foundlings of the city was negligible, and the taxing of the Catholic community for the support of the Protestant minister, and the 'perversion' of the abandoned Catholic infants of the city was a major grievance. The local Protestant vestry had traditionally the charge of providing for children found destitute or abandoned within its parish boundaries; in practice it was impossible to provide sufficient Protestant nurses for these infants, and in one particular instance thirty-seven young children had been left in the care of Catholic nurses, who had taken matters into their own hands and had the children baptized Catholics.[10] The time had now come when they were to be brought to the South Dublin Union to be registered as Protestants, as the families were too poor to undertake their care without state assistance.

> St Brigid's was, at this time, still in its infancy, without funds, character, or credit, still willing to take charge of the thirty-seven children. But the nurses knew not St Brigid's, and how could they trust that payment would be forthcoming from the Orphanage? In this difficulty, the Parish Priest of St Nicholas', Francis Street [Canon McCabe], stood in the gap and saved the children. He sent for the country people, who were having some refreshment in the inns about Francis Street after their long journey, before bringing the Children to the poorhouse, pledged his word that St Brigid would not fail to pay them every half year, and induced them to return home with their charge. The Priest's word was kept, the Orphanage did not fail to pay, and all these children were reared Catholics.[11]

These '*enfants trouvés*, the poor deserted tho' innocent children' were accepted by St Brigid's as, its managers claimed, no other Catholic institution in the city existed which could admit them.[12]

To be fair to Paul Cullen, once the orphanage was established he backed Margaret entirely, granting St Brigid's his special approbation in 1859, and urging the clergy and 'the good ladies of the city' especially 'to associate and work under the banner of St Brigid for our holy Faith.' He invited the city's Confraternity men to work on behalf of St Brigid's, placing an awesome responsibility before them: 'Out of the Catholic Church they may obtain trades, secular knowledge, riches, power, but not everlasting salvation.'[13]

ADMISSIONS POLICY

The arrival of the thirty-seven Wicklow orphans was exceptional; most children were admitted singly or in twos and threes, often with young brothers and sisters. Applications were made 'from clergymen, communities, societies and from the poor themselves, who come to the door without any recommendation' but Margaret insisted that the managers (herself, Ada Allingham and John Gowan) be left free to make their own investigations and decide whom to admit, pointedly thanking the friends of the charity 'very sincerely, for leaving us at liberty to accept or reject the cases which they sometimes presented'. Children were directed to the institution by a great diversity of persons, including nuns such as Mother Rose, the Mercy sister who ran St Joseph's Night Asylum, Sr Mary Stanislaus, a Dominican sister in Cabra, and Sr Josephine Virien, the first manager of the Daughters of Charity orphanage in North William Street, with which community Margaret had a long and complex involvement (see Chapter 5).[14] The Vincent de Paul Society, including the Belfast branch, was another source of recommendations, along with employers, fellow employees, and local clergy. Pressure from individual clergy to receive particular cases could be immense, and led to bitter and generally unreasonable criticism by some priests.[15]

Only children baptized as Catholics could be received ('the greater number having had both parents Catholic'), and 'the outcast, lying in its blood, naked often and sick', most obviously 'in danger of loss of faith' and in great material need, was to be taken in preference to the child with funds, for whom provision could safely be made in other Catholic institutions.[16] 'The Orphan and destitute child upon whom the double calamity of physical and spiritual destitution has fallen' was regarded as the 'special object of St Brigid's Charity'.[17]

Although based in Dublin, St Brigid's advertized itself as truly an all-Ireland charity, receiving 'a considerable number' of children directly from other counties, and even Britain, while those with Dublin addresses were often newly arrived in the metropolis, 'their poor parents, unable to live at home, or perhaps, uprooted from that home of their childhood and their affections, drag their weary bones to Dublin', where 'flung to wither in the pestilential courtyards of this city', they die 'and leave us their orphans'.[18]

St Brigid's would receive only those who could not be cared for among their relatives, convinced that 'the separation of parent and child is one of the greatest social evils, and that in all cases where it is possible, the parent ought to support and bring up his own child.'[19]

> Do not advise poor widows or widowers to put their children into any Orphanage; two evils arise from this: society is injured by weakening or dissolving family ties, and the poor parent loses the support of the child in old age, for children reared in Orphanages do not usually feel the obligation of supporting their parents. When both parents die it is better to provide for them among their uncles or aunts, for thus they will grow up in their own families, and help them in their old age. By following these directions Catholic Orphanages will be relieved of undue pressure, and a greater number of children will be saved.[20]

While strenuous efforts were made to secure some financial support for individual children, for example from a well-to-do lady who had taken an interest in a particular child's fate, or from guildsmen seeking admission for one of their local 'cases', or from surviving relatives, 'no one has been denied admission merely for want of money, and in fact ninety per cent have not and do not pay.'[21] The register entries are punctuated with notes such as 'mother in great poverty', 'wretchedly poor', 'in great distress', 'starving', 'very badly off and bad health' and occasionally 'all fearfully wild and neglected'.

Margaret took great pride in the fact that St Brigid's never refused a child on the basis of poor health or disability. Considering that 'Some have come to us all covered with sores and filth; a great many were weak and sickly', some even 'in a dying state', the low mortality was remarkable, and due credit heaped on the foster mothers involved.[22] In direct competition with the Protestant Orphan Union (which targeted the orphans of inter-denominational marriages), St Brigid's was quick to point out that the admission paper of their competitors directed the attention of medical practitioners to 'the necessity of careful examination of every child presented to them, in order to prevent children being received who would prove a burden to the society.' A more significant restraint on the numbers St Brigid's could admit was the level of funding: in 1866 the number of applications was 'totally beyond the means of the Institution to receive or accommodate', and in the report for 1877 it is made clear that children are only received 'to the extent that there is a fair prospect of meeting the debt'.[23] Table 2 illustrates the correlation between the number of children accepted and the number taken 'off the books' in any one

Number of Children

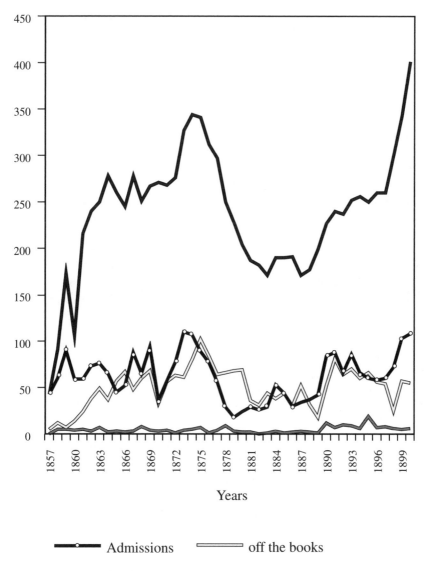

Years

Table 2: St Brigid's Orphanage, 1857–1900

year.[24] A peak of 110 children was received in 1873, which was followed over the next six years by fewer admissions, while the numbers 'off the books' is consistently higher in the period 1875–83. In 1879 only eighteen children were accepted, the smallest number admitted in the period under review, but it already had responsibility for 263. A year of 'calamity and distress the Orphan has, to some extent, shared in the general depression'; without funds many were refused, 'lest the whole work should collapse'.[25]

The admission of foundlings was always characteristic of the institution, although the number was small relative to the overall figures. Nevertheless, the abandonment of infants was a feature of Dublin poverty in the 1850s, the situation facing young unmarried mothers being especially pitiable. Under English law (from 1844) a father could be compelled to pay maintenance money for the support of his illegitimate offspring, which in 1872 was fixed at five shillings per week, and could extend up to 16 years of age. While this failed to provide satisfactorily for unmarried mothers in England, it was still well in advance of the situation in Ireland, where more restrictive legislation 'exonerated the reputed father from punishment or contribution', effectively leaving only poor law guardians the power to sue the father, and then only in respect of destitute and pauper children, whose maintenance would otherwise fall totally on the rates.[26] The care of children born outside marriage was therefore in law the sole charge of the mother, excepting only where she 'burdened' the poor law union with their maintenance. The case of a five-week old infant admitted in November 1858 is typical, and illustrates the urgent need that existed for child care and parental support:

> Mother's name Byrne – this child was left in a wad of straw in the middle of the road – child was born in the Coombe Lying-In Hospital. Mother was found and prosecuted – refused to take the child, said she could not support it – appeared almost dying.[27]

Margaret gave foundling children admitted to St Brigid's whose parents remained unknown the surname 'Vincent' after St Vincent de Paul, a marked improvement on the contemporary Dublin practice of naming such children after the street or church door at which they were found.

With its avowed aim of rescuing children from the clutches of proselytizing institutions, Margaret actively involved St Brigid's in controversy from the outset. Register entries include information on the movements of zealous Protestant missionaries, such as Mrs Ellen Smyly who had shown great anxiety about the two children of Matilda Geraghty, now 'leading a bad life' in Mabbot Street. When Ms Geraghty was operating as a prostitute from an 'improper house' in North William street, 'Mrs Smyly called on her in her own carriage', offered her '£5 for the two children, and 8s. a week to turn Protestant', at least according to Margaret's summary.[28] Mrs Smyly, and her co-workers, it was claimed, regularly made offers to poor women of childcare and schooling, of training and employment, on the understanding that they would adopt the Protestant tradition. Once accepted, it was most difficult to extricate oneself from the situation, as for example the Smyly homes sought to be refunded for the cost of childcare if a child was removed by a Catholic parent or other relative.[29] The nature of these claims, and the names and addresses of all involved, are carefully noted, and corroborate the public disclosures made by Margaret Aylward and other Roman Catholic activists of an extensive campaign of proselytism among the poorest and most vulnerable, namely destitute parents unable to provide for their children. It is also certain that threats of handing a child over to Protestant individuals or institutions were used to try and force St Brigid's to admit children. William Kealy's mother, now remarried to a soldier in Dover, abandoned her child to its aunt, with the instruction that it could go to a Mrs Lish of 13 Pembroke Road, 'who will bring him up a Protestant or else to do what they please with him.'[30]

As Margaret was so thoroughly acquainted with the methods of the English evangelical missions, the substantial means at their disposal, and considering the prize at stake – nothing less than eternal salvation – it is not surprising that she took what could be termed a highly pro-active stance. In this she was joined by other Roman Catholic activists, who though not formally part of her charity networks regarded St Brigid's as a safe asylum for Catholic children 'in danger of loss of faith'. The standard register details of date of admission, register number, name, age, parents' details, residence, contact addresses, and place of child's baptism, are often supplemented by detailed notes on the circumstances which led to the child's admission. One recurring theme is the parent's or guardian's acute poverty and the consequent likelihood of being 'protestantized'; in the case of Robert de Gud, rescue from such a fate required rapid action, and is one of the more dramatic and lengthy entries in the orphan register. The father, who was 'old and sickly' was confined in Simpson's hospital when his child was 'stolen' by Protestant relatives. The police were summoned, to no avail. A legal guardian was appointed, and with the father visited the child. The register entry continues in breathless fashion: this gentleman

> 'took the child in his arms to caress him with becoming affection and darted like a lightening flash with the hatless child in his arms out of the shop (seeing this the shortest way to win *Habeas Corpus Acts*, summonsed to save the child) running with him as far as his speed would allow a long distance then having a car, he drove as hard as he could and deposited his charge at St Bridget's, in the good saint's care.'

The father died shortly after, 'the exertion of saving the child &c was too much for him.'[31] Although such dramatic 'rescues' were the exception rather than the rule, Margaret clearly approved of placing all one's energies and ingenuity, even cunning, at the service of preserving the faith of Catholic children, and was ready to support those who took bold (but still legal) steps to that end.

BOARDING-OUT POLICY

The 'boarding-out' system of rearing young deserted children in families had been greatly discredited under the Dublin Foundling Hospital (1703–1838). Repeated parliamentary investigations in the eighteenth and early nineteenth century exposed scandalous neglect and excessive mortality among the infants, the destitution of the foster-mothers and the irregularity of their payment, the disinterest of the governors, and a failure to keep correct records so that thousands of children were quite simply unaccounted for.[32] With the passing of the Poor Law (Ireland) Act of 1838 responsibility for deserted and destitute children became the charge of the poorhouse, which in its turn attempted to have children under two years of age nursed by country mothers, but was initially very reluctant to allow older children this advantage.

The relative merits and demerits of boarding out charity children was a major topic of public debate throughout the British Isles, one which involved financial considerations as well as human welfare, since the level of poor law rates and the disbursement of these funds interested every rate payer to some extent.[33] The mortality of young children committed to the workhouse was repeatedly exposed as scandalous. At a meeting of the North Dublin Union in 1857 a resolution was passed requesting the police commissioners, who were seeking admission for a number of foundlings in their care, 'to have the children kept for the present, as it would be nearly certain death to receive them into this house.'[34] But there was also the serious question as to whether a sufficient number of good homes could be found for all those in need of childcare.

St Brigid's constantly and very publicly compared its system with that of the poor law union, stating for example that the mortality rate among children under seven years of age in the workhouse was 60 per cent, while St Brigid's, despite accepting sick children, could boast a rate of under 12 per cent.[35] The children who survived to seven years of age in the workhouse then risked 'scrofula, ophthalmia and pulmonary complaints' and were 'spiritless, dwarfed and prematurely old.' St Brigid's children, on the contrary, were 'playing and bounding in the green fields, the limbs lithe, the chest expanded and the rose in the cheek.'[36] The passing of the Poor Law Amendment Act 1862 allowed boards of guardians to board out orphan and deserted workhouse children up to five years of age. St Brigid's played a significant role in enabling the union to take advantage of this relaxation in the iron prescriptions of the poor law, accepting the charge of fifty-eight children aged 1–2 years in the year 1869 alone.[37] The foster care of these children was not in any way exceptional: they were nursed in families which had either previously nursed St Brigid's children, or were located in an area where some children were already at nurse. However, for final destination, 'restored to guardians' or 'dead' are the only entries.

St Brigid's well-publicized abhorrence of the workhouse system did not prevent it from co-operating with the poor law guardians where it could benefit children. However, Margaret relentlessly pressed on for what was generally termed 'the family system of rearing children, adopted in its entirety, for the entire of the natural limit of guardianship by nurture – fourteen years.'[38] Progress was made slowly but steadily, so that by 1869 workhouse children could be boarded-out up to ten years of age, at which stage the child had to be returned to the workhouse, if not retained without further payment, by the foster parents.[39] The debate concerning the relative merits of boarding-out and indoor rearing, and the associated matters of industrial and reformatory schools, continued throughout the 1880s and 1890s.[40] By this time St Brigid's had been in operation over twenty years, and was regularly held up as a model institution, on both sides of the Irish Sea.

Margaret Aylward's system of 'family rearing' was comprehensive and closely regulated, and within a few years on a scale far larger than that of any of the other orphan societies based in Dublin and operating this system, such as the Protestant Orphan Society and the Presbyterian Orphan Society. As it differed radically from the institutional orphanages already established and the temporary outdoor childcare system operated by the Birds' Nest,[41] it was necessary to publicize in some detail the characteristics of the system she had created. Because of its reliance on voluntary subscriptions it was vital that the public were fully aware of how well conducted a charity St Brigid's was. This was achieved through the annual meetings and published reports, which give the official statistics, outline and expand on the Institution's philosophy, list subscribers of over 10s. and serve as advertising material. Other means of publicizing its policies were charity sermons, letters to the newspapers, and the personal recommendation of many friends of the institution, including many clergy. The unpublished orphanage materials, in particular an orphan notebook for 1874–75, record the day-to-day management of the institute.[42] Ada Allingham, who was to prove the most loyal of Margaret's early women co-workers and saw to a huge amount of the orphanage administration, wrote in queries as they arose, and Margaret entered brief replies. Commitment to 'family rearing' was its guiding vision, and was reiterated in countless ways:

> The chief hope of this system is that the children are reared in family. God has been pleased to make this arrangement for (we may say) the whole human race, and so it must be good. Indeed, it is hard to compensate for the loss of a father's protection, a mother's love, and the endearments of a family circle.[43]

This system had also the advantage of rearing boys and girls together, 'a happiness nearly impossible to us in any other arrangement'.[44] The primary requirement was good 'nurses' or foster mothers, recommended in writing by the local clergy (or by another nurse), and willing to 'act towards St Brigid's children as if they were her own and be a true mother to them'.[45] 'They are all small farmers, except one, all in possession of more or less land, with a greater or less stock of cows.'[46] The earliest register entries detail the family and economic circumstances of each nurse, for example, 'Nurse Mrs Anne McEvoy, sister to Mrs Carroll, Ballintubber; 4 cows, 4 acres & ½ inside land, 3 young cattle, ass; 5 boys & a girl; Kylebeg, Blessington; recomd. by Mrs McCreedy.'[47] The supply of milk for St Brigid's children was an important consideration hence the preference given to families with even one cow, while there was a constant struggle to prevent the children from being fostered by the very poorest families where it was inevitable that St Brigid's money would be thinly spread maintaining both existing and foster children. And as these were the families most anxious to board children it was not at all a simple matter.

Rough notes from Margaret to Ada illustrate the day to day struggles in the placement and maintenance of individual children. Although St Brigid's was to become by far the largest boarding-out charity in the country, it was neither the first nor the only source of nurse children. Mrs Leahy of Saggard who had adopted one of St Brigid's children 'wants to know will she get any more children as if not she wishes to apply elsewhere.'[48] 'No definite time or promise' is the response, but other replies were more emphatic: 'don't give any child to Mrs Crawley – she is poor – nor to Mrs McNally, one is if possible too much for either. Forget Casey altogether for the present, I do not think well to give her a child.'[49] Families with a foster child generally recommended others, but they had to meet Miss Aylward's exacting standards first. John Lacken of Blessington was asked to send up a nurse for an infant, but warned 'not to send any person with whom a child died – or from whom a child was removed or any one that I find fault with' and in particular not to dare send his daughter, as the child she had minded returned with fleas '& I will remove every child who is not perfectly clean'.[50] Close supervision of the families tried to ensure the children were well cared for, with 'unannounced visits that the lady visitor might see everything in their real, everyday state' for 'then there can be no making up'.[51] The principal control however was through twice annual general inspections, the award of premiums, the fining or withholding of the nurse's money in cases of neglect, and the removal of children to other nurses.[52]

The orphanage's ability, within its first three years, to attract 'a superior class' of foster parents[53] was important to its success, as was the fact that

> There is always a large demand for our Orphans and this places it in our power to select the most competent and the most painstaking, and thus, every year, the less competent are cast aside, and in this way it becomes obvious to the country people that there is no means of securing our patronage but by constant attention to the Orphans.[54]

The institution made every effort to pay the nurses on time and maintain its good standing, 'for it is of great importance for if they once began to think that we were failing them there would be no end to the trouble with them.'[55] The financial commitments weighed heavily; by 1886 Margaret writes that 'the orphans are so numerous, about 200, and the payments are so heavy' that much more than £500 is now required to make the half yearly payments to St Brigid's 'little colonies'.[56] It could not serve those for whom it was intended if its resources were imposed upon unfairly, and much time had to be spent following up promised sums of money which were not forthcoming: 'Tell Mrs Donnelly that Miss Aylward has been paying this long time for the support of her child & that she has directed you to write and tell her that you want to speak to her – she I suppose could not support it but something she must give – How long is Norbert in, how much money has been paid and when?'[57] The occasional opportunity of securing substantial sums of money was not to be by-passed; a wealthy man from Co. Dublin fathered an illegitimate infant and wished to have it placed quietly in St Brigid's; on enquiring how much the orphanage would require of him Margaret writes: '£100 or how much could he pay?'[58]

RURAL LOCATIONS

The popular vision of the city slums as nests of infamy and disease was shared by Margaret Aylward, based on extensive first-hand knowledge of cellar and attic dwellings. With straw for beds and little beyond a dirty rug or great-coat for covering, she was in no doubt that whatever the patient resignation and deep faith of the Dublin poor, their home environments were not conducive to physical or moral health. These particular children, many of whom on admission were 'weak, pale, emaciated, diseased full of sores' having spent their infancy 'in the courts and back lanes of the city, at the rears of which quantities of organic matter are allowed to accumulate, and putrefy, and infect the atmosphere'[59] needed 'healthy' locations, a requirement which was understood in both medical and moral terms:

> The children are reared at a distance from large towns, in isolated country places, where there is the least amount of vice, and the least amount of danger of contamination. The children are located likewise in small groups, four being the

largest number in any one house, and this only in three or four cases, where
usually the nurses have no children of their own, and where they have proved
themselves capable of taking great care of them.[60]

In case of epidemic, either physical or moral, their isolation in very small bodies
is a happy security.[61]

Scattered over an area of four counties the managers can choose between
the 'seaboard, the hillside, the glen and the plain' and if a child does not
thrive in one locality, it can easily be transferred to another.[62]

During the period 1868–74 the orphanage accepted between 64 and 100
new children annually, and had an average of 292 in its care at any one time.
Analysis of the orphan register and payment notebooks reveal a well-defined
geographical spread (Figure 9).[63] There were two distinct settlements in north
county Dublin, focusing on Swords and Cloghran, with the children largely
concentrated in adjoining townlands: St Doulagh's, Rathangle, Lispapple,
Springhill, Rahulk, and Middleton. To the west, on the county border with
Kildare, were similar colonies in Celbridge, Hazelhatch, Newcastle and
Rathcoole, continuing to the border with County Wicklow at Brittas. Saggard
was the focus of one of the largest groupings, stretching southwards to
Ballinascorney, and including Slade, Royal Garter, Boherboy, and Crooksling,
which was later to be noted for its TB sanatorium. The valley of Glenasmole,
south of Tallaght, was another important concentration of St Brigid's nurse
children. This was a particularly remote area, quite self-contained both
physically and socially in the nineteenth century, and considered ideal for child
rearing. William Nolan's geographical study of this valley reveals close knit
kinship groups, the careful control of subdivision so that individual tenancies
were viable, and the labour intensive reclamation of marginal land throughout
the nineteenth century,[64] all factors which influenced the readiness of the
families to take in nurse children and the willingness of the orphanage to entrust
them to their care. The final most significant south Dublin concentration was
along a line from Rathfarnham to Glencullen, moving from the foothills of
the Dublin mountains towards the higher land of Wicklow. Significant
County Wicklow concentrations were in Blessington and Lacken, with a small
scattering of other individual families, as in Corrigane in Delgany, Moyne in
Rathdrum, and in County Kildare at Larah near Kilcock. Only one child was
at nurse in Dublin city, at 9 Lower Mount Street. That the orphanage operated
within clearly defined districts is also evident from the division of 'Children
Ready to be Placed' into three groupings: Cloghran, Saggard, and Newcastle/
Celbridge districts, in a further document relating to 1874.[65]

While rural locations were chosen primarily to benefit city slum children,
St Brigid's also saw itself as supporting, in a modest way, the social and
economic fabric of country areas:

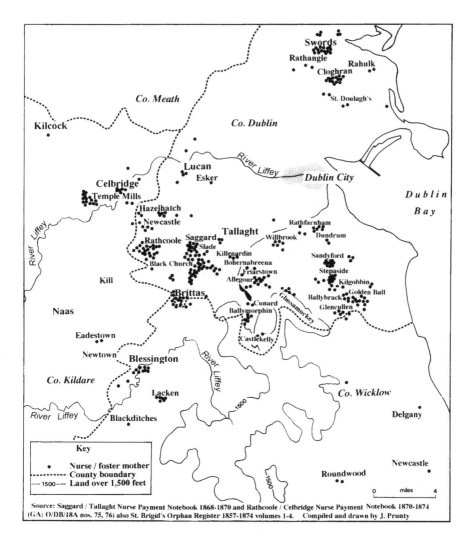

Figure 9: St Brigid's Nurses, 1868–1874

> The money of the Orphanage does, so to speak, double work: it supports the Orphans and helps their foster-parents. During the past three years of unfavourable weather and bad harvests, it was a great boon to small farmers to receive a considerable portion of the rent each year. And this money, as everybody knows, does far more good than mere alms, because they receive it as their due, and we may add, very justly so. Many think that a special blessing attends St Bridget's money. Indeed, Mrs Osborne expressed the feelings of many of her neighbours when she said to her nurse-child one day, 'Now, Malachy Thomas, you brought a blessing to my house, for when you came I had only one cow, and now, thanks be to God, I have three.'[66]

The children were valued for their contribution to family labour as well as the difference their funds made to the family budget. The orphans were to be employed about the farm and home, as were the children of the family, with the stipulation that 'no person shall, however, attempt to put labour upon any child above its strength, or to treat it cruelly'.[67] 'The Irish peasantry, though blessed with genuine affection, are yet no fools. They know well the help little boys and girls can give them in light work such as caring their stock, weeding their crops, going of messages, etc.'[68] Children were seen as a significant source of labour, not alone by St Brigid's managers and nurses, but more generally by the poor law commissioners who constantly exhorted the workhouse managers to provide training and employment for the children under their care.[69] Acutely aware of the migration streams from rural areas to Dublin and beyond, Margaret presented this positive aspect of the institution to its subscribers:

> The country is benefited, because, by emigration to foreign countries and migration to the cities the rural parts are left with a population insufficient to the work. Every pair of arms therefore that is given to the country enriches it.[70]

SUPERVISION OF CHILDREN

While 'unannounced' visits were one means of ensuring the children were well cared for, Margaret's principal control was through twice-annual general inspections, at which premiums were awarded and the nurse was paid, while the seasonal visit was also designed 'to receive the accounts of the School Masters and School Mistresses concerning their regularity of attendance and improvement'. In cases of neglect the money due could be withheld and the child or children speedily removed to other nurses.[71] The fact that the managers of the orphanage travelled to the localities to conduct these public examinations and to pay the nurses was 'a great convenience to the country people, as it saves them the time and expense of coming to Dublin.' However, it had other, subtler advantages:

It makes the people pay attention to the children lest they should be censured before the neighbours, a thing which the country people feel as a disgrace or calamity. On the other hand, it gives them heart and happiness when their Orphans get premiums. This practice of calling them together gives also the opportunity to the Priest of instructing both nurses and children in their duties.[72]

Premiums of ten shillings were awarded at each step: when the child knows his/her prayers, passes a catechism test, receives Confirmation, and can 'read fairly' and 'writes a legible hand, and knows figures enough for house-keeping, fair and market.' These bonuses were considered 'really substantial' and 'worth striving for', a 'solid incentive to exertion'. They were not however competitive, 'thus in reading for example it is not the child that is best of a dozen that obtains the prize, but if the twelve read well, they all win the premium'. 'What we aim at is not precisely the stimulation of the talent of the gifted few, but the education of all according to their state.'[73]

The withholding of payment and removal of children when matters were not satisfactory was no idle threat; Miss Aylward had set fair standards and expected them to be kept. Money was evidently withheld from a nurse Mrs Jones because of her charge's absence from school; Margaret's reply is 'If she gets Certificate from school may be paid – fine will not be paid until he answers well'. Odd notes and letters to Ada are in the same clear style: 'Tell [Mrs Ledwidge] to bring in Mary Carroll with her clothes on the next Saturday that is Saturday week – tell her to have her hair perfectly clean and herself also, otherwise I will be much displeased – Tell her that I will probably be soon sending for little Murray to see how she is thriving.'[74] Concerning another child, Helen Boland, at nurse in Killenardin, Ada is to 'enquire if the itch is quite gone – she was looking very delicate – I mean to remove her.'[75] The nurses' payment books 1868–74 detail a few more such occasions when part of the money due was held back for a month to allow the nurse one chance to remedy some minor neglect, and several instances of a child's removal due to 'incapacity', or 'not thriving'[76] but by far the most frequent reason for relocating orphans was 'for better school accommodation'.[77]

FINAL PLACEMENTS

The orphan registers from 1857 include family histories, entered in Margaret's or Ada's handwriting (or very often a mixture of both). Analysis of admissions for a sample period 1868–75 reveals that the vast bulk, just over 75 per cent, of the children admitted, were the charge of women caring alone, who through widowhood, desertion, or illness were unable to provide for their children, at least for a given period. This also explains the large percentage of children each year 'restored to mother' or other relative; few of the children were orphans in the sense of having neither parent. The genuine affection that grew up between many foster families and their nurse-children very often led to adoption among those 'who are never inquired after by those who placed them in the orphanage'.[78]

This happy outcome, the extent of which could not have been foreseen, was given extensive publicity on every possible occasion:

> This is the most satisfactory result of our work, for it is appalling to think of the danger of a poor Orphan thrown alone into society without family ties to bind him, without family reputation to uphold, and without family authority to be responsible to. It is yet more appalling to think of his danger when he loses or is dismissed (from) his situation.[79]

Wherever possible, children were provided for among their relatives, or if in service somewhere near their former nurse, so that they would be able to maintain these family links.[80] Margaret took endless care with applications from prospective employers, fearing lest the children be exploited; in one handwritten list of requests for children from persons seeking servants such as 'a girl to mind a baby', or help in the poultry trade or laundry, practically all were refused, despite evidence that there were at least 15 children then 'ready to be placed'.[81]

The founding principle of 'family rearing' required, in the first place, that children be supported in their own homes among their own family circle as far as possible. Such assistance was organized from Eccles Street on a small scale; its account books are separate to those of the Ladies of Charity and the orphanage itself, and are not as detailed, but they do testify to the quiet weekly support of parents in distress, which was extended through the medium of St Brigid's schools for the poor (chapter 7).[82] In a memo from *c.*1866 Margaret warns how 'attractive' Catholic institutions could in fact undermine the family unit, cautioning her volunteer co-workers 'not to encourage the poor Catholic parent to part with her child upon the pleas of her own distress or of its being better provided for in Catholic institutions. Experience shows that the breaking of these natural ties is generally attended with disastrous consequences both for parent and child.'[83] That St Brigid's made great efforts to keep children out of residential care is evident in countless written instructions to the ever-patient Ada: give one woman '2/– for a basket', another 'one of the new blankets in yr. press and a bit of carpet that would cover a bed', and another '2/– weekly for 3 weeks'. Nor should one lose track of what outdoor assistance has previously been dispensed; Ada reports that 'Mrs Church says her little girls have no boots and that Mrs Harris is poorly – she wants money to buy them and would show the bills.' Margaret's sharp reply is 'tell her about pledging the other girl's boots'.

SUPPORT OF ST BRIGID'S ORPHANAGE

The orphanage met with widespread initial approbation, Margaret reporting to Cullen in Rome that 'Priests and people seem greatly pleased with St Bridget's work – The monthly receipts are *very good* thanks be to God.'[84] St Brigid's Orphanage was hailed as the 'chief bulwark in Dublin against the multiplied machinations' of the proselytisers, and, along with the Ladies' Association, received special mention in Cullen's pastorals, their services being 'above all praise.'[85] The archbishop of Armagh, Joseph Dixon, longed for an institution such as St Brigid's ('over which Miss Aylward so worthily presides') to be opened in Belfast or some other Ulster town, to meet the many similar cases in danger.[86] Its system of 'outdoor rearing' received many favourable reviews in London periodicals such as *The Workman* and *The Month*:[87]

> The idea is so grand in its simplicity and has proved itself to be so powerful in its practical working, that, as we have said, we are quite conquered by it. Our plans and rules, our trusts, our legal documents – the hundred and fifty different things that are at once so necessary and so ponderous, have never existed in St Brigid's orphanage. It seems to us as airy as a vision, but it is as firm as a rock, and works out the will of God, which is, that none of these little ones should perish, with perseverance and success. If we could adopt this idea in England, and work it, say by divisions of dioceses, the good that might be done would be quite incalculable.[88]

Fanny Taylor, who had so ably opposed English funding of Protestant missions in Ireland, could not speak highly enough of St Brigid's; she commended it for economy, and for the way in which the children become integrated into families and local communities, preventing them 'from ever becoming such waifs and strays of humanity as poor orphans often run a chance of becoming'. Finally, St Brigid's rearing leaves the children 'more fitted for the rough path in life they have to pursue':

> The child in the orphanage is brought up too tenderly; her life flows on in an easy routine; she is under the care of kind and gentle teachers, striving to be just in all their dealings with her; food and clothing come to her without any trouble. It is true she is taught to work for the general good but not for her own individual wants and needs, and all this produces a tendency to helplessness. When she goes out of the peaceful convent, and hears rough words, and meets the petty injustice, thoughtlessness, and selfishness which those in the world must meet, she is dismayed, frets to get back again, and gives up in dismay.[89]

Such success demanded exceptional administrative and diplomatic skills of its lady manager, for St Brigid's was entirely reliant on public fundraising and goodwill in a city that was already stretched to support a myriad of competing charities. The active support of the clergy was crucial, as a favourable word from the altar, or better still, a charity sermon, could provide substantial funds, while it was very often through the clergy that suitable 'cases' were directed. Rose Gaughren reported that Margaret 'visited almost all the Archbishops and Bishops of Ireland who afterwards became subscribers to the Orphanage and good friends as long as they lived.'[90] As with the fundraising for the 'sick poor' Margaret approached the matters of raffles, bazaars and charity sermons (Figure 11) in a professional manner, securing the services of Dr Murray to preach and the Lord Mayor, Mr Pianos, Mr Devereux and other prominent citizens to take up the collection at one of her many charity sermons.[91] In the summer of 1860 she undertook a tour of some of the southern counties including Cork city, where she distributed copies of the archbishop's pastoral on proselytism along with St Brigid's Orphanage annual report, in what she called a 'tedious' undertaking 'particularly for one who does not know this city'.[92] Wills made in favour of the orphanage had to be followed up lest the executors fail to meet the wishes of the deceased and St Brigid's be the loser; a scrapbook collection of newspaper cuttings from 1869–78 includes 89 bequests, many made in care of Dr Cullen.[93] As the numbers 'on the books' increased (Table 2) the scale of the finances required mounted, so that by July 1870 Margaret writes 'the examination and payments begin this week hundreds of pounds we must have ready for this time to pay the nurses'.[94] Cullen directed a steady flow of monies of which he had the stewardship to Margaret; he also forwarded donations from members of his own family, and directed the attentions of some generous donors to St Brigid's. He delegated to Margaret the care of many of the orphan cases which were brought to his attention, writing to her 'If you would be so good as to read the enclosed letters – I could not get through them – they are all about children.'[95] In 1859 following on her intense lobbying, Cullen directed the confraternities of the Metropolitan Church 'to assist Miss Aylward in collecting funds to support the orphanage of St Brigid. The members of the Confraternities cannot engage in a more meritorious work.'[96] In 1869 Margaret redoubled her efforts to get Confraternity collectors through Cullen's encouragement, focusing especially on Westland Row parish, 'that great parish of riches, misery and proselytism' from which she was repeatedly asked to accept children; 'Add to this if Priests from the Parish would kindly make a door-to-door collection for the orphanage amongst the wealthier classes who are giving largely to other Priests and Bishops' dioceses and the children of their own parish being lost in numbers, something worthwhile would be got and many souls saved to the church.'[97]

GUILDSMEN

Margaret's most successful funding move was the establishment of guilds of men (and, less numerously, of women), who undertook to support St Brigid's in every possible sense, regarding themselves as active co-workers essential to its mission, as indeed was to be the case. In a memorandum to Dr Cullen on St Patrick's Guild *c*.1866, Margaret explains that its role is to support St Brigid's Orphanage, its final purpose being 'to honor God in the protection of Orphans and destitute Children in danger of loss of faith'. The president of each guild receives new members 'according to his judgement and discretion', appointing the duties of each, and with power to remove members, though he himself is entirely subject to the archbishop and removable at his request. Once the membership of any guild reaches twenty-four, four members will break off and form the nucleus of a new group, 'the president of the parent guild naming the president of the new.' Based solidly on 'the eternal and immutable principle that out of the Catholic Church there is no salvation', the members were to use their best endeavours 'to widen and deepen in Ireland the faith of St Peter and St Patrick', through their own good example (each to be 'a person of good morals and practical faith') and through prayer (on behalf of 'poor infants in danger of loss of faith'), superintendence and the collection of alms. 'Superintendence' was wide-ranging, including a requirement that guildsmen explore the situation of Catholic children in the workhouses, Protestant Orphanages 'and like institutions', watch lest poor children of their own district go to Protestant day-schools, take an active interest in the faith of children of 'mixed marriages', and promote the election or appointment of Catholics to civil offices which deal with destitute infants. In all cases they were to 'inculcate everywhere the inestimable value of faith and show the poor their folly and extreme guilt in bartering the souls of their dear infants for a little lucre'.[98] The matter of collecting subscriptions was covered in a few lines; though obviously an essential element, these men were recruited for a much larger task.

The most extraordinary supporter among many excellent guildsmen, was John Joseph Steiner (1832–1916), a German convert to Catholicism and shoemaker by trade, who found work in North King Street, Dublin about 1857; his employer, Mr Reynolds, was already a weekly collector for the newly-founded St Brigid's and introduced Steiner to the charity. After about twelve years as a member of St Patrick's guild, and an ardent supporter of 'the good and great Miss Aylward', he saw in this orphanage the kind of religious work to which he might devote his entire life.[99] In 1872 he formally requested to be allowed 'to give all my time to St Bridget's institution hoping to be able to work for it until the very last day of my life', without any reward or recompense whatsoever, 'as I wish to do this work entirely for the Glory of God, the salvation of poor Children and my own sanctification.'[100] The fulfilment of this resolution on a full-time basis was delayed by several attacks of illness, and also by responsibilities towards his elderly employer; but

Figure 10: John Joseph Steiner, 1832–1916

finally, in August 1878, he resolved to embark upon the task full time, travelling the length and breadth of the island on foot, publicising the mission of St Brigid's and the Sisters of the Holy Faith, and collecting quite literally the pennies of the poor, along with the crowns and half-crowns of the well-to-do.[101] Unsalaried but allowed his expenses (which were minimal), his generosity enabled 'the Institution preserve the still glorious privilege of being manned by volunteers'.[102] A prolific and polished writer, his reports to the Eccles Street headquarters as he trudged around country lanes are full of local detail, historical anecdotes, and theological reflections. Margaret Aylward is a constant theme of his writing ('a bright pattern for each succeeding superioress', 'a great and noble mind'), from the evening of her imprisonment when the men collectors assembled gloomily in Eccles Street to hold their usual meeting (left without a president, feeling 'like Children without a Mother'), through to the celebratory visit in September 1866 of the newly-elevated cardinal, Paul Cullen, flanked by his secretaries, bringing the 'confirmation of the Order of the Holy Faith', and receiving an address from the 'Brothers of the Guilds'.[103] Reminiscences about Margaret's own collecting days in Cork and the south east, her inspection of orphans in Saggart, and the numerous persons of all classes who claimed some acquaintance with her, and continued faithfully to subscribe to the orphanage, are scattered throughout his correspondence.[104] His fifty-eight years of service to St Brigid's as a volunteer collector went well beyond the founding era under Margaret Aylward, John Gowan and Ada Allingham; he reflects back the regard in which many ordinary people held the managers of St Brigid's, and makes the connections for successive leaderships with the earlier period.[105]

CONCLUSION

St Brigid's Orphanage, Margaret's brain-child and a cause for which she was to suffer, went against the flow of practically every contemporary movement. While she was placing children in small family groups and arranging personal visits, all around the diocese monumental institutions were under construction, in a great wave of Catholic building. Although she did not have the capital costs of those charities which were building residences to house their charges, they at least had children on site who could be readily assembled, inspected and displayed, and the buildings themselves testified to the good works in hand. Operating much less visibly from modest committee rooms in Eccles Street, St Brigid's was nevertheless one of the largest and most complex charitable child-care organizations in the country, with its volunteer collectors, guildsmen, subscribers, clerical and other supporters, nurse families and lady visitors, and by the time of Margaret's death in 1889 had undertaken the long-term care of 2,717 children. Infants accepted would be 'on the books' until aged 15, so their care was on-going; the immense pressure to provide extra places must be set against the constant struggle to provide for those for whom responsibility had already been assumed. As an institution St Brigid's made a major contribution to the formulation of child care policy. It demonstrated in practice how 'boarding out' of charity children could be carried out successfully, when closely supervized, to the advantage of all parties concerned: children, foster families, rate-payers and subscribers. The system was reliant on the parenting skills and good will of the foster parents, and the possibility of neglect or maltreatment was therefore always present, as is evident from references to children being removed because they were not kept

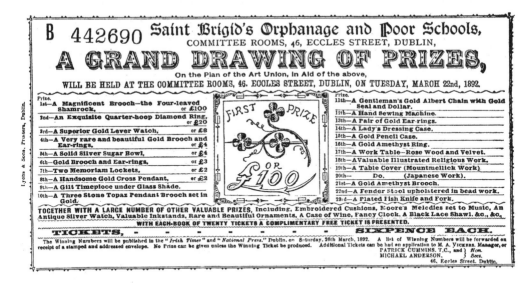

Figure 11: Raffle ticket, 1892

clean, or failed to 'thrive'. However, where the child was well cared for, it was a markedly better system than the monotonous and restrained workhouse regime, and was extolled as such by a wide variety of observers.

Margaret's early years as founder and manager of St Brigid's were to be dominated by two major struggles: painstaking diplomatic moves from 1856–58 to place the orphanage under the supervizion of a religious community (chapter 5), the bitter disappointment of which was rapidly overtaken by the scandal and strain of legal proceedings, directed against the lady manager (chapter 6). The depth of Margaret Aylward's commitment to the

5

Troubling Paris

Securing the direction of the Ladies' Association of Charity, the long-term good of St Brigid's Orphanage, and the establishment of much-needed schools for the poor, were the hopes which involved Margaret Aylward in protracted negotiations to bring the Paris-based Sisters of Charity to Dublin. From the foundation of the metropolitan branch of the Ladies' Association of Charity in 1851 Margaret cherished the hope that this lay charity would in a short time come under the direction of the sisterhood also founded by St Vincent de Paul and, as on the continent, 'in the charity of a common parent', they would mutually aid each other 'in working out the ends and purposes for which they were respectively founded.'[1] After four years in operation, with 'numbers for Active Service between fifty and sixty ladies', she complains that 'we have for years anxiously looked forward to having the co-operation of the *Sœurs Grises* with us in the work and we understood that upon their arrival in Dublin they would attend our meetings, work with us amongst the Poor and give us the advantage of their experience and advice – and vain as yet has been our hope.'[2] In a draft summary of the predicament she faces in 1855, she lists the financial and visitation demands which this successful venture has created; however, in a final note she states as 'chief case: I have been charged with the office of Superior in this Charity since its commencement – the latter has been rather much – I am not quite equal to it now.'[3]

Margaret could see immense potential for good in the collaboration of an organization of lay women with a community of sisters, while her own pre-carious state of health gave a real urgency to the establishment of such arrangements. 'Most anxious to give solidity, stability and permanency to this little work by attaching it to some religious congregation',[4] a joint venture would ensure the financial security of the orphanage in particular: 'Once it becomes known that it is in the hands of the Sisters every kind of aid will be given to it.'[5] The transfer of Catholic lay charities to religious congregations was common in the Dublin diocese throughout the nineteenth century, for reasons of organization, funding and continuity.[6] However, in this case it was not envisaged as a takeover, but rather as the grafting on of a religious congregation to an existing lay association, the cement to be their common Vincentian heritage.

The first record of Margaret's efforts to bring the Daughters of Charity to Dublin is a letter from Fr Philip Dowley, Vincentian provincial, dated 15 January 1851, nine days after Margaret had convened a preliminary meeting in Gardiner Street church with a view to establishing the Ladies' Association of Charity in the parish of St Mary's. The new archbishop, Paul Cullen, was resolutely opposed to the matter at first, and Fr Dowley warned Margaret against further lobbying as Cullen, currently 'so entirely engaged with public projects of the highest importance to the interests of religion and the country' and particularly anxious re depressed *local resources*' might take it 'as rather a troublesome intrusion, having so latterly decided against it so strongly'.[7] However, Dowley's reluctance to reopen the matter with Cullen did little to dim Margaret's enthusiasm for the project, and in September of that year she was in direct communication with the Vincentian superior general, Père Etienne, whom she had met once before on a visit to Castleknock. He warmly praised her zeal, foresight, and perseverance despite obstacles, and promised sisters as soon as the house which she intends for them shall be ready.[8]

The opposition of Dr Cullen was not overcome for several years, nor was her spiritual director, Fr John Gowan, too encouraging. He himself was barely settling into his new role as a Vincentian priest, having recently transferred from the diocesan ministry. Although he supported Margaret's project of providing a 'home resting place' for the lay women who managed the charities, in 1853 he advised that it was best not to think of Paris for the present.[9] Publicly Margaret kept up the pressure on Cullen through the medium of the annual reports which expressed the hope 'that ere long it may be given to us to welcome them to this land, as children of a common parent, and claim from them their counsel and their aid.'[10] Fr MacNamara of Phibsborough added to the pressure on Cullen, suggesting in April 1855 that Cullen call personally on the Vincentian superior in Paris during a forthcoming visit to the continent, to press the case for the establishment of the Sisters of Charity in Ireland.[11] Further communications with Père Etienne assured Margaret that he continued 'quite well disposed to make this foundation as soon as possible' and awaited only 'the hour of the Divine Providence, when she will provide means to the subject'. As far as Etienne was concerned, four sisters would be sent 'as soon as the things shall be ready', that is, a house for their use and some annual income for their maintenance.[12] Never one to delay where the will of God appeared to manifest itself so plainly, by the summer of 1855 Margaret had decided on a suitable house for the sisters, requested the archbishop to purchase it, and had already bargained with the owner and brought the price down 'But we have got to see if he will not take less still – three thousand five hundred pounds is what he asks now'. The choice of location was crucial for with much power vested in the clergy there was a real danger that these religious women and their charities would be overlooked unless they were strategically located. Hence Eccles Street was chosen:

> a highly respectable and healthy street, under the shadow of the Archbishop's Palace – the house that I am so anxious to have secured for them being exactly opposite His Grace's – This situation *is most desirable* – being very near the Church and establishment of your good Fathers at St Peter's, Phibsboro: I long to have the head house in this place – the Sisters would become known here – they would be here in the way of getting good subjects with fortunes – add to this the Archbishop – it is but reasonable to hope he would feel a deep interest in them, and would introduce them to the notice of the large number of ecclesiastics who are daily calling on him from various parts of the country, thus would they be known and thus would their spread *thro' all Ireland* be facilitated to them'.[13]

Margaret strenuously objected to the possibility of the sisters being first located in Kingstown, which Thomas Kelly CM was urging on the archbishop, for:

> It appears to me much more reasonable for the good working of the thing, to have the first Establishment, where the most advantages are to be gained, where they will be in the way of all necessary help, where the widest field will be for the development of their works, and where they shall be the most thoroughly appreciated – All this is not for the good of the Sisters' sake, but for the sake of the good works for which they are needed and in which they will be engaged.[14]

The surest way to move the project forward rapidly, Margaret maintained, was to install the sisters temporarily in a house in Phisboro pending a decision about their final location, 'their presence will necessitate quick decision and vanish timidity, and will be found the surest way to secure their Establishment.'[15] Undoubtedly it would. However, her ambitions to have the sisters so ideally (and speedily) located in the 'ecclesiastical heart' of Dublin, or even temporarily in nearby Phibsboro, came to nothing and a year later there are further communications between Dublin and Paris, this time concerning the proposed removal of the Carmelite Community and their orphanage in North William Street to Sandymount, and the granting of the premises to the French sisters. The Vincentian provincial was directed by Paris to convoke his council to reconsider the matter, this time based on the William Street proposal, and to focus especially on the question of whether 'there is any *sure hope* of creating a comitee [*sic*] of zealous and charitable ladies to get money in order to support the school and the visit of the poor'.[16] Although the transfer of the North William Street house to the new community was to go ahead, there were continuing difficulties in this long running saga, involving Margaret in very sensitive and confidential negotiations conducted *en Français* and in English, between the Vincentian clerical authorities in Paris and Dublin, the active members of her Ladies of Charity who were

Figure 12: Daughters of Charity (*Catholic Home Almanac*, 1885)

sponsoring this community, the Carmelite prioress and 'Reverend Guardian' of the North William Street convent, and the archbishop. The number of Vincentian clergy who were actively involved in making arrangements at the local level compounded her difficulties: Frs Dowley, MacNamara, and Lynch each conducted bilateral (but rarely multi-lateral) discussions, while Fr Edward McCabe, first as curate in Marlborough Street, later as parish priest in Francis Street and always a strong ally of Margaret Aylward, was appointed during the crisis summer of 1857 to direct the newly-launched 'collaborative' orphanage.[17] And all the time the persons most immediately involved, the individual Daughters of Charity who were to place this Dublin mission on a firm footing, were sidelined in the negotiations conducted on their behalf. At no stage did Margaret Aylward have direct communication with the sisters or their female superiors in the Paris mother-house, a weak link in the chain of events that was to have serious repercussions.

The prolonged occupation of the Carmelites of their convent in North William Street brought everything to a 'dead stand', these sisters being unsatisfied about the arrangements being made for the orphans in their care, and with the delay in paying them a sum of money promised by the Archbishop.[18] A further difficulty was 'the subject of signing an engagement in the part of the [Ladies'] Association to pay the *rent* and *taxes* of William Street for the French Sisters on condition of their taking up the Orphanage'.[19] When Margaret first broached the project to some of the Ladies of Charity they '*willingly* consented' but reasonably requested that they be 'acquainted with all details, they believe that in justice to the body for whom they act and whom they represent must be conversant with all details relative to the foundation.' Draft 'treaties' were drawn up between Fr Dowley and the French sisters, and between the French sisters and the archbishop; the Ladies of Charity 'not being contracting parties to these Articles' refused to put their signature to either, despite being pressurized by Fr Lynch CM.[20] They were willing to pay the annual rent of £50 but 'will not be satisfied to be charged with firing, lighting or repairs – with them they will have nothing to do' nor would they agree to being charged with the support of a servant.[21] The Ladies' association drew up their own version of the agreement, which they forwarded to Fr Dowley, and some further discussion ensued; in some final clarifications he stated that relations between the Ladies of Charity and the sisters regarding the 'internal management and government of the orphanage' should be 'exactly similar to the conditions and arrangements which exist between the Committee for the C[atholic] Instruction of Deaf and Dumb and the Ladies of St Mary's Convent, Cabra.'[22] A signed treaty was eventually forwarded directly to Père Etienne in Paris, and Margaret sighed in relief that at last 'the long looked-for foundation will now so soon be made here' and the sisters 'are now enabled to commence their works here under such cheering prospects', in 'our poor persecuted but faithful country'.[23] In an undated memo she writes that the archbishop is to support the Dublin foundation of the 'Sisters of St Vincent' with an annual grant of £100, 'this with a house rent-free and the probability of getting subjects to join them with good means, leaves grounds for regarding this as a good and desirable foundation.'[24] Her relief and delight at the prospect of their arrival was however to be short-lived.

Future difficulties were foreshadowed in the suggestions of the ladies' committee that 'before coming the Sisters should be made aware that the 2 works for which they are brought over – are the Poor Schools, and the Orphanage – any leisure time they have they are free of course to go amongst the Sick if they like.' They also requested that a copy of 'the Address of the Committee of St Brigid's Orphanage should be sent to Paris at once and let them see the work *they are wanted for*'.[25] Lack of clarity in this area undoubtedly contributed to intractable problems on the sisters' arrival; Margaret Aylward had made her group's position eminently clear in letters to Fr Dowley well in advance of the foundation, and St Brigid's orphanage was by definition a boarding-out establishment, a founding principle which could not be compromised. There is no evidence that Dowley or any other Vincentian priest passed on this vital information to the sisters who were to come. It had been agreed that the Ladies of Charity 'will exclusively select the orphans, present them for admission, provide the means for their maintenance, and regulate their removal according to the rules and terms laid down'.[26] Such an agreement was dangerously open to misinterpretation, if the founding principle of 'boarding out' had not been grasped. The Dublin ladies were also concerned at the small number of sisters proposed for this first Dublin colony, and above all the impact this would have on the future of their fledgling outdoor orphanage:

> The Ladies of Charity require that whatever nuns take the charge of their orphanage should do that work well, and this they believe to be simply *impossible* if 4 Sisters come over to undertake 3 heavy works – if in France they go to mind an hospital surely they don't go to visit the Sick and mind poor schools – it is better that they should simply know and be satisfied to undertake what they are brought over for.[27]

Margaret's great anxiety that the first Dublin community of the 'Sœurs' should be successful, and her characteristic directness, prompted her to speak boldly, even bluntly, to Père Etienne on how 'the Sisters for the first foundations in Dublin will require to be educated with a kind and winning manner, they must know a good deal of schools, a great want for the poor – so much will be expected from them here.' Margaret completes most of these letters with the postscript 'You will excuse the frankness with which I write, I believe it best to be plain in doing business.'[28] However well that style suited dealings with the French superior general it was not at all designed to foster harmonious relations with the first superior of the North William Street foundation.

Margaret's excellent grasp of financial affairs and of the necessity of winning popular support was an important element in this as in all her undertakings. Having secured £3,000 from Cardinal Cullen towards the establishment and maintenance of the French sisters, she proposed in 1856 that they utilize the premises in North William Street as a school for the blind, not alone a great necessity but a charity which was assured of great support financially, with some donations already received.[29] Indeed, as the space demands of a boarding-out orphanage were minimal, the North William Street premises gave great scope for other good works.

The strain of trying to satisfy all the parties involved was immense, and the constant delays particularly trying. Fr Dowley, apparently in an attempt to reassure her, writes 'You have gone as near as it is desirable to the point of pleasing everybody – what more on the grounds of success need be desired? Energy and activity seem to have been born with you and what state of mind or health could you hope to enjoy, if those blessed energies were not brought into and kept in constant play.'[30] Three years later it is Fr Dowley who appears to be finding it all too much, especially 'the new and complicated difficulties that make their appearance every other day', and confides to Margaret: 'I beg to assure you that *you* are not more uneasy or troubled by this blessed concern than *I* am.' The only positive gloss he can put is that 'I suppose that annoyance given here to all the parties concerned ought to be taken as evidence that it is the work of God and that it will succeed.'[31] The unwavering support of Père Etienne in Paris for her special mission of introducing the 'second family of St Vincent to Ireland' was one of the few constants over several years of set-backs and complications.[32] By nature Margaret was active and efficient; once a thing was decided there seemed to her no advantage in delay, and she appeals to others to speed up the process: 'If you would think well of urging in your letters quick movements about it I believe it would be advantageous.'[33]

Margaret held great ambitions for the Daughters of Charity and the blessing they would be to the Dublin poor. Even while negotiating the principal worry, the charge of St Brigid's Orphanage, she considered expanding their proposed role in Dublin both in terms of ministry and geography. In consultation with the newly appointed parish priest of Francis Street, Fr McCabe, where 'proselytism raged', Margaret suggested to him the advantages of placing the '*Sœurs*' in charge of the local poorly-run Catholic 'ragged' school, 'he approved of it, and worked for it zealously' Margaret promising that 'A glorious work lies before them, they will see poverty, rags, misery, wretchedness, such as I do believe they never saw before.'[34]

The French sisters were never to come to Francis Street parish, but a group of five sisters arrived to take charge of the convent in North William Street on 14 May 1857, while on that same afternoon a further group of five sisters took up residence in Richmond (Fairview) where they were to establish a hospital, a foundation with which Margaret had not been involved, but an area of service for which they were internationally esteemed (Figure 12).[35] Serious strains between the new arrivals in North William Street, Dublin and their lady benefactor and local collaborator, Miss Aylward, were immediately evident. Within days Fr Lynch CM was advising Margaret 'to see all things, hear all things and say as little as possible', as it became clear that there would be no meeting of minds between the welcoming group of lady associates and the new community.[36] Sr Josephine Virien intended that her institution would cater for girls only; Margaret expected them to take St Brigid's orphans on a co-ed basis, and had already ascertained with Père Etienne that this would not be a problem.[37] More seriously, the new community was clearly committed to operating an indoor orphanage of the type with which they were already familiar, and embarked on this project with considerable energy. The 'Cabra' model of organization, whereby lady associates raised and supervized the funds for the Deaf and Dumb institution, but the nuns had entire freedom in its management, had been presented in good faith by Philip Dowley as the type of relationship which should subsist between the Ladies and Daughters of Charity in the North William Street project.[38] Where the mode of operation was entirely at variance with what the lady associates expected or could support, there was little they could do, and the constant recourse of Josephine Virien to the Cabra model served only to further polarize what were supposed to be collaborating parties.

In a lengthy conference with the French superior soon after the sisters' arrival, the very different stances held by the two women were exposed. Sr Josephine Virien saw her position in very clear terms: the undoubtedly zealous and generous Miss Aylward had held preliminary discussions with Fr Dowley about the care of the orphans, but now that the Daughters of Charity had taken charge of the institution all further planning should be left between the French sisters and their own Vincentian superiors. In fact, even in that department it was not so simple, as is clarified by Fr MacNamara CM for the archbishop some years later in reference to their relationship with the priests of the Irish province of the Vincentians: 'the Sisters of Charity have a government of their own distinct from us and they are not required to consult us in their projects or the conduct of their works'.[39] This situation undoubtedly further muddied the waters of the North William Street foundation. Regretting that 'we cannot agree on a work which commands our mutual sympathy', Sr Josephine saw that new negotiations with the Dublin parties were necessary.[40] Problems had arisen due to an 'inadequate understanding' between the two groups; however, these could be settled amicably by exchanging binding documents on either side, and so allow the excellent and very necessary work to proceed.[41]

Sr Josephine understood that the relationship between her sisters and Margaret Aylward's lay group was to model that of the Cabra Deaf and Dumb institution, arrangements of proven excellence; Margaret demanded changes in the proposed 'Cabra model' before acceding to it, and refused point-blank to sign a written document.[42] Sr Josephine, on reflection, held ever most trenchantly to the Cabra model, convinced that 'we cannot depart from this precision which establishes a greater security in our relationship', reminding Margaret yet again that 'the terms of the Cabra institution have been found by all to be very satisfactory and I am not free to look elsewhere for my line of conduct'.[43] Margaret's repeated claim that 'If any good priest of your order made any promise that we should adopt the "Deaf Mutes" as our Standard or Model, we were not party to it and never entered into such a contract' was entirely ignored. The French arrivals were fully convinced that such an agreement had been made on their behalf – did they not have a signed document in their Paris mother-house as proof? If, in charity, there had been some misunderstanding, the best move now was to tie down this overbearing and even insolent woman benefactor to such ideal terms by insisting on written contracts. And all future plans should also be in writing, 'in order to avoid all misunderstanding'.[44]

From May to August 1857 the stress mounted as each side tried to implement fairly an impossible arrangement. Sr Josephine informed Miss Aylward that 'the type of food, clothes, furnishings on which we will agree together will be provided for the children and each month or each quarter we will furnish an account of these expenses which your charitable Association will be good enough to pay', begging pardon for the 'business-like approach which has been necessary because of our inadequate understanding concerning the matter'.[45] At least one child was placed by Margaret in the institution, but a fortnight later relations with the new management had deteriorated so much that she was requested to remove this child, with the bitter addition, 'and also all the furniture, utensils and clothes which are left here'.[46] A few days later the request to remove St Brigid's child was repeated, and all monies which had been subscribed to North William Street for this purpose were returned, with the assurance that any future contributions to St Brigid's would be immediately dispatched to Miss Aylward. A postscript makes it plain that no hopes of any common mission are now entertained on the Virien side: 'I will send the box as soon as I can get a workman to remove it from the wall.'[47] The Vincentian priests who had done so much to facilitate the new venture could do little except to urge 'patience and mutual forbearance'.[48] Each woman claimed to be 'acting according to the wisest and most legitimate advice' but such consultations merely hastened the erosion of whatever common ground had been between them.[49] The scheduled June 1857 annual meeting of the Ladies of Charity was postponed as the crisis continued. Margaret Aylward laid the matter before Dr Cullen in July, showing him the considerable file of correspondence to date; both he and Fr Edward McCabe advised her not to accede to the terms of the French sisters. In yet another exchange with Sr Josephine, Margaret adds the loaded statement, 'Your last letter [to M. Aylward] especially displeased them very much and I do not wish to tell you the alternative the archbishop spoke of, in case that you still continue to mar the prospects of the charity by raising difficulties as unexpected as they are unreasonable.'[50] While obviously echoing the sentiments expressed by their own Vincentian provincial, the thinly-disguised threat did nothing to endear her to the French sisters, and the compromize agreement that the Ladies of Charity will support children in the new institutional orphanage (at £9 each per annum, more costly than St Brigid's), and supervize the monthly accounts, is not likely to be accepted. Margaret's additional note, that 'We expect the Sisterhood will take up the work cordially and do all in their power to make it popular because its success depends on popular sympathy' could also be read as too-personal criticism.

A very final end was put to the Aylward/Virien project in August 1857, with a letter from Sr Josephine formally 'bringing to an end our relationship with you', after the 'trial experience' had been further soured by Aylward's appeal to Cullen, convinced 'it is evident that we will not be able to take charge of the orphans in a way which is satisfactory for you and at the same time to maintain the degree of freedom which is essential in the fulfilling of our works.' On a final, more kindly note, she credits Margaret Aylward with being 'inspired by the best of intentions' always, and that as Daughters of St Vincent de Paul, 'we will always respect your zeal for the poor, and we will never forget your kind welcome on our arrival in Dublin.'[51]

The parting of the ways was complete. Margaret Aylward, encouraged by Vincentian priests such as John Lynch and John Gowan, was to work out her Vincentian vocation unhampered by formal ties with the Vincentian sisters. In December 1857 the sixth annual public meeting of the Ladies' Association of Charity, postponed from June, was held. The first formal report for St Brigid's Orphanage was published as an addendum to the Ladies' report, noting that forty-three children were now boarded-out by the new institution. There is no longer any mention of entrusting this mission to a religious community, but in a spirited rallying of support, the founding (boarding-out) principles are stated with conviction, and great confidence expressed in the future:

> Our work is simple in its working, has a broad foundation, and is capable of immense extension, and if our unworthiness do not place obstacles, is destined to do something for God's glory and the Irish Church.[52]

A strong emphasis on the Irishness of this institution (see Figure 8), nurtured in the heart of 'the beautiful Irish Church, the Church of St Patrick and St Bridget, the witness of Catholic faith in the West', may be read as a reaction to the too-recent painful experiences with the continental community:

> In God's name, and our Lady's and St Bridget's, Irish Catholics must do this thing. Let us therefore, take heart, and begin anew.[53]

The Daughters of Charity embarked on their new mission in North William Street with energy. Their 'works' as listed for May 1857 were 'the visitation and relief of the Poor in their own homes' and 'teaching the poor children'. They took over an infant school and small girls' school, which at Cullen's request they withdrew from the National Board, greatly enlarged and reorganized, to cater for over 500 children.[54] Concerned with the 'plague' of child proselytism, the 'conspiracy against the Catholic faith of Ireland and against the common sense of mankind', which having 'spread like a net-work over the country' made its headquarters in Dublin, they worked to combat the evil in a practical and well-informed manner.[55] The orphanage work, the cause of so much misunderstanding, was launched as 'St Vincent's Female Orphanage' on 28 December 1858, with Fr James Dixon CM credited with fundraising, and their own 'ladies committee' meeting each week to decide on applications to the orphanage.[56] A model institution of its type, the children were trained in 'industrial works' as well as receiving general schooling, with the 'services of a very clever French woman who bore an Irish name, Mlle Emma Donovan' credited with introducing flower-making. The final end of the children, a worry for every group involved in child-care, was uppermost: 'Ma Soeur Virien always found excellent positions for them, very often in families in France, personally known to herself, and she provided them with an excellent outfit.'[57]

The many-pronged negotiations in the 1850s between Margaret Aylward and the several parties concerned with establishing the Daughters of Charity in Dublin are revealing. Most tellingly, they demonstrate Margaret's enthusiasm, and indeed impetuosity, when embarked upon a path which she is convinced can only lead to good. Her linguistic skills, sound business head, grasp of the many complexities involved and sheer tenacity reveal her to be an exceptional diplomat, who was not to be underestimated. Her fidelity to her women co-workers as she negotiated on their behalf, returning repeatedly with questions for clarification and counter-proposals and signing nothing until she was sure of their full backing, is very much to her credit, although from the Vincentian perspective it made for very trying negotiations. The correspondence also provides very useful insights into the ecclesiastical and lay power structures within which all philanthropic women had to steer a course if, like Margaret, they were convinced that the end was worth pursuing relentlessly. The exclusion of the Daughters of Charity from all the early stages of planning had painful but inevitable consequences. Had Josephine Virien and Margaret Aylward corresponded directly from the outset how very differently might matters have evolved.

In terms of public acclaim, Margaret's role in bringing the Daughters of Charity to Dublin has been almost entirely blotted out of history to date. Josephine Virien was, understandably, relieved to draw a line firmly under the Margaret Aylward connection. Absolutely nothing of their extensive correspondence is preserved in the Daughters of Charity provincial archive, Dunardagh, though admittedly there are many possible reasons for its absence, as the founding days of the Dublin houses are on the whole poorly represented. There are no public pronouncements on Margaret Aylward's part, just a traditional memory in the community she went on to found (Holy Faith Sisters) that Margaret had brought the French sisters to Dublin to run St Brigid's but that they would not work the boarding-out system. It was almost as if the encounters between the two women, and their respective communities, were too painful to be recalled even by their contemporaries. The Daughters of Charity community annals record only that 'His Grace the Archbishop, Dr Cullen, personally appealed to the Superiors of the Company in Paris and the Father General, Monsieur Etienne appointed five Sisters with Sr Virien in charge.'[58] Margaret Aylward was removed from the memory of the Daughters of Charity as effectively as her collecting box was prised out of the wall of the North William Street convent and the space cemented over.

6

Prison Trials

On 23 November 1860, Margaret Aylward was confined by the Court of Queen's Bench to six months imprisonment, and ordered to pay all costs. The controversial case, centred around the abduction of an infant, had been closely followed on both sides of the Irish Sea, and was to continue to provide the media with drama and debate throughout the six-month sentence. The incarceration in a common jail of a prominent lady of high social standing, following on the dismissal of the charge against her (kidnapping), was in itself worthy of coverage, but the added interests of a major Church/State dispute, and claims of collusion between the prosecuting party and a prominent English evangelical society, not to mention the questions surrounding the fitness of the judge to officiate, provided excellent media material. It also epitomized the denominational, legal and political struggles which surrounded the care of charity children in Ireland throughout the nineteenth century, struggles about which seemingly every person felt compelled to provide an opinion. Only eight months had elapsed between Margaret's final tortuous break with the Daughters of Charity and the beginning of the Mathews case (April 1858), so that the institution under fire, St Brigid's, must still be considered very much a fledgling operation.

A child, Mary Mathews, the offspring of a marriage between Henry Mathews and Maria née Johnston, was entrusted to the care of St Brigid's Orphanage on 3 April 1858. The father was Catholic and a native of Dublin; the mother was an English Protestant who converted to Catholicism before her marriage. The wedding ceremony had been held in Dublin, in Francis Street parish church, where the child Mary Mathews was also baptized.[1] The couple moved to England, where Henry, a chain maker, had hoped to obtain work, but the marriage was in serious difficulties, and in October 1857 Maria took their youngest child, leaving England to take up a position as nursemaid in the family of Governor Bayley, Nassau, the Bahamas. Mathews described his dilemma: 'left with 2 children in a horid sity wicke London' he tried every avenue to have his other children reared as Catholics. However, despite assurances from 'a Lady, one of the comete' that 'when the ladys woud sit the woud do all in her power get in the 2 children which woud be a good job for them and me' there was no way the 'rule of the scole' (sic) requiring

5*s.* per week for two children, and security, could be waived. Mathews had no option but to return to his native Dublin, where his former employer Mr Jordan of Chancery Lane had promised to reemploy him, and although in poor health hoped that 'God will leave me so as to do for them.'[2]

However, shortly after arriving in Dublin, Mathews was confined to Sir Patrick Dun's hospital, and from here he committed his two children to the care of his former employer's wife, Mary Jordan, giving verbal instructions that they were to be reared as Catholics. The father died in January 1858. The boy, also Henry, was brought to Fr Fay's Catholic orphanage in Brown Street,[3] the girl, Mary, was admitted to St Brigid's and sent to nurse with a Mrs Kenny in Saggart on 3 April 1858. That same month the mother, Maria, was expelled from Nassau, Bahamas on the instructions of Governor Bayley, who stated that during 'the whole of her stay here she had exhibited continued bad temper' and had 'grossly neglected' the child she was employed to mind; 'her conduct was characterized by capriciousness, impertinence and sullenness, which could only be explained on the supposition that she was given to drink and that on the evening on which she was discharged, she was certainly intoxicated'.[4] She was deported to England on 12 January.[5] When four months had elapsed she began to enquire after her children, sponsored, it was repeatedly claimed by the opposing parties, by the Smyly family of the Irish Church Missions. Tracing them to Dublin she removed the boy from Brown Street Orphanage and sought to have the girl returned from St Brigid's. However, aware of the possible removal of the child from St Brigid's, a third party took upon himself her protection and sent a forged note to the nurse in Saggart, purporting to be from Miss Aylward, and demanding the child be delivered into the custody of the messenger. The infant could not be traced, and as it emerged years later had been spirited away, first to North Great Georges Street, then to France and later to Belgium.[6] The first Margaret knew of the abduction was eleven days later when the nurse visited Dublin to express her regret at the loss of the child. Lengthy legal proceedings were instituted by the mother and under a writ of *habeas corpus* Margaret Aylward was ordered to produce the child in court.

The fact that she had not, on hearing of the child's removal, immediately reported the matter to the police was held against her, and her claim that the police had exhibited nothing but disinterest and incompetence on a previous occasion where a child was illegally removed from the care of the orphanage was discounted. Opposing counsel also rejected outright her protestations that she had no means of tracing the self-appointed guardian of the child, and berated her for her passivity.[7] The fact that the child was known as 'Mary Farrell' in her foster home laid Margaret Aylward wide open to the accusation of purposely thwarting the efforts of any Protestant relatives who might seek at a later date to trace her. Margaret certainly knew on the child's admission that she was likely to be 'protestantized' if returned to her mother or other relatives, and the unusual step of changing the name was consciously done to ensure that the child would not be easily located.[8] The father's verbal instructions, although witnessed by a woman visitor and by a nurse, were not acceptable as evidence. On no other occasion had St Brigid's failed to return a child to relatives, Protestant or otherwise, on request, although in the case of 'losing' a Catholic child to Protestantism this would be accompanied by outpourings of concern for their eternal salvation; in the case of Mary Mathews, the abduction by a third party removed all possibility of returning the child, no matter what the court ordered.

The mother's delay in making any inquiries after her children after her return from the West Indies and her previous neglect of them, according to counsel for Miss Aylward, made it 'plain, therefore, that the mother was not the moving party here. The question was between a Roman Catholic Institution and a Protestant Institution.'[9] Judge Lefroy, who although now aged eighty-four years was still stubbornly holding office,[10] had a family interest in this case, his sisters' involvement as collectors for a branch of the Irish Church Missions having received special mention in St Brigid's report of 1859.[11] The first court appearance was 29 May 1858, from which date the possibility of Margaret Aylward going to prison was widely discussed, with friends such as Philip Dowley, the Vincentian provincial, expressing the hope 'We shall, I trust in God, prevail so far as not to see and visit you in chains.'[12] Numerous affidavits were sworn by all the parties implicated, and sentence was finally delivered on 7 November 1860.[13] The court found her innocent of kidnapping and complicity but sentenced her to six months imprisonment on the lesser charge of contempt of court. Margaret conveyed her own assurance: 'The persecution against me is they say against St Bridget's Orphanage – the thorn in their side – Chief Justice Lefroy wanted to have me imprisoned for 2 years.'[14]

The case received widespread coverage over the two and a half years between first court appearances and imprisonment, the *Freeman's Journal* reporting on each step of the proceedings. The fact that a lady of 'high respectability, of high social standing'[15] was to be interred with convicted prisoners, resulted in sensational editorials in all the major newspapers, including the London *Times*. The newly-formed *Irish Times* was merciless in its attack:

> A sentence of this extent, passed upon a semi-nun seems, at first sight, to be severe; but it sinks into insignificance when compared with the misery Miss Aylward has inflicted on a mother, and, possibly, upon her child. There was a harshness and cruelty manifested in her conduct towards the mother hitherto unparalleled even in similar cases. Setting herself, a woman who never knew the strength of domestic ties, or what it is to feel a mother's love for her offspring, as

the judge of all human relations and the arbitress of domestic life, she violated not only the law of the land but the first duties of humanity. For more than two years she has baffled justice. There was not an individual in court yesterday who was not morally certain that she knew where the child was concealed, and could produce it in a moment. Yet to the 'interrogatories' she gave evasive or deficient answers, and at last acted the 'Mortara' case over again, and replied to the inquiries of the court but *ignoramus* or *non-possumus*. It was high time that the law should interfere, not only to punish the past, but to deter for the future.[16]

The Dublin *Morning News* defended her, seeing it as an attack on the rights of Catholics and depicting her as a martyr. The *Morning News* was among those who ridiculed the judges' error in first condemning her to Richmond Bridewell, a male penitentiary, so that the governor there had to accommodate her in his own apartments for two days until the judges committed her to Grangegorman.[17]

But to send a lady to a prison where none but males were to be incarcerated was a violation of the common decencies of life. The judges of the Queen's Bench admitted so much when they revoked their order, when they were re-called from those regions of abstraction where their souls walked in imagination down to the stern facts of prison rules and the orders in Council.[18]

The confinement of a woman to the Bridewell, a prison popularly known as 'Cease to do Evil Learn to Do Well' from the inscription over the entrance, also provoked much vulgar banter on the streets of her native Waterford:

In some courts in this land some injustice prevails
But the Court of Queen's Bench is both prudent and mild
It sentenced Miss Aylward to a prison for males
As the very best mode of producing a child.
How she'll do it 'twill puzzle Creation to tell
If she cease to do evil and learn to do well
And if in six months without hard labour confined
She produces a child, 'twill astonish mankind.[19]

Impassioned speeches in her defence were made, and many letters of support arrived in Eccles Street and at the prison including letters from Lady Georgina Fullerton, in London, John Curtis SJ, Gardiner Street, Dr Kirby in Rome and Fr Tully in Maynooth,[20] Bishops Leahy, Gilhooly, Furlong, Flannery, Kilduff; and many priests, religious and lay people around the country and in England.[21] Archbishop Dixon of Armagh was visiting Rome and reported the circumstances of the case to Pius IX, who sent '*la poveretta*' his blessing and a cameo of the Mother of Sorrows as a token of his support.[22] St Brigid's Defence Committee was established with her long-standing ally Fr Edward McCabe, along with the Catholic activist Ignatius

Kennedy, as secretaries. Public subscription lists were opened to defray the heavy expenses of the legal proceedings and 'prove that Catholic Ireland regards her conduct with admiration, and esteems her as a martyr of charity'.[23] Margaret described Dr Cullen as 'most supportive and kind'.[24] The prison visits by clergymen friends including the archbishop provoked the London *Times* to claim that 'since her committal her faith has been sustained and her martyrdom sweetened by the visitation of the most notorious among the priestly zealots of her creed'.[25]

During her imprisonment she directed arrangements for the fourth annual meeting of St Brigid's Orphanage, which was rescheduled for 16 January 1861. It was a provocative display of clerical support, with Archbishop Cullen in the chair, flanked by the bishops of Kerry and Dromore, and an impressive array of high-ranking clergymen. Ostensibly to launch the fourth report and encourage the members in their charitable endeavours, it was an occasion to publicly show support for the imprisoned 'lady manager' and a platform for speeches defending St Brigid's against counter-charges of proselytism. Margaret planned the meeting from her prison cell.[26] The printed report included these speeches, as well as Margaret's 'Statistics of Proselytism' which had created a storm the previous year. Naming individuals and quoting extensively from the published reports of various Protestant missionary and charitable associations which she accused of proselytism was inflammatory. Margaret clearly signaled that the attack on the proselytizing societies was still in full force. The proceedings were widely reported in the press, and the *Freeman's Journal* printed the full text of the speeches.[27] The response from the opposing camp was outrage, led by the London *Times*, and now particularly directed against Dr Cullen:

> Dr Cullen, the Titular Archbishop whom nothing daunts – Dr Cullen, the great embroiderer of damaged escutcheons – Dr Cullen, the athletic Catholic white-washer, advances, in confident conviction of Protestant gullibility, to call down the sympathy of the world for the poor prisoner Margaret Aylward. Why urge on these poor, weak, fanatical women to go a child-stealing for the glory of the Church? Is it not rank cowardice in a man to tell a feeble, superstitious body of women, that they will 'have their merit' in conduct which has brought one woman into gaol, and has fixed upon the Church of Rome in Ireland the stigma of an odious crime against the human affections?[28]

Yet another source of controversy was the fact that the judges refused to rule on the conditions under which Margaret should be held, but left that to the discretion of the Board of Superintendence of the Prisons.[29] This inde-cision caused numerous divisions in the prison administration, some members objecting to the harsh conditions under which she was held: 'the Board acted most *bravely* and independently about me. Yesterday the Inspector General attended, and I think was against me. Some of the Gentlemen of the Board declared that if they acted against me they would resign their places at the Board.'[30] However, the board members need not have troubled themselves on her behalf, for a far more significant person was to be countered in the person of Marian Rawlins, the prison matron, a formidable woman who was able to block any of the rights granted by the board.[31] Mrs Rawlins' submissions to the Board include outright fabrications, such as explaining how 'A yard adjoining the room Miss Aylward occupies is suitable for air and exercise'[32] without of course adding that she is making sure Miss Aylward never gets to see it. Similarly she claimed to have 'selected the Board Room for her to receive her friends, as it would be most objectionable and unprecedented for strangers to be frequently passing through the interior of the prison'[33] which was equally distant from the truth. As if the restrictions of prison life were not sufficiently demeaning, Margaret spent most of her term in a futile struggle to obtain the conditions allowed her by the Board, and of which the Board believed her to be possessed.

Her imprisonment had repercussions for, among others, the prison governor, Thomas Synnott, who was accused of displaying 'a strong sense of partisanship' and became the subject of a decided campaign to have him removed, surviving five years of complaints which proved to be mostly petty or untrue, before finally being dismissed.[34] In response to the claims of the *Daily Express* that Margaret has been living in style, 'rules supreme' and 'holds levees' the *Morning News* of 6 April 1861, wrote

> She has been confined in an hospital, and here, inhaling the miasma of the sick, dying and dead, she has lain for four months. But it is not an ordinary hospital. Some of the poor patients are idiotic, some are epileptic, and some are lunatic. Their piteous cries and piercing screams would rend the hardest hearts.

The injustice of the situation rankled, and in a fit of spleen Margaret wrote a fiery letter to Mrs Mary O'Carroll, deputy matron, finishing with the retort 'Forget my request now and may you enjoy every happiness in the room you have refused me', although on recovering her temper she evidently thought better of it, for she notes in the corner that it was not sent.[35] She took her attorney, Laurence Mooney, to task for the slowness with which he appeared to be dealing with her case.[36] In January 1861 Fr Gowan appealed to her to 'be very prudent in the transaction of your business. Weigh all before God. Be not precipite in anything' and in the matter of her imprisonment 'Be grateful to everyone especially to those who oppose you. Do not speak of their opposition except to prudent advisers and then without feeling. If others speak endeavour to let it pass quietly.'

Shortly afterwards, however, Margaret presented Gowan with a paper outlining the prison conditions she had been enduring, and he noted that the question had narrowed itself to whether or not the prisons board had the legal authority or not to dismiss Matron Rawlins. He appealed to Margaret to write to the board only if she can prove that the board had that power, and was himself 'decidedly of opinion that you ought not to write to the Board unless some of them ask explanations from you'.[37] Under such pressure Margaret again held back, but not for long. Dreading the dark,[38] and now deprived by the board of 'the assistance of a female attendant at a time when I most need her attendance, viz., at night, and that was a privilege the Chief Justice particularly ordered' she appealed directly to the Lord Lieutenant.[39] In February she wrote directly to both the Lord Lieutenant and the Chief Justice, stating that her health was fast failing and that a prolongation of her confinement would have a permanently injurious effect,[40] a letter which received the curt reply that Miss Aylward 'had better consult her legal advisers upon the proper form to be observed in any application'.[41]

Other minor but nevertheless aggravating events were the demands of her opposing attorney, Martin, who walked into her prison cell and demanded the legal costs, and the landlord of 46 Eccles Street who wrote to the prison to know when she would pay him his half year's rent.[42] A month before her release she signed and had distributed a printed circular addressed from Grangegorman Prison in defence of her case.[43] But above all, the enforced inaction as calumnies continued to be circulated about her, rankled most.

While Margaret considered herself greatly constrained by the prison regime she in fact succeeded in completing an immense amount of daily business, staying up regularly to 2 a.m., directing the outdoor relief efforts of the Ladies' Association and the multifarious concerns of St Brigid's. In the numerous letters to her friend and co-worker Ada Allingham, who at first was denied access visits, there are requests that various account and collecting books be brought to the prison, instructions about signing cheques, bank lodgements, the separation of the Sick Poor account from that of the Orphanage, and the canvassing of subscribers.[44] Countless individual cases are dealt with in staccato style: 'will you try if there be any of the new blankets in yr. press and say how many – have you a bit of carpet that would cover a bed if so mark it and one of the blankets with M. Malone and leave it at the office'.[45] While she was out of circulation two unknown 'ladies in black' had undertaken to 'collect' for St Brigid's; suspecting (rightly) that they were exploiting St Brigid's to line their own pockets, Margaret had it checked out, including a note telling Fr McCabe 'to pay a man if necessary to find out who they are *entre nous*'.[46] In a similar vein a collector named Humphreys is to be told that 'you have reason to know that he has been collecting without authority and that is a *very* serious thing and that the consequences might be very unpleasant for him – so stop it *at once*'.[47] From Grangegorman Margaret also organized a 'Grand Raffle' which necessitated newspaper advertisements, securing the promised prizes, the wheel, and printing 10s. and £1 books of tickets.[48] And never one to bypass an opportunity to expose wrongs, she noted the number of her fellow prisoners who were former inmates of the South Dublin Union workhouse and requested Cullen to have a person named Maguire call officially on the prison governor and get a statement on the matter.[49] In Cullen's submission to the Select Committee on Poor Relief the following month he exposes the South Dublin Union's mean practice of forcing girls of 16 or 17 years of age to leave the workhouse, without any regard for how they might maintain themselves, and then refusing to readmit them, so that 'exposed to very great danger in a large city, without house or friend' it was not surprizing that they featured prominently in the prison numbers.[50] Margaret had not wasted what must be considered an exceptional opportunity for field research; it was her names and numbers that were used to contradict the 'official' account.

One further aspect of this crisis period was the intensive campaign Margaret conducted from early 1860 and throughout her imprisonment to have Fr John Gowan CM (1817–97) appointed as spiritual director of St Brigid's. Gowan, 'holy, self-sacrificing and devoted' already familiar with its internal workings and, more importantly, fully supportive of its spirit and purposes, was the ideal candidate. Despite the support of Dr Cullen, and Edward McCabe's assertion that Gowan with his 'unpretending, unassuming manner' would be well received by the diocesan clergy, and the warm sympathy Philip Dowley CM had already extended to the imprisoned manager, the Vincentian provincial would not grant permission.[51] Gowan himself was in no position to insist. Relations between the diocesan clergy and the Vincentians were strained at the time and Cullen was anxious not to antagonize Dowley. Cullen suggested Margaret should take the matter into her own hands and apply directly to the Vincentian provincial in Castleknock. Here she found the provincial, as she had expected, 'not inclined to entertain the subject' and acridly remarks 'The wonder of it is that if a *mitre* be offered in that Congregation to the Fathers no difficulty is ever made by the heads.'[52] From prison, the orphanage work having attained 'gigantic proportions' and its position increasingly perilous, she petitioned her old Waterford friend, Dr Kirby, president of the Irish College in Rome.[53] Ever alert to the intricacies of ecclesiastical power struggles Margaret wondered if Dr Kirby could get the pope to appoint Fr Gowan 'Apostolic Missioner' and so bypass the provincial. This innovative stratagem did not appear at all advisable to Kirby who feared 'it might prejudice the matter very much if we attempted here to carry it by force' and he advised persevering diplomacy allied with patience.[54] By the following February she was near desperation, but following Kirby's 'prudent advice' she instead petitioned Cullen to write to the Vincentian Superior General, Père Etienne, requesting that John Gowan be appointed full-time to the works of the orphanage.[55] Frustratingly familiar with the snail's pace of church bureaucracy she even drafted the letter, 'which embodies all that is necessary', directing Cullen to send it open via Mr Dowley to avoid alienating the provincial any further, and with repeated urgings to act with haste.[56] The well-crafted letter had the desired effect, and within three weeks Père Etienne instructed the Irish provincial to inform Dr Cullen of the reservations the Vincentians had to Gowan's appointment, but to accede to the archbishop's request if he insisted that it was necessary 'for the good of religion', and as an example of the spirit of obedience to ecclesiastical authority that should characterize all Vincentian operations.[57] By the time Gowan was finally assigned in April 1861 yet another influential church dignitary, Dr Dixon, archbishop of Armagh and primate of Ireland, had also been drafted in by Margaret to press the case.[58]

This appointment was of huge personal importance to Margaret. From the surviving correspondence (which regrettably consists almost solely of Gowan's replies to letters she wrote) we learn of her shadow side, the scrupulosity, vulnerability and feelings of inadequacy under which she laboured, and though most exposed during the time in Grangegorman were to continue during much of her life. The most frequent theme of John Gowan's replies, 'endeavour to be patient under your sufferings whether they come from within or without' had a particular aptness during this time of imprisonment, but also point to Margaret's enduring spiritual turmoils.[59]

The most serious personal outcome of the imprisonment was the effect on Margaret's health. With a characteristic lack of self-pity Margaret admitted that 'My health has got a little shake here, but when my day comes for being emancipated I hope to be quite well again.'[60] John Gowan recorded that 'First her teeth became loosened and fell out. Next her two arms became paralysed and the head Matron was obliged to lend her the assistance of one of the ordinary prisoners to cut her daily bread.'[61]

An important consequence of the trial and imprisonment was the break-up of the Daughters of St Brigid, the lay community of six women, unmarried and widowed, who were living in 42 Eccles Street and formed the core of the Ladies of Charity and the Committee of Management of St Brigid's Orphanage.[62] The annual report covering June 1859–June 1860 was presented in January of the following year, during the imprisonment, with an apology for the delay and the hope that 'the storms which have kept us out of harbour are nearly over and that we may be permitted to give our account each year at the proper time'; two years later 'some want of vigour and a little chilliness' in the assocation was noted.[63] The illness and death of Mrs Frances Murray, one of the first and most generous volunteers, before Margaret's release from prison, had been a most serious blow.[64] Mrs Mara and Miss Seaver now left, as did Mrs Allingham. Her daughter Ada, aged 22, stayed and ran the orphanage for the duration of Margaret's imprisonment, according to Margaret's detailed daily instructions. Mrs Allingham's decision to sever links with St Brigid's left Ada in a difficult situation; while quite literally working around the clock to keep the institution afloat for the present, she had to discern her own future path in the midst of upheaval and scandal. Could it be alongside the imprisoned and maligned Miss Aylward? Or with dear Mama who leaned so heavily on her?[65] The other person to stay was the elderly home-maker Eliza Monahan, the stable centre at an othewise chaotic time; she was never to take religious vows even when Margaret and Ada and some later followers determined upon that road.[66]

Margaret left Grangegorman Female Penitentiary at 6 a.m. on the morning of 5 May 1861, having completed the full course of her sentence to the very day. After Mass in Arran Quay church she returned to Eccles Street to a simple but 'most hearty welcome' from Ada and Eliza, and the two servant girls, 'the latter had the front hall strewn with green rushes to greet her return'.[67]

7

Schools of St Brigid

Upon this one thing, the education of the poor, depends
the future of Ireland and the future of society.[1]

The time in prison determined Margaret Aylward on the path she would
pursue on her release: the education of 'the more abandoned more destitute
children' of her adopted city of Dublin, carrying the schooling 'into the poor
localities, to the doors of the room-keepers and inhabitants of cellars'.[2] As
with St Brigid's Orphanage, the schools were planned as a direct offensive in
the battle with the Irish Church Missions and other evangelical societies; as
early as 1852 she could produce substantial field evidence to back up her
claim that 'Alike in the streets and by-lanes, in respectable looking buildings,
bearing their date of erection in legible characters, and in back rooms and
decaying houses, is the work of proselytism stealthily carried out.'[3] St Brigid's
schools had been proposed in advance of her imprisonment, as is evident from
correspondence during the summer of 1860 when she prays 'for new hands
to help at St Bridget's; I long for the schools', but the Grangegorman
interlude provided ample time for reflection and strategic planning.[4] She
credits John Gowan CM with the initial inspiration, and he was to play a
major role in their development, acting as school inspector and checking out
the feasibility of responding to invitations to establish schools in particular
areas. Writing to Margaret who was fundraising in Cork in July 1860, he
reports on how the newly-arrived Ada though 'lonesome without you', is
nevertheless 'strong and well pleased with her work; if you could bring a
couple like her from Cork we might set up school at once, "St Brigid's
Catholic Schools".'[5] Margaret's own interest in schools was also long
standing, from her first experience as a volunteer lay teacher in the
Presentation poor schools in her native Waterford, to the adult catechism
classes in Gardiner Street and first communion classes in the parish schools
of St Michan's under the care of the Ladies of Charity.[6] Within five months
of her release, and now aged 51 years, she opened 10 Crow Street, in the
heart of the Temple Bar district of central Dublin, as the first Catholic School
of St Brigid. A new chapter had begun.

SCHOOL PHILOSOPHY

> The schools are free in the full sense of the word: they are free to the poor, in fact
> the poorest have the first claim to admittance; they are free also from government
> control, and the demoralizing effects of mixed education. They are named Catholic
> schools, being entirely under the guidance of the Church and under the control
> only of her authority.[7]

The philosophy formulated by Margaret Aylward and presented at the
annual public meetings was therefore threefold: her schools were to be Roman
Catholic, for the Catholic poor, and independent of State control.

The impact of this contribution can only be understood within the climate
of suspicion and animosity which surrounded the issue of state-controlled
primary education in Ireland in the mid and later nineteenth century. The
establishment in 1831 of the Commissioners of National Education introduced
a state-sponsored system of mass education to the country for the first time.
With a founding principle of separating religious from literary instruction, so
that 'mixed' schooling would be achieved in all areas excepting religion, it was
vehemently opposed by each of the Christian churches. The initial response
of the Catholic Church in Dublin under Archbishop Murray was one of
cautious cooperation: the need for elementary mass schooling was indisputable, and the Church had neither the human nor material resources to
respond adequately; it would also provide some protection against certain
state-funded proselytizing educational societies.[8] For the protection of Catholic
interests it would be much more expedient to be part of the controlling
system than outside it. The National system could in fact be shaped towards
its own denominational requirements, if carefully handled. The Catholic
Church had one overwhelming advantage: the weight of its numbers, providing the vast majority of the potential pupils, and by extension the great
bulk of their teachers. However, confidence was quickly eroded, and the
foundation by Margaret Aylward of the Catholic Schools of St Brigid, its
philosophy eloquently articulated by John Gowan under the pseudonym
'Testis' and in stirring nationalistic contributions to the published annual
reports,[9] coincided exactly with a period of outright hostility to the state
system, championed by Paul Cullen, appointed Archbishop of Armagh in 1849
and of Dublin in 1852.

1   *Roman Catholic*

In the case of St Brigid's Schools the principal distinguishing feature
enunciated by Margaret Aylward and John Gowan was the place afforded to
religious instruction, so that 'these schools will be always Schools of Faith'

where the children will be 'made strong in Faith – a Faith that is living and operative'.[10] St Brigid's schools always held a crucifix and 'other emblems of religion', the children 'begin and end their work with prayer, and the teachers, while giving secular instruction, can remind the children how all should conduce to their last end and be referred to God', all practices expressly forbidden in the national schools.[11] The criticism that 'the teaching of religion in the schools consumes too much time' and 'impedes the children in their secular studies' was denied: while the catechism lesson 'certainly takes up some little time, but no Catholic would deny that this is necessary', the training of the children 'to blend religion with their daily work' requires little time. 'As to the objection of giving the children too much of religion, every well trained teacher knows well that over-dosing the children with piety defeats the end in view.'[12]

2 Poor

The schools were to be for the poor, which immediately committed Margaret Aylward and her co-workers to securing food and clothing for the poorest pupils. However, such a move laid them open to much criticism. Some considered the education of the poorest a matter of 'wasting' resources; others that St Brigid's schools were no better than the proselytizing institutions they opposed; still others that the only way of effecting the betterment of children of the 'criminal classes' was to confine them in secure reformatories. Margaret defended St Brigid's position at the public meetings in Marlborough Street held to launch the annual reports. She pointed to the utter necessity of providing for these children, orphaned, abandoned or neglected by parents, and independent of any home care from perhaps nine years of age. Refused admission to 'ordinary schools' because they are 'squalid and naked', the provision of food and clothing was essential for 'How can a child stay four or five hours in school that has had no breakfast?' She regularly cited the economic worth of educating the poor, and the great saving in taxes for jails and reformatories that schools such as hers could effect. Worst of all was the great injustice of leaving these children, without knowledge or practice of religion, prey to proselytizers. 'It would be worth a large sum to save these children, make them good Catholics, self supporting men and women, as in fact they are, after spending three or four years in the schools.'[13]

To the charge that 'the practice of giving food for attendance at school demoralizes the poor' Margaret invited 'those good people who make the objection' to 'set up an alms-house near each of these schools, and maintain it', to the eternal gratitude of the sisters; however, until that was the case, the sisters would continue to feed and clothe their charges.[14] Her first move on taking over the Ragged Schools in the Coombe was to rename them: 'She could never be induced to adopt the name ragged. She said that Irish children, though poor, have a certain hereditary nobility of mind that resents degradation.'[15]

It was constantly emphasized that the children were amenable to instruction, and 'if the charitable public only knew how kindly these poor children take to learning their prayers and catechism' there would be no shortage of funds:

> One would not be surprized if these children, many of whom were gathered off the street, were intractable and hard to be taught. No: these wild little boys take to the school-drill wonderfully, and after a few months become steady and obedient. Many of them learn quickly and well. There is no difficulty in getting them to confession. By means of the religious and secular teaching constantly blended, and especially by the moral discipline, they are induced to the practice of obedience, truthfulness, honesty, and fidelity to religious duties, they are raised up and fitted to take a worthy place in society, and in fact many of them, now young men and women, are in respectable employments and far in advance of their poor parents. This is how society is renewed, purified, and lifted up.[16]

The reformatory and industrial school approach to the education of destitute children was actively opposed by St Brigid's schools. St Brigid's Orphanage had been founded on the principle that no institution could substitute for family care, and had taken great risks to maintain this founding ethos.[17] Similarly the schools were strongly opposed to the ready separation of child from parent, and their incarceration in correctional institutions:

> It is commonly supposed that the very poor children of Dublin, who run half-naked about the streets, are corrupt and almost irreclaimable, and that the only way to reform and civilize them is to commit them to the reformatory or Industrial School. No doubt there are subjects among them for both places. But most of them require only care and instruction, for they are naturally intelligent, quick, and amenable to discipline. It would be a blunder as well as a sin to seize poor children and deprive them of their liberty for five or seven years without a crime on their part, on the pretext of reforming them. Men are seldom reformed by coercion. In the ordinary providence of God, human beings are made good by enlightening the mind and directing the will. It is quite right to reform those who, by their misdeeds, have forfeited their liberty. But it is a totally different thing to take away liberty lest a bad use should be made of it. Experience proves the evil consequences of such experiments. Hence the surest and least expensive way of making Christian men and women of these poor hungry children, is to entice them to good schools by a little food and clothing.[18]

The schools were to enlist the active cooperation of the parents, 'and for this purpose, a little book of directions and regulations is given to each parent that presents a child for admission'. Teachers were not to usurp parental responsibilities, 'but care is taken that the children shall go to discharge their religious duties with the leave and under the directions of their parents'.[19]

School lending libraries were promoted from 1875 as an outreach to the families, simultaneously promoting both literacy and religious knowledge. A book was borrowed for the weekend and read 'especially on a Sunday evening, by the child, or some other member, for the family'; appeals for further donations of books especially 'Lives of the Saints, histories of the Church, good religious tales and suchlike' were regularly made.[20]

While pride was taken in the achievements of children in advancing from one level to the next, and especially in the successes of past pupils, with notes of the employment secured, there was a commitment to trying 'to fit the children for their position in society', to teach 'reading, writing, and some ciphering, and the girls as much sewing as will enable them to mend and make for an humble family'. 'What we aim at is not precisely the stimulation of the talent of the gifted few, but the education of all according to their state.'[21] The children were to be prepared to make their way in the rather harsh real world that awaited them, Margaret warning that 'Over-education fills the poor with illusory hopes, and for one who succeeds, it leaves thousands prowling about the outskirts of the professions, filled with the bitterness of disappointment, angry with their fellow-man, railing against authority, assailing religion, and, at last, gnawing in their despair the very bonds of society.'[22]

3 Independent of State Control

The decision to remain independent from the Board of National Education and to by-pass such a ready source of revenue, was a political as well as religious stance, and continually needed to be rationalized:

> English statesmen present a subsidy education with one hand, and a manacle with the other; he who accepts the one, is bound fast by the other, and becomes a slave. Coming events should be read by the light of the past, and independence, especially in primary education, secured by any sacrifice.[23]

The most objectionable aspect of the national system as upheld by Margaret Aylward and John Gowan was 'the possession by a non-Catholic or anti-Catholic government of the supreme control over education', and the abuse they made of this position 'in the establishment of so many model schools, in the publication and circulation of so many anti-Catholic books, the enactment of so many "Rules and Regulations" favourable to heresy'. Above all was 'the attempt made by their chief agent, Dr Whately, to convert the whole system of national education into a huge engine of proselytism.'[24] Background to such claims was the well-publicized and long-running battle between the teachers of Phibsboro National Schools, Dublin and the National Board for allowing the children make the sign of the cross when the clock struck the hour,[25] combined with the very active involvement of his wife and daughters in the Irish Church Missions/Smyly schools (chapter 3), and claims by Whately's daughter in her father's biography that he relied on the national schools for the defeat of popery, all served to further increase the suspicion with which many Catholic activists, including Margaret Aylward and John Gowan, viewed the national system. State-controlled education, perceived as a way of subverting the traditional right of the Catholic church to educate its own adherents, also provided grounds for suspicion. 'To the state is given power to rule society, but to the Church God has given a commission to teach'; St Brigid's schools therefore will be 'absolutely and unreservedly under the Church ... believing that she alone can command the swelling waves of human passions, reach the heart, form the man, and save society'.[26]

By operating only through English, even where Irish was the living and sole vernacular of the people, and by omitting material of a distinctively Irish nature, the National system had the insidious effect of weakening the cultural identity of both pupils and teachers, a fact noted by contemporary critics but very difficult to withstand.[27] How otherwise could school books be procured at no cost, in a situation where very few of the pupils could aspire to purchasing such luxuries? By opting to provide the students with education of a distinctively Irish flavour, St Brigid's schools was a politically subversive force, well in advance of the establishment of the Gaelic League and the resurgence of interest in the language and traditions which made such cultural revivalism popular. The 'cause' of Catholic education was presented especially by John Gowan as an urgent nationalistic issue:

> Ireland stands in the crisis of her destiny. A glorious future lies before her. She is forgetting her internal feuds. Under her bishops she is growing in strength within and in respect without. Let us say it not in boast but in thankfulness: she leads Europe in the cause of innocence, truth and practice, and the greatest man on this earth, Pius IX, commends her for her veracity. Our duty therefore is to stand firm in the cause of Catholic education.[28]

There was also the challenge of demonstrating, 'by facts and experience, that good Catholic schools for the masses can be maintained at a comparatively trifling cost, and can, in fact, be made very nearly self-supporting'.[29] By proving that privately-funded education for the very poorest of society could be well-run and methodologically advanced, St Brigid's intended to subvert the claim that only the state could provide this, confounding the sceptics, including many Catholic priests. Margaret had seen how the Christian Brothers, after experimenting with operations under the National Board, made a policy decision to stay aloof from the State system, with the strains of relying on charity more than offset by the moral support and total freedom they exercised over the running of their schools.[30] 'We take and will take *no* money from the National Board, ours are on the plan of the Christian Brothers, we use their books, their present Superior General has helped me a little in arranging our first – we will have schools also for boys.'[31] From the outset therefore St Brigid's Schools were to be similarly reliant on public funds and good will for their survival and expansion, and as a corollary were to be both open and accountable.

The Child's First Spelling Book in Use at St Brigid's Schools of the Holy Faith was a typically innovative production, spanning the entire primary school period, and thus facilitating the very great range of children found in any class especially where numbers of years of schooling varied radically.[32] With multiplication tables, general rules for spelling, tables for shillings and pence, and 'proverbs, counsels and maxims' ranged in order of difficulty and providing texts for reading and writing practice, it was designed as a single essential in acquiring basic literacy and numeracy. Its cheapness ensured even the poorest child could be supplied with a copy.

The decision to operate independently of the National Board led to very real strains, and St Brigid's and the Christian Brothers schools were not the only ones to take this difficult path. And whatever about taking a bold stand for religious and political reasons in the 1850s and 1860s, the state system was becoming *de facto* denominational with the progress of time. The Sisters of Charity, who ran a convent poor school in Gardiner Street independent of the Board, applied to Dr Cullen in 1884 for approval to become a vested school, subject to the Board's rules and regulations. The request by Sr M.S. Lyons speaks of how the annual grant would be a 'great boon'; the sole drawback she could foresee was that in the unlikely event of a Protestant child attending, the parson could insist on coming to instruct him, a danger she faces good-humouredly: 'Protestants never come to us, and supposing they did, I don't know what Parson would trust himself among a lot of Nuns!'[33] By the 1880s Margaret's insistence on remaining outside the system was becoming more difficult to justify; continuing to go against the grain of popular opinion, and the practice of other religious congregations, is evidence of her deeply-rooted commitment to the principles upon which the schools were opened.

POOR SCHOOL NETWORK: DUBLIN CITY

The efforts 'to carry the schooling into the poor localities, to the doors of the room-keepers and the inhabitants of cellars', progressed steadily in Dublin (Figures 13, 14). There was nothing elaborate about the founding ambition: 'to take a large room or floor in the midst of the poor, set up a statue of the Blessed Virgin, and begin'.[34] The first establishment, 10 Crow Street, was opened exactly on that model, in meeting rooms donated rent-free by the

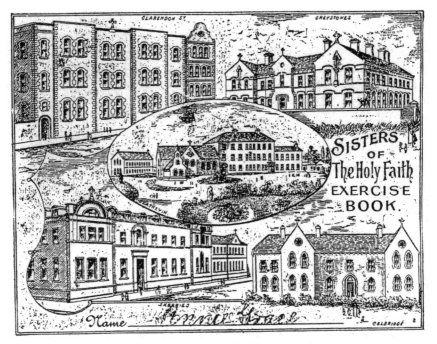

Figure 13: Copybook Cover, *c.*1906

Oblate fathers, while a 'charitable gentleman', on hearing of the project, 'most kindly thanked us for being permitted to furnish the school-room, and asked no earthly return but the concealment of his name.' On 7 October 1860, 'without any formality save the blessing of God' the school was opened for business, Ada Allingham and Margaret Aylward entering the names of fifty girls and infant boys, the first pupils; the earliest report claims that 'the strictest discipline is maintained, and they are learning rapidly'.[35] No. 14 Great Strand Street followed in 1863, directly opposite the Christian Brothers schools, and in the heart of the markets district; the £300 required for building and fitting out was collected by Ignatius Kennedy, the lay activist who had supported Margaret in prison, while John Gowan CM had also secured contributions.[36] Each of the poor schools operated an outdoor relief system, while it was claimed some of the schools 'are the refuge of the poorest children in Dublin, and in fact many of them are kept alive by the food and clothing given them at these schools'.[37] The network expanded gradually: West Park Street, the Coombe (1865), Glasnevin (1865), 65 Lower Jervis Street and Clarendon Street (1870).

The Clarendon Street foundation was in response to a meeting held by St Teresa's confraternity men, attached to the Carmelite church, and chaired by Fr Henry P. Kelly ODC, in January 1869, 'for the purpose of establishing schools for the children of this locality', a great necessity, as 'Clarendon Street is about the centre of a district containing not less than 20,000 inhabitants, and within that district there is not one catholic school; while there are three proselytizing schools doing their infamous work silently but too well'.[38] In this case the children were not of the destitute class, 'food and clothing were not given, because these children did not want it'.[39]

Although nothing whatsoever of the fabric of Crow Street, in the Temple Bar district, survives, a journal kept by Cecilia Donovan allows some of the highlights of the school year to be reconstructed for 1861–72.[40] The distribution of 'premiums', a feature of the orphanage, was also characteristic of the schools at the annual mid-summer and Christmas examinations. Following on the two-day examination of each class, conducted by Fr Gowan and sisters from other houses, an assembly was held, presided over by Miss Aylward, at which books, beads, statues, sweet-meats, pictures, medals, story books, ornaments and toys all feature, the wholesome mixture of pious objects with playthings being exactly what one would expect of St Brigid's, with (usually) every child in attendance receiving something. Such occasions were rounded off with hymn singing, always with the observation 'accompanied by the harmonium'. First confession, first communion, and confirmation in Westland Row church, with dates, numbers and (usually) names, were also recorded, while the establishment of the Children of Mary sodality (8 December 1868), its preparatory branch, the Association of the Holy Angels (8 December 1869), and the first enrolment of children in the Brown Scapular (21 November 1870) were also noteworthy events. The usual school minutiae ('each one being received was told to bring in 8 ¼*d*. it being the price of the ribbon, medal and rule-book for each one', 8 December 1870) is interspersed with accounts of colourful enrolment ceremonies, and Blessed Sacrament and Marian processions in the grounds of Glasnevin convent for the children of the city schools. On 7 May 1868 Dr Cullen, now Cardinal, accompanied by Father Mullally, visited the schools, yet another supportive gesture towards Margaret Aylward and her co-workers: 'he remained about 20 minutes, examined some of the children in their catechism, and gave them his blessing; the children sang a hymn and a song for him' in which they were accompanied on the much-prized harmonium.[41]

Crow Street premises was directly opposite the Medical School of the newly-founded Catholic University; Rose Gaughren recalls how boisterous medical students on one occasion rushed in as several children and the teachers swept out the room at the end of the day; one student grabbed a brush 'and began to sweep the floor vociferously, the other took down a pointer and made the children stand around him in a class and began to hear them spelling'.[42] Threatened with lusty calls for the police they departed as quickly as they had entered, but continued their persecution on other

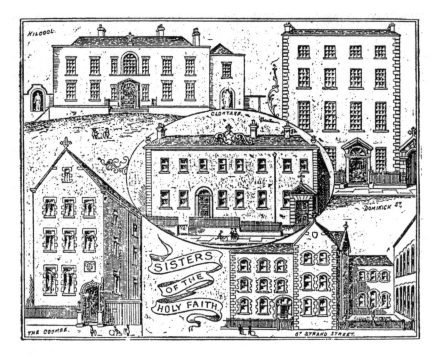

Figure 14: Copybook Cover, *c.*1906

occasions, throwing a dead rat into the schoolroom another morning.[43] The student pranks were inconsequential; of more interest to Margaret Aylward was the intelligence that the medical school building was to be let by the Catholic University in 1871, she 'would get it on better terms than any one else', presumably through Dr Cullen's influence, and if she could only get up 'a decent subscription list' there was a generous individual ready to contribute substantially to the transfer of St Brigid's Catholic Schools to these fine premises.[44] While the Crow Street school was very overcrowded, by 1870 the first purpose-built convent and schoolhouse were in operation in nearby Clarendon Street, and it was more economic to integrate existing and new pupils at this site.

John Gowan's day-to-day involvement in all of these schools is significant, and allowed him to put his own considerable teaching skills to good use. Reporting to Margaret who was *en route* to Rome in September 1864, he found the schools in a satisfactory state, 'but I think the boys are now the best, and Sr Mary Scholastica [Jane Fagan, Margaret's sister], appears to be developing into a woman of sense and energy. She is almost in rude health'. He recommended that the newly-arrived Julia Conran be sent to Crow Street schools, 'should she be well minded she'll make a very good teacher', while the skills of Ellen Maguire (Sr Magdalen), who was keeping order in Crow Street, were deserving of all praise, 'she shows really good sense and great power with the boys'.[45]

WEST PARK STREET SCHOOLS, THE COOMBE

Margaret Aylward had a very special attachment to the West Park Street schools in the Coombe, judging from the coverage these received in the annual reports. These schools also exactly fulfilled her criteria for action: they provided for the very poorest of the poor children of the city, and were situated in the heart of a district ravaged by proselytism. They were also the most populous of St Brigid's schools, with the most extensive and sophisticated daily outdoor relief system.[46] In October 1865 when they were opened under the title of St Brigid's Catholic Schools of the Seven Dolours, there were 54 boys and 104 girls present. This number increased steadily, so that in December 1901, 1099 children were examined in catechism; in 1915 there were 1100 children in attendance and eighteen sisters teaching.[47] Entirely reliant on the charity of the Catholic public, Margaret exploited all possible contacts for its support, with a number of local business people particularly generous supporters. A Mr Ward merited special praise, 'As he did everything at the suggestion of the sisters who knew best what would be most useful for the School, he was a real Benefactor.'[48] At the opening 'Not having means of procuring hot water in order to give the children a more comfortable breakfast, Mr Farrington (baker) offered to supply hot water and the sisters with two of the boys went every morning to carry the hot water from the bakery to the schools.' The school journals record similar instances on an almost daily basis. A Mr Hughes, who had spent most of his life in France, returned home to retire and 'secure sepulture in holy Ireland' looked into the schools and 'was amazed to see so many bare feet and such scanty bodily clothing' and from time to time gave 'large bundles of new and substantial material, which was made into suitable clothing, partly by the little girls, but chiefly by the Sisters'[49] while he also 'gave largely to the children for their parcels: coal, tea and sugar'.[50] 'Distribution days' were usually held twice yearly, at midsummer and Christmas, and also served as concert days and prize-giving, as in the Crow Street schools.

A greater number of families benefited by food relief than were clothed. Cecilia Donovan, first principal of the school, recounts that on arrival to open up the sisters would often meet 'a row of little boys standing by the wall in their caps to keep the feet warm while waiting at the school door',[51] the first of the breakfast queue. About 200 children were provided with breakfast in school in the opening years and sent home with a loaf of bread, a very real incentive to scholarly exertion; there were also periodic distributions of food (tea, sugar, bread), to these families, and a reliable relief order at Christmas. However, the provision of relief was only one of the problems the teachers had to face each day. A particular impediment to the girls' advancement was the amount of child-care they were expected to provide. 'Little girls come to school with their infant sisters or brothers in their arms. The mother is washing or charing to earn a shilling, and if the infant is not admitted, the girl is kept at home without any instruction whatsoever, and in danger of being sent to the proselytizing school.'[52]

The original accommodation in the Coombe was soon grossly inadequate, but the problem here became legal rather than financial: a suitable site, with proper title, could not be obtained for a Catholic school, 'simply because all the parish practically belonged to the Earl of Meath, a Protestant'. A benefactor of the Orphan Refuge, Circular Road, one of the Protestant asylums publicly exposed by Margaret as notoriously proselytizing, it is unlikely that he regarded her with anything other than hostility.[53]

> The fabric which had been a fine old mansion of the old style was then (1865) in a dilapidated condition. Notwithstanding, the Sisters of Faith conducted the schools here for twenty years or more. As years went by the old school was falling to ruin, oftentimes pools of water would be on the floor after a rainy night, and the windows and doors as well as the floors were in a very shaky condition. The number of children too had increased very much, so the juniors had to be taught in the school yard, on a fine day, and sitting on the school floor on other days. The yard was overlooked by tenement houses and often the occupants would lean out of their windows to inspect the classes, which of course distracted both teacher and children.[54]

There are homely details, such as the perilous journey down a rickety stairs to the cellar to procure fuel each morning as there were no heating pipes or caretaker to light fires; using the water pipe to soften the hard bread brought for lunch; and the excitement in the packed school yard when a cat carrying kittens was spotted on the top of the surrounding ten foot wall 'apparently removing her family to safer lodgings'. The fortitude of both children and teachers under such harsh conditions is evidence of the importance attached to education by both parents and teachers. There was no separate apartment for a breakfast room, but 'it would have been ungrateful to complain'; the sister teaching in the yard protested, but 'Of course she did her best in the circumstances, there was no immediate remedy but patience.' Cecilia Donovan, against charges that the sisters had a 'dreary time' in the old premises claimed that the situation was quite the contrary: there was 'a charm about the old place and an attraction towards the poor children', so that she could not help thinking how appropriate were Fr Gowan's words: 'An Irishman loves his native land in proportion to what he suffered in it or for it.'[55]

The accommodation crisis in West Park Street was one of the more intractable problems that Margaret had to face, along with the struggle to meet ever-escalating daily running costs. In 1886 Mr Myers, an unmarried cooper, donated the site of 117 The Coombe to Miss Aylward, with funds and assistance immediately forthcoming from Edward McCabe, former parish priest and now cardinal archbishop of Dublin. Praised by Cecilia Donovan as a 'wideawake man', Myers was the sole owner of his dwelling house 'and a lovely strip of ground reaching from the rere to New Row which was not included in the Earl of Meath's estate':

> Here he had carried on for some years a large cooperage business and had massed sufficient means to support himself and his sister, so that he decided to retire from business. He had been offered £1000 purchase money for same. Having sufficient means he was not avaricious, and as he had no further need of all these premises, he was in doubt as to how he could dispose of it in a manner that would benefit his soul.[56]

The good neighbourliness of Mr Parkes, who owned the adjoining site and 'general merchant' business, and the active help of the parish clergy, Canon Daniel and Fr Hickey, as well as the work of the architects and builders, are all recalled, down to the polishing up of the old desks for their new home, and marching the children in order to take possession on St Mark's Day, 1887.[57]

> Between Mr Myers' dwelling house 117 and the schools 115 there were two old tenement houses. These Miss Aylward purchased for the sum of £700, a large amount then but the site was much needed for a convent as the sisters were obliged to walk from Strand Street or from Glasnevin to the Coombe. The sisters longed to be in the midst of the poor. The convent being finished 1890 four sisters were installed there by Sr Superior, Sr M. Agnes Vickers, first superior general of the Institute.[58]

The convent was followed by the addition of a breakfast hall at the rear of the schools, so that the full length of the narrow plot was now filled, leaving a long passage as the only playground. This hall was paid for out of surplus funds contributed to erect a stained glass window to the memory of the late Canon Daniel, parish priest, including a 'commodious hall with range and boilers'. Canon Scally 'finished the hall with tables, pictures and statues'.[59]

It was the mixture of very poor and slightly better off children that, it was claimed, effected the transformation of the 'wild and apparently untameable children into steady and self-respecting boys and girls':

> How can this be done? It is really not very difficult. All the children of the schools are poor, but not all of the wild class. Somewhat more than half are the children of good, though poor, parents. And be it observed, that the poor of Dublin, who

love their religion and practise it faithfully, are the best Catholics in the world. Well: when the wild children are admitted they do, after a little time, as their betters do. They must obey the click of the signal or the word of the Sister instantly. They cannot do anything or go anywhere out of the ordinary routine without asking leave. They must learn their prayers and say them. The moment the clock strikes there is perfect silence, and each looks up to the Crucifix, blesses himself and says the Ave Maria. They are instructed and prepared for confession, and sent to it in company with steady children. They are prepared for first Communion with care, and afterwards prepare for and make it several times in the year. Care is taken that they go to Mass on Sundays and Holidays, and in fact some of them get up early and assist at Mass on week-days, before the school opens. Thus the Sacrifice, the Sacraments, the Liturgy and the pious practices of the Catholic Church are active agents in the education of these children.[60]

There was the oft-mentioned effect of 'civilizing' the children, Archbishop Walsh reporting on his return from a visit how he was 'delighted with all I saw today. Everyone who was at the schools was talking of the graceful bearing of the children' and that the work 'plainly is bringing a great blessing on that poor neighbourhood'.[61] Despite pressure from clergy to open many more such Catholic schools throughout the city, Margaret Aylward proceeded slowly, needing more recruits.[62]

RURAL SCHOOLS

St Brigid's schools were not to be separated from the first St Brigid's mission, the boarding-out orphanage, and it was partly concern for the schooling of these children 'at nurse' that led Margaret to the decision to found 'village schools'. Requirements – once an invitation was extended from the parish – were relatively simple: 'All that will be ordinarily required will be the use of a plain dwelling-house, and school-rooms free of charge, and, if possible, a plot of ground, for which a fair rent will be paid.' Village schools were also founded with a view to recruiting teachers. The poor schools could be maintained and extended only with large numbers of committed persons, unlike the orphanage which even at its most populous required only a small management team. Rural schools would, it was hoped, 'foster and develop religious vocations among the daughters of the Irish farmers', who were regarded as the most promising material for teaching in the city schools as they have 'enthusiasm and buoyancy and mental power and strength of constitution, and withal a simplicity of character'.[63] This wish was in fact to be fulfilled, with Mullinavat, Co. Kilkenny, proving to be the most successful in that regard (*see* chapter 8).

The setting-up of the short-lived Kilcullen schools on 30 June 1873 can be followed from Margaret's innumerable instructions. This move from

Dublin to Co. Kildare was undertaken in a truly pioneering spirit: the clock to be well-packed with hay in a clothes basket ('also wanted') and Crone the carrier instructed to bring it and 'the little hair mattresses and little iron bedsteads if they not be gone'; the young Rose Gaughren was reminded to be sure to send up the larger hair mattresses in their place.[64] Rose Gaughren's own invaluable account of that mission speaks of the cottage 'situated on the bank of the Liffey with a nice meadow or lawn in front and a good vegetable and fruit garden at the back', the sisters' work to consist of two pension schools, charge of the choir and sacristy and to teach Catechism in the church on Sundays. The departure of the sisters from this scenic location was due to the refusal of the landlord ('Mr Blacker, a bigoted Protestant') to renew the lease, while the owner of an nearby old house, with some land, refused to sell it to Margaret as he had his own plans for the village. His daughter was then a postulant with the Cross and Passion nuns who were 'very anxious to make a foundation in Ireland, and Mr Quinn, knowing this, gave the old house and land as a dowry to his daughter.' Dr Cullen refused to allow this religious order to move in for as long as his friend Miss Aylward wanted her community there, but she had little choice, and the house was closed in August 1878. Celbridge, which was to provide for the many St Brigid's children at nurse in the area, was a very happy alternative. The building of Celbridge convent predates Margaret's involvement; there were proposals in 1854 from the local parish priest, James Lynch, that adjoining the Chapel grounds 'there is what is called the Brewery Yard containing about 2 acres with building materials &c., most eligible for a Convent and Chapel to be had at very reasonable terms if applied for by a *lay party*'.[65] The convent on this site was built for the Mercy Sisters of Naas, who were to take charge of the workhouse, 'but they declined to take it up as their number at the time was very small'.[66] Other village schools to be opened in Margaret's lifetime included Skerries (1875), John Gowan's birthplace, and Mullinavat (1879, *see* chapter 10).

FEE-PAYING SCHOOLS

Explicit mention is made of fee-paying schools in the request for congregational status made by Margaret Aylward to Dr Cullen in 1866, when she follows a description of the congregation's mission as 'endeavouring to defend the Holy Faith in the persons of poor Catholic orphans and destitute children', with the intention that

> If it please God we shall not confine our efforts to the teaching of the poor, but found schools for higher classes, the profits of which shall be applied to the

maintenance of schools for the poor – our chief care being the poor, and our principal object the defence of the Faith.[67]

In the published report for 1869 St Brigid's schools are described as 'partly self-supporting and will it is hoped be wholly so with the aid of middle schools which are about being established'.[68] Within a few years it was announced that pay schools would be opened at the request of 'parents in good circumstances' who sought the benefits of 'unmixed' Catholic education for their children. In 1879 it was reported that a 'middle school was opened for them in the Convent, Clarendon Street' with the note that 'it is reasonable that those who are able should pay for the education of their children'.[69] The fees, though modest, enabled the sisters to continue working gratuitously in the poor schools. That the middle class had been poorly provided for to date is noted in an offer from the Mercy sisters to open a pay school in the vicinity of Marlborough Street for Catholic children 'of a class who do not wish to mix with the very poor and are not able to pay at the expensive day schools'; Cullen's encouragement of the expansion of the Holy Faith network into the private sphere is for precisely the same class reasons.[70]

Glasnevin Boarding School, opened 1873, for 'respectable girls', was warmly welcomed 'for the farmers' daughters, the parents of whom dread sending their children to a regular young ladies school, it so turns their heads'!'[71] The account book of the Boarding School of Our Lady of the Angels Convent Glasnevin lists the expenses involved in its establishment (1873–4), including the erection of a partition between school room and dormitory, the printing of 500 prospectuses and the cost of newspaper advertisements, the purchase of bedsteads, palliasses and feather bolsters, 12 Windsor chairs, fabric for table cloths, cutlery and delph for about 30 persons, and a second-hand piano. The student body was drawn from a wide geographical area, attracting the daughters of business families from small towns such as Bailieborough, Ballinasloe, Carrick-on-Suir and Skerries and, to a lesser extent, from Dublin city and suburbs. Farming families are, understandably, the largest group represented, with the counties nearest to Dublin (Meath, Kildare, Westmeath) as well as Dublin county itself providing students, along with Cork, Waterford, Mayo and Tipperary.[72] The basic pension in the 1870s was £20 per annum with additional fees for tuition in music, drawing, French, dancing, singing and 'fancy work', while the costs of clothing, school-books and stationery were also supplementary. As would be expected of any Aylward venture, the boarding school accounts were meticulously kept, all school expenses separated from the convent account (although they shared the one premises), with regular contributions from the school monies towards 'building the new convent, Glasnevin'.[73]

A newspaper clipping from *The Leader* speaks stirringly of the 'Irish education given to Irish girls' of the middle and upper classes by the Holy Faith sisters in Glasnevin boarding school:

After God and his laws they are taught to love their native land, her language, her traditions, her history, and her poetry. Their plays are all Irish in sentiment, in history and in plot; their songs are all Irish in genius and in feeling, and the impression made on a visitor is most pleasing. In a school like this, the impressions made on the youthful minds and hearts are Irish of the Irish. They grow up with a love of their native land, and when these girls go out into the world and become mothers of families and mistresses of houses it is not likely they or their children's children will ever be ashamed of the grand traditions and history of their race.[74]

While Glasnevin is held up as a model establishment from an Irish perspective, other named convents are derided for their blindness in continuing their 'West British game' and making their convents 'vehicles of Saxon manners and education', contributing to the creation of a 'mongrel class who were neither fish nor flesh – neither Irish nor Saxon – and who burdened this country with the useless encumbrances of shoneens and cads'.[75]

EXPANSION OF THE SCHOOL NETWORK

While it was the evolving network of 'poor schools' which took up the greater part of Margaret's attention, the principles on which all her schools were founded were not to be diluted, as illustrated in the negotiations regarding the establishment of houses outside Dublin. Requests from Donegal and Westport were turned down; from Headford, Co. Galway, the parish priest assured Margaret that the schools were ready, 'statues placed in them – up to the sisters to come and teach in them', but that invitation was also declined, as the schools were under the National Board.[76]

Negotiations for a school in Letterfrack, Co. Galway had progressed much further before that project was also abandoned. The demand for schooling in the western diocese of Tuam was immense, due mainly to the obdurate refusal of the long-reigning archbishop of Tuam, Dr McHale, to countenance the development of the national system in any shape or form; the very small number of religious in Connacht meant that there were few alternatives.[77] The Irish Church Missions in particular had targeted the region in search of converts (chapter 3); the attraction of food, clothing and schooling to a famished and dispirited people was understandable.

In December 1883 John McEvilly, who succeeded Dr MacHale as archbishop of Tuam (1834–1881) made 'a truly generous offer' favoured with many 'temporal advantages' of a foundation in Letterfrack.[78] The prospect appealed greatly to Margaret, as Letterfrack was among the poorest of the western districts, greatly in need of Catholic schools 'and the great good derivable therefrom to the poor people'.[79] It seemed to encapsulate exactly where she felt her community should be: 'it would give me much pleasure to be able to do anything for the poor people of the West, as I think they need it, the Soupers plied their trade there artfully.'[80] She had turned down innumerable requests for her 'Sisters of Faith' to work on 'foreign missions', believing that 'our Mission should be in Ireland, and in the most ignorant, necessitous and abandoned parts of this poor country', and what better place than the west? This house seemed to fulfil all the criteria, and while there was a shortage of personnel, Margaret hoped that 'by the time the Lawyers have done all that is necessary' Divine Providence 'by sending us additional help will enable me to withdraw from other houses those subjects suitable for the proposed work'.[81] Two months later she was arranging for 'a friend' (John Gowan) to inspect the premises on her behalf, checking on the 'shortest and easiest route' by train and car, discussing house repairs and hoping a caretaker was on the premises in the interval. 'In three months from this I expect to have in Letterfrack a colony of the Sisters of Faith, if that time would suit your Grace's wishes.'[82] Then 'a difficulty cropped up': McEvilly 'had no idea on earth' that her schools were not connected with the National Board, 'like most of the convents and schools through Ireland'.[83] He himself 'had introduced the National Schools into all my convents as I found it worked so well in Galway etc., and in every other Diocese in Ireland' and would now 'be in rather a false position if I introduced nuns' schools for the poor different from all the nuns' schools in the Diocese'. His commitment to collaborating with the national board can be judged from the way in which he informed Archbishop McCabe in 1879 of his intention to support new national schools with diocesan funds and threatening to appeal to Rome if he was thwarted in this resolve.[84] The independent stance of St Brigid's schools was to him incomprehensible. He appealed that an exception might be made in this instance and the new schools placed under the national board, citing its inspection system as a 'security or guarantee' as to their efficiency. Long term continuity was also an issue: while 'praying a long life' for both Margaret Aylward and John Gowan he assured them it was not likely they would live for ever, 'not is it quite certain that I will either'![85] But the answer from Dublin was unequivocal: 'we could not on any account accept the proposed foundation in Letterfrack and have our Schools in connection with the National Board', closing 'our correspondence on this subject' with the wish 'that our decision thereon will not make us the less friendly nor sincere well wishers of Your Grace and of your pious undertaking' and assuring him he will have no difficulty in getting another community for the Letterfrack foundation 'who will accept the authority of the National Board'.[86]

Invitations to expand the Holy Faith network to other parts of the British Empire were extended in 1884 by the then elderly John Curtis SJ. His request that the 'Daughters of the Faith who owe their origins as a religious order to St Brigid' might take on the challenge of 'making the true faith known and loved to the most distant boundaries of the earth' was turned down by Margaret Aylward, under the pressure of existing commitments in Ireland. While accepting that it was currently impossible for her to take on the proposed project, Curtis however urged her to keep an open mind:

> I would sow the little mustard seed and allow it to grow as far as Divine Providence might favour it, content in doing some good though not all I could desire. It would seem to me that such is the case with the Church of God.[87]

John Curtis had followed Margaret Aylward's struggles for over thirty years, from the first meeting of the Ladies of Charity, which he had chaired; he more than most could testify to the remarkable development of St Brigid's work. For him its extension overseas was but the next logical step; though under considerable pressure, Margaret reiterated that her mission was still to 'the most ignorant, necessitous and abandoned parts of this poor country'.[88]

CONCLUSION

Margaret Aylward's attachment to independent status limited the geographical spread of her poor schools and also the size of her sisterhood as country areas and small towns were better recruiting grounds than the Dublin metropolis. By her death in 1889 there was only one foundation outside the Dublin archdiocese, Mullinavat in Ossory (Chapter 10). However, within the parishes where the schools operated they made a significant local impact. The fine premises in which, after much hardship, the schools were accommodated, is illustrated in copybook covers from *c*.1906 (Figures 13, 14). The schools became part of the physical fabric of the city, but more importantly contributed to the building-up of the city's social fabric. The sisterhood which emerged to run these schools did so with considerable lay support, and through the combination of varied services which they provided in the parishes, such as the provision of Christmas dinners in Jervis Street, night classes for working girls in Clarendon Street and Strand Street, sodalities in Crow Street, and food and clothing in the Coombe, along with daily schools free to the poor, they made an important contribution to the local community. They proved that the 'street arabs' could be educated and formed into useful citizens, and constantly supported the care of children within the local community in preference to the institutionalizing of industrial schools and reformatories.

> During the last twenty years, about three thousand children passed through the schools at the Coombe. Of these five, that had spent less than a year in the school, were brought before the magistrate and punished; one that had been in the school two years was similarly punished. But of those who had been under the discipline of the school three years or more, none are known to have become criminals.[89]

Through the platform of the annual reports and action at the local level these schools undoubtedly affected the activities of the Irish Church Missions and other evangelical societies which engaged in proselytism. However, proselytism continued to be a major challenge to the Catholic church in Dublin, as evidenced in the Walsh papers for 1913 which include 'statistics of proselytism', black lists of institutions accused of involvement, and accounts of 'raids' by Catholic activists on the 'proselytising schools' of Lurgan Street, Rath Row, Grand Canal Street and the Coombe,[90] all reminiscent of Margaret Aylward's crusade launched sixty years earlier.

As far as the disparate nature of the records allow one to judge, the academic standards in the schools founded by Margaret Aylward were good, and certainly reached those who would otherwise have had no schooling at all. St Brigid's schools contributed to the development of an Irish curriculum in their adoption of the texts produced by the Christian Brothers, but also in the production of their own texts and teaching aids. To the extent that one can measure the religious and moral success of any school, these institutions did all in their power to ensure each child was 'taught their catechism, and trained to the faithful performance of their religious duties'.[91]

8

Sisters of the Holy Faith

Margaret Aylward's sustained efforts from at least 1851 to bring the
Daughters of Charity to Dublin, and her subsequent disappointment in the
summer of 1857 when she realized that her ambitions to provide them with
a ready-made lay branch complete with an established if young ministry – St
Brigid's boarding-out orphanage – were not going to work out, threw her
back to the drawing board yet again. Imprisonment, for obvious reasons,
placed some plans on hold, though it did allow her vision to crystalize, and
she left Grangegorman convinced that the Catholic schools of St Brigid were
really the road to travel. Within months Crow Street had opened, followed
quickly by others (chapter 7). But the problems of long-term staffing and
management of the existing charities, now extended to this new venture, had
not been resolved. Reluctant to take on the role of foundress of a new
congregation, and indeed, in her early fifties, with two unsuccessful novitiate
attempts behind her, media notoriety, and poor health, she was an unlikely
candidate for such a role.

Margaret's decision to allow her group be formed into a religious
congregation was intimately bound up with her hopes for the enlargement of
this Catholic poor school network, and her determination to maintain the
unpaid character of all her charitable work. To ensure stability the voluntary
services of like-minded women who would bind themselves permanently to
this mission was required, and a religious congregation could make this
possible. The idea evolved gradually. The earliest reference is found in a
letter to Cullen dated 29 December 1858, when Margaret expresses the hope
that 'a few Ladies will come and live with me and devote their time to our
charities. They will be under no tie whatsoever, in fact it is done by way of
trial, and if it please the Almighty thro' our Lady's and St Bridget's inter-
cession He will give form and permanence to it.'[1] During her confinement in
Grangegorman Margaret received several applications from women who were
interested in joining her in the work of St Brigid's Orphanage (while,
ironically, the little lay group in Eccles Street was rapidly disbanding and the
whole project teetered on the brink of collapse).[2] It was the worry of 'who is
to mould and form them for that work?' that prompted her to press for the
appointment of Fr John Gowan as spiritual director, a move supported by

Cullen; and it was Gowan's eventual appointment and agreement to take charge of spiritual formation that led Margaret to acquiesce to Cullen's urgings to found a religious congregation.[3] In 1863 John Gowan, signing himself as 'director', described 'St Brigid's Society' as a collection of 'thirteen pious maidens', who 'direct the work of the Orphanage, established by Miss Aylward, foundress of the Society of St Brigid, AD 1857'.[4] In June 1864 a Ligourian sister congratulates 'dear Miss Aylward' on being foundress of a new congregation, remarking 'Through what thorny paths must walk those who are called to be foundation stones of those great edifices which reach from Heaven few better than you can tell!', and assuring her of her prayers for St Bridget's work, 'the grain of mustard seed truly, which will flourish throughout the green Isle your virtue casts so bright a halo over'.[5] In 1886 the Institute of the Sisters of the Holy Faith, described as 'founded and directed' by Margaret Aylward, was granted an apostolic blessing, and commended for its rapid growth, flourishing spiritual state, and zeal for youth.[6] The stream of applicants was to be small, and losses due to persons leaving and deaths often cancelled out the gains of any single year, but the total number of permanently committed members rose gradually (Table 3). Once the path was agreed upon, the transformation from a lay community to a religious congregation was remarkably rapid, taking about seven years.

It was Cullen who in June 1866 'kindly told me to write the application' to Rome that 'it may be made a religious congregation or at least that the first steps thereto may be taken that it may receive the sanction and approbation of the Church.' However, while Cullen had requested that it be erected '*for his own Diocese*', it was Margaret who questions if it would not however be better to make it 'general *not* local'.[7] The question of diocesan *vs.* pontifical control was not new to Margaret; as early as 1840 when she was exploring the possibility of establishing a house of the Irish Sisters of Charity in her home city of Waterford, and had their constitutions ('carefully sealed') delivered to her 'without any danger of observation or remark', she was advised that the sisters 'would be more desirable provided they were established on the same footing as the other Convents, *dependent on the Bishop and subject to no other control*'.[8] Now facing the same question in relation to her own community, it appears most likely that it was Dr Kirby in the Irish College in Rome who endorsed her preference for a central authority; a letter marked 'Copy' is an explicit request to be erected 'into a Congregation for Your Grace's Archdiocese' and is most probably the text which Kirby critiques a fortnight later.[9] Whatever the background politics, the congregation came under the direct control of Rome (subject only to the ordinary authority of the bishop of the diocese), a matter of much consequence later.

The first group of ladies living in community had disbanded during the prison episode, excepting Ada Allingham and Eliza Monahan. However, one

Total number of entrants per annum

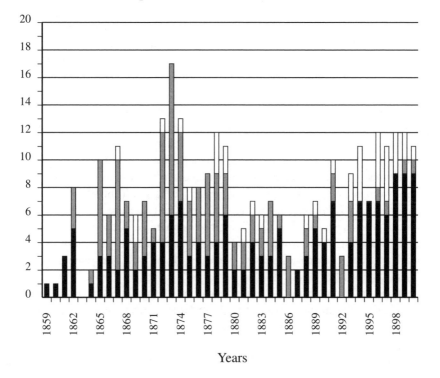

Years

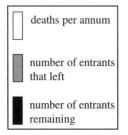

Table 3: Entrants to Holy Faith Congregation 1859–1900

year later, in 1862, Margaret was able to report: 'Eight of us live together now, we have a little Chapel in the house – and we follow a simple rule.'[10] The following year 'St Brigid's Society' was described as numbering thirteen 'pious ladies' living a communal life, whose first concern is 'to apply themselves to their own sanctification', and secondly, 'with the approval of the Catholic authorities, to devote themselves totally to the work of snatching orphans and poor Catholics from the plots of the heretics, and of keeping them safe in the holy Catholic Faith.'[11] In 1869 Margaret reported 'At our convent of "The Sisters of Faith" Glasnevin we number 27. A large number made their vows on the great feast of the Assumption, the vows are made by his Eminence's desire for three years first, and then for life.'[12] In practice, the founding group and their successors renewed temporary vows at three-year intervals up until 15 August 1904, when perpetual vows were taken for the first time.[13] Eliza Monahan, the first named in the list of members, was the only woman not to take vows, but continued as a full member of the young congregation. Of indeterminate age ('she was old, her age not known'), in the Obituary it is stated that she 'kept the orphanage accounts and helped in every way but never wore the religious habit'. She acted as homemaker in Eccles Street, cooking and caring for the sick, as well as managing the house finances, until her death in 1869.[14]

The rapid and thorough transformation of the founding group must be largely credited to the energy of Fr John Gowan, who, once embarked on the road of directing a new religious congregation, devoted himself to it with his customary zeal, that the Institute might be recognizably religious, and its members 'real' nuns. The specific criteria which had to be met to fulfil this end can be gleaned from the 'query sheets' which congregations of religious women had to complete and return to the diocesan ordinary; surviving sheets completed by Margaret Aylward for 1869 trace the origins of the congregation from the Ladies' Association of Charity, and summarize its ministries, properties, income, the formation of novices, its relationship with 'externs', the role and duties of the chaplain, adherence to various church regulations, and precise details relating to the reservation of the Blessed Sacrament, sacred vessels, and the proper celebration of Mass.[15] In response to the inquiry on the constitutions and statutes under which this order operates, Margaret explains:

> In the commencement of the Institute but few Rules were necessary. In process of time and according as necessity required it, other Rules were added. During the present year a Code of Rules has been drawn up extracted chiefly from the Rule of St Ignatius. These the Sisters have begun to observe and as soon as time shall have found their perfect adaptation to our manner of life, they shall be submitted to the Church for approbation.[16]

John Gowan formulated the first draft rule of 1858, followed by an order of day.[17] In 1863 he described how the 'pious ladies' of St Brigid's Society 'rise at five, are free for one hour and a half for mental prayer, recite the Rosary daily, make three examinations of consciences each day, and practise other exercises of piety.'[18] By 1866 Margaret explains that over the preceding seven years the group has 'observed the ordinary rules and practises the ordinary observances of Community life'. In her outline of the daily routine she describes how the morning half-hour's meditation is supplemented by another hour's meditation from 12–1 p.m. for those sisters who do not teach in school, 'during which they usually do needlework'; the school sisters make good this absence 'by recollection walking to and from school', besides which:

> All assist daily at Holy Mass, make a Visit besides to the Blessed Sacrament, make two examens of Conscience general and particular each day, have reading at meals, accuse themselves in presence of each other of some of their outward faults each Friday evening, go to Confession once a week, and observe silence except in times of recreation.[19]

John Gowan's Sunday sermon and weekly 'spiritual conferences on the duties of Religious Life' were the central elements in the community's formation; several hundreds of his sermons and spiritual addresses to the sisters survive, many written up by the sisters directly following the address.[20] Practices such as the Chapter of Faults, as described above, were introduced under his direction.[21] He also contributed to teacher training, his role of giving 'Instructions to the Sisters on the Method of Teaching' specified as one of his principal duties in the returns of 1869. The title 'Holy Faith' was adopted at his suggestion.[22]

Religious names were first adopted 15 May 1864, as Margaret Gaughren (Sr M. Rose), who joined in September 1861 aged sixteen years, describes:

> One Saturday evening Miss Aylward came up to the community room in St Brigid's Eccles Street after tea as she very often used to do and said 'To him that conquers I will give a new name'. On the next day, Sunday, she came with Fr Gowan as he often did on Sundays after his instruction in the Oratory. He took a small leather bag and told each of us to put in the name of a saint, only woman saints at the time. He said that if anyone did not get the name she wished it would be a pleasure for her to see it with another. Even Miss Aylward did not get her choice for she put in St Therese but drew out St Agatha.[23]

The religious name M. Agatha was used by John Gowan in letters addressed to Margaret from this date, but no one else appears to have made the change, and Margaret herself continued to use her own name with the sole exception of signing her vow formula.

The adoption of religious dress was even more important, placing an indisputable distance between the 'lay' and 'religious' life and bringing with it an appropriate code of behaviour. The first members of the new Holy Faith congregation wore a sober secular dress: 'plain black dress, black bead collar, a chenille veil on head in the home, black straw bonnet trimmed with ribbon in the school, and walking in the street a black lace veil and black woollen shawl'. Shortly after the adoption of religious names, St Patrick's Day 1863, the shawls were replaced with 'black cloaks of black cloth and very long, a black cashmere cape with buttons in front. Fr Gowan was greatly pleased to see the members wearing a more religious dress, each one had to turn round to let him see the cloak on'. The outfits were made 'with the greatest care for Miss Aylward was exceedingly particular about the dress of the sisters, everything should be extremely neat ... to a hairsbreadth like the given pattern no matter how often it had to be taken asunder'.[24] This was clearly as far as Margaret intended to go in the matter of a religious habit, but there was further pressure. Rose Gaughren writes that:

> For a long time Miss Aylward did not intend to let the community have any other dress than that mentioned above, but in 1869, by advice of Cardinal Cullen, on 15th August Miss Aylward, M. Allingham. M. Vickers, M. Maguire, M. Fagan (sister of foundress, widow), M. Graves, M. O'Brien, M. McKeogh, and M. Gaughren made the three vows of religion before Father Gowan in the Oratory, Glasnevin, now used as a Refectory by the Boarders – had their hair cut off and wore black bonnet lined with white and long black veil and gamp and silver cross.[25]

While conversion to a religious congregation was now largely complete, Margaret herself did not wear religious dress again, according to Rose Gaughren because she had 'so much public business to transact, regarding the Orphanage etc'.[26]

Although John Gowan played a major role in the creation of the sisterhood, Margaret Aylward, foundress and first superior, was not a bystander in the process. Her own emerging vision of religious life can be gleaned from references in business letters and in letters home from the continent, short pieces in the annual reports of the orphanage and schools, and from the membership register of the new congregation. Wherever she travelled she checked out the charitable institutions and convents, and does not spare her criticisms of some orders, such as one in Aix-les-Bains, where she has been sent in 1864 to drink 'hideous waters'. She notes in a general way that 'the religious are dressed here and in all France most strangely – black night caps close to the head, and white linen showing out under the lower part – black veils getting in and out of railway carriages'.[27] In a later letter from the same spa town she notes again that 'the nuns are here in all imaginable costumes – too many altogether'.[28] One particular instance had come to her notice:

> A young lady of this house goes to a convent next week and such preparation! – silver fork, silver handled knife – and drinking cup, gilt inside – white watered silk dress with a bouquet of orange flowers new made for the reception – not 20 years of age yet – & well off.[29]

In Aix-la-Chapelle (Aachen) she was impressed with the Nuns of the Poor of St Francis whose work was gratuitously 'attending and relieving the sick poor in their houses'. She notes that they take perpetual vows, 'go on the streets alone', and most importantly, have no lay sisters, 'all are of the same ~~rank~~ class (*sic*) – some of better position than others, some with fortune some without it'.[30]

The main elements of Margaret Aylward's plan are contained in these comments: dowries will not be necessary for admission; there will be no division in the community as existed in almost all convents in Ireland at the time between 'lay' and 'choir' sisters; the sisters will be 'walking nuns' untrammelled by cloister; the visitation of the sick poor will continue; and the kind of extravagances exhibited by the presence of fine food, silver-handled cutlery and watered silk dresses would ill befit the daughters of St Brigid. In a description of the group as it stood in 1866, she explains how 'Some have considerable fortunes, and some have little or none – all have given their services gratuitously to the works of the Institution', trusting that 'from the experience of the past, and the goodness of Almighty God', our Lady and the saints, 'there are grounds to hope that material resources shall not fail the little Congregation.'[31] She directs in 1872 that the sisters 'live in an ordinary house attached to the school, and go to Mass like the rest of the faithful ... there will be no need of a chaplain nor of walls of enclosure nor of any ornamentation, and the schools in most localities will be self supporting[32] and in reference to the take-over of a house in Jervis Street that year says 'The sisters will live here as in Clarendon Street, in the midst of the poor, looking after their children.'[33] The full divine office, as sung by cloistered nuns, and choir sisters in apostolic congregations such as the Presentation convents, would not be required. In response to an enquiry as to whether this community had 'long prayers' Margaret replies 'I told him we had not, that of our work we should make a prayer.'[34]

Analysis of the community 'Register of Membership' reveals the extent to which Margaret's plans were carried out, and modified, as time passed (Table 4). Of the first forty-one entrants, 1859–67, only five brought money: Ada Allingham brought the exceptional sum of £1000; Jane Fagan, Margaret's sister, whose husband had deserted her, came to live in Eccles Street bringing an income of £50 per annum; three other women brought dowers of £100, £25 and £40 respectively.[35] Over time dowers became increasingly common, but even by 1879 still fewer than half of the entrants brought dowers, and a substantial number of these are quite modest, as low as £20. By 1889, Margaret's death, most entrants brought money, and there is a clear target of £100 dower money and £14 to cover clothing. Allowance is still made for persons with no means who wished to join, although some contribution, at least towards the cost of clothing and noviceship 'pension', is now expected.

Number of entrants

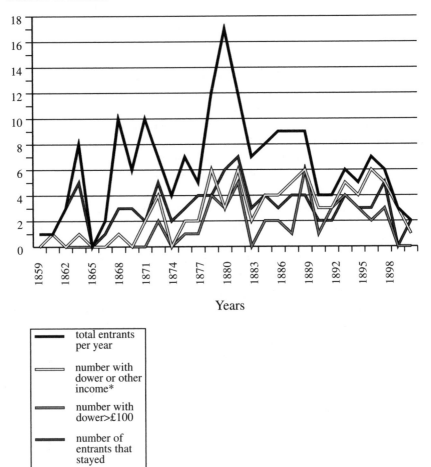

Years

total entrants
per year

number with
dower or other
income*

number with
dower>£100

number of
entrants that
stayed

Table 4: Holy Faith entrants 1859–1900, dowers and other income

To place this in perspective, Caitríona Clear in her study of Irish convents reports that the minimum for acceptance as a choir nun to the Presentation Convent, Galway in the early nineteenth century was £500; the lowest dowry accepted in the Galway Mercy from 1840–1857 was £200, while the average was £375; and occasional larger sums were not uncommon in many convents, even as large as £35,000 from a postulant in the Loreto Convent, Rathfarnham.[36]

The new Holy Faith community, with its relatively modest dower, and the accompanying flexibility, brought religious life within the reach of some women who wished to enter and teach, but were excluded from many of the longer-established convents unless they were prepared to lower their sights and become lay sisters. Lay sisters, who either brought no dower, or a small one, performed the domestic work of the convent, cooking, scrubbing, serving, gardening, washing.[37] Regarded by many as a necessary substitute for servants, Margaret's decision to disallow such divisions went against the prevailing wisdom. There could of course be persons who might choose to devote themselves to domestic work rather than teach or administer the orphanage, but all who taught were to contribute to the housework, even taking turns at milking cows in Glasnevin before heading off to teach in city schools.[38] Rose Gaughren's account of the first days of the community explains this evolution:

> There were two servants in the house so there was no manual work assigned to the members except the making of their beds., &c. After some months the servants were dismissed and one woman who did not lodge in the house employed to open the hall door during the day. The Community then did the cleaning of the house, the washing etc.[39]

Each member was to take her turn with the various household duties under a rota system, with Saturday duties ranging from scouring the stairs to washing out the refectory; Margaret directed operations even when convalescing at a remove from Eccles Street, with orders to those on floor-washing duty to put sacks or 'a coarse rubber' under their knees, and 'to mind the oil cloth and not to let *any* soda or much soap touch it'.[40] In the midst of such mundane matters she reminds the young recruits to be 'very gay and cheerful', and that 'It is a great honour and happiness to be allowed to do any little menial work for God in His house.'[41]

Several religious congregations directed postulants without means or with relatively small dowers to Glasnevin once the new congregation had become well established.[42] The Presentation Convent, Carrick-on-Suir, sent a welcome stream of ten postulants between 1879 and 1889, starting with the niece of the Presentation superioress, Mary Josephine Phelan (Sr M. Regis). The register provides scrappy but valuable family details on the type of persons who entered, particularly if they stayed. Note is made of possessions and money, as these had to be returned to the woman if she left the community. The aforementioned Mary Josephine Phelan is typical: 'no dower, £10 has been paid for her outfit and £12 per annum for 3 years. She brought a hat and jacket also some clothes in a carpet bag and £1.12.3 in purse'. The elderly Catherine Colclough (Sr Lucy), 1868, aged sixty-four was one of several widows who joined; Catherine's son was a solicitor in Dame Street and her married daughter Mrs Spain lived in 15 Eccles Street so she was evidently a woman of substance, paying at the rate of £150 per annum out of her yearly income, 'as she is old and has no dower to leave to the Community'. More typical was Maggie Coughlan (Sr M. Bonaventure), 1878, nearly sixteen, no dower, but had £10 for outfit and 'also brought a purse with 7/6 in it. A little underclothing in a black leather bag – no trunk – a hat and black shawl'. Brigid Coughlan (Sr M. Gabriel), 1883, aged seventeen had no dower but 'brought £10 for her outfit and 2/– worth of stamps'. Ellen Byrne, about twenty years, from Roundwood, arrived in 1880 with 'a good dress fashionably made, a good jacket and hat – very little underclothing and a small fancy bag'. She seems to have found life in Glasnevin too demanding, as within a month she leaves, 'as she thought she was too delicate'.

Previous occupation is mentioned in a few instances, mainly service, shopwork, or governess. Rose Maloney (Sr Mary Borgia), 1876, aged eighteen, was from Westmeath and had worked as a governess in Longford; although without a dower she arrived well equipped, with 'a pretty good supply of clothing and a trunk, £3.0.6 in her purse'. Both Margaret Carroll (Sr Mary Camillus), aged '27 or 29', 1877, and Mary Jane Dowling (Sr M. Peter), aged thirty-eight, 1878, were in 'trustworthy situations', at a draper's and confectioner's respectively, and arrived without dowers but otherwise well set up, Mary Jane bringing an income of £18 per year from house property, 'a good supply of clothing and books, a writing-desk, work box and trunk'. One of the best off was Teresa Lenehan, Rathfarnham (Sr M. Benedict), 1879, aged nineteen, whose mother was in the provision business, and came with a dower of £300.

Past pupils of the boarding school in Glasnevin, founded 1873, numbered among the entrants from 1884, providing a reliable source of moneyed and educated girls.[43] Of far more significance in terms of recruitment in the 1880s was Mount St Joseph, Mullinavat, founded in May 1880 and which between 1882 and 1885 sent twelve postulants to Glasnevin, nine of whom stayed.[44] Within this group there was a wide range of social classes, from the wealthiest arriving with a dower of £300, followed by four more with dowers of £100 or more, down to the poorest, whose father had promised £30, £15 of which 'will be paid next harvest'. The other women entered with sums between £40 and £60.[45]

The number of entrants per decade (Table 3) is greater than in the convents in Limerick and Galway which form the basis of Clear's study; however, the percentage loss in Holy Faith, at over 50 per cent in the 1860s and 1870s, is considerably greater than losses in the Galway Mercy at 20 per cent, or the Limerick Good Shepherd at 18 per cent.[46] Of the 96 who left, 15 were sent home because of delicate health or a tendency towards consumption; 26 were sent away as unsuitable, one girl was taken away by her father 'without consulting her wishes',[47] two were dispensed from their vows, while the majority, 52, left of their own desire, though after some is also noted that they were unsuitable, and presumably would have been encouraged to leave had they not made up their own minds on the matter.

Margaret's readiness to accept those without income led initially to a distinctive pattern of recruitment and internal organization, which set it apart from the majority of nineteenth-century teaching congregations in Ireland. As the new congregation became more established, and particularly after Margaret's death, the original distinctions between Holy Faith and the majority of other religious congregations operating in Ireland became less notable, although a crisis in 1903 highlights the energy with which some of the distinctive founding principles continued to be defended. The Holy See withheld approval of the new constitutions until a specified dowry for the admission of a postulant was agreed on and entered.[48] Sr Agnes Vickers, superior general, based on this tradition, and on the practical matter that 'a postulant possessed of a superior education is more advantageous than one possessing a large fortune' in a community which is engaged in teaching, insisted on maintaining an 'opt-out' clause, so that both educated and otherwise useful persons could always be accepted without a dowry, and the issue was finally conceded by Rome in 1907.[49]

Margaret Aylward's other ambitions for the community, that they would not be cloistered, could continue their visitation of the sick poor, have a simple form of prayer, and live without any great fuss, were bound up with the increasingly 'regular' form the community was to take, under the combined efforts of various ecclesiastics who took an active part in encouraging, and indeed marshalling, the young institute 'into line' with the accepted, and very specific, patterns of religious practice and behaviour. One small example was the requirement to specify the austerities in use in the convent, and the penances or reparations usually required for offences against discipline; Margaret replied 'No peculiar austerities; occasional deprivation of recreation, kissing the floor and acknowledging one's faults in the Refectory are the only penances'. Similarly required to detail how the rule of silence was observed, she explains that, apart from the hour's recreation allowed after lunch and again after dinner, 'conversation is occasionally at supper to receive an account of the schools and to discuss matters connected with them'. When compared with contemporary, longer-established communities, religious life as lived in the new Holy Faith community was quite simple and uncluttered; its lay community origins however had been very definitely overtaken in the founding decade.

GLASNEVIN

In 1865, at the behest of Cullen, Glasnevin House and accompanying 45 statute acres (Figure 15) was purchased by Margaret from the Sacred Heart sisters who after twelve years occupation found it too small for their needs and relocated south of the city to Mount Anville, Dundrum.[50] Glasnevin was extolled as a 'paradise' with its beautiful grounds and historic associations with Irish monks.[51] The task of securing a suitable house for the Institute had been beset with difficulties,[52] but this place was beyond all Margaret's hopes:

> Apart from everything – away from all and in the midst of hermitages, grottoes, waterfalls, where the saints would love to dwell and as St Canice, St Kieran and others trod this ground it is well to touch the sod that bore them. I was never a poet but Glasnevin would almost make a body one.[53]

Enchantment with Glasnevin House did not blind Margaret to the business aspects of the transaction, and on taking possession she was quick to notice that the property she had purchased in good faith on 18 August 1865 had been stripped of certain 'Fixtures' by the previous occupants since the date of the sale – some window shutters, sashes, small doors, presses in the clothes room and *Dépense*, along with a glass roof over a passage. In her usual forthright fashion she itemised the articles and pursued their return, or reimbursement totalling £28 19s. 6d.[54] Her requests being ignored, she sent a demand for payment through her solicitor. Madame Julia Scully, superior of the Sacred Heart sisters, immediately appealed to Cullen, for after all 'from the beginning it was to please your Grace that we were induced to accept her offer which was much lower than what we had every reason to expect from others'.[55] While Madame Scully complained bitterly of such an issue being made of 'a trifle of about £25' by the very person to whom 'we really made many concessions leaving her things gratuitously or at a nominal value', she was entirely out of her depth.[56] What she presented as a 'feminine little dispute' between two religious communities over which it was 'absurd' to 'go to law',[57] was to Margaret, as an accomplished business woman, an annoying breach of contract which had best be settled quickly and definitely.

Much more wearing than the dispute with the former occupants was the long-running saga with the Catholic Cemeteries Committee over the purchase of six acres of land adjoining the convent grounds known as Violet Hill (and formerly part of the Lindsay estate). A 'somewhat unreasonable' price of £240 per acre was demanded by the cemetery committee, but payment of same was only the beginning of Margaret's troubles; failure to deliver the deeds of conveyance, and the refusal to erect a new boundary wall as promised verbally, led to endless tiresome letter-writing and house calls on individual committee members, from 1877–82.[58] Having access to the other side of the

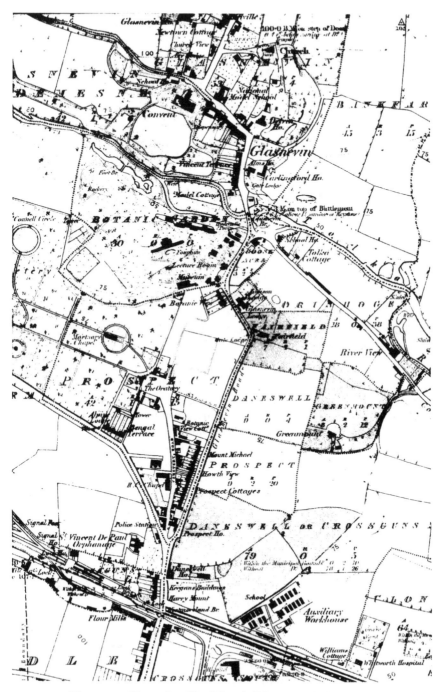

Figure 15: Glasnevin 1885 (Thom's Directory, six-inch OS)

negotiations through a woman friend, Sarah Atkinson, the wife of a cemetery committee member, Dr George Atkinson, was at least some encouragement to Margaret to persevere in what she knew was only just. Sarah reports volubly after each committee meeting on every move and counter-move of certain 'troublesome and extortionate committee men' and of one particularly 'fearful foe'; after five years of time-wasting complaints, 'hounded from intrussion of sheep etc.' (*sic*), Sarah rejoices with Margaret that the end is in sight, 'I hope soon to hear of a bonfire on the heights above the historic [river] Tolka in commemoration of the building of the boundary wall and final settlement with the C.C.C.!'[59] While refusing to build the wall themselves, or to assist by allowing stones to be carted through its own property, the cemeteries committee grudgingly voted Margaret Aylward £140 to cover the costs of construction.[60]

However, problems with the fabric of Glasnevin House (Figure 13, p. 108) and the grounds were relatively minor; the real challenge was to provide such community structures as would ensure the effectiveness and continuity of the mission in hand, the purpose for which this very beautiful new headquarters had been secured. In 1866 Margaret made a formal request to Dr Cullen, on behalf of herself and fifteen companions, for congregational status, that a superior might be appointed, and its members granted 'the privilege of making the simple vows of chastity, poverty, obedience and constancy'.[61] In the published annual report that year it was announced that

> Almighty God, to mark his approbation of this work [the orphanage and schools], has brought together a number of young ladies who purpose to devote their lives to it. They are now formed canonically through his Eminence's great kindness into a religious sisterhood, under the beautiful title of Sisters of the Holy Faith, with permission to take the usual vows of Religious.[62]

Margaret and the first sisters 'tried in every way to have St Brigid's name brought in the name of the Institute and could not succeed'; 'however, as the defence of the faith in the persons of little children seems the end for which (without any seeking on our part) we were called into existence the name [Holy Faith] was thought appropriate – to Father Gowan we are indebted for the thought.'[63] Writing from Rome, John Gowan marvels with others that:

> the name *Sisters of Faith* had been left unappropriated during so many centuries in the Church. I hope Almighty God will bestow upon us the grace to be and to act in some way worthy of the name. I think we ought to have great confidence in God and not fear to undertake anything and everything that his majesty will require of us for the defence and nurture of Holy Faith.[64]

Now with its own motherhouse, novitiate, title, habit, and religious names the institute was very rapidly taking on all the outward structures of a religious congregation.

Within the day-to-day life of the congregation Margaret continued to wear secular dress, travel, solicit funds and audit accounts, directing the development of the school network, and the continuing work of the orphanage, and especially seeing to the ever-increasing burden of correspondence. She played a central role in all of the household matters in the 1860s and 1870s, from instructing the young sisters in housework, and the care of the Chapel ('the curtains should be handled very carefully lest they be torn down frill and all'),[65] ordering a feastday treat for the novices ('apples and raisins to be there – rice pudding *with currants etc. at dinner*')[66] directing the cutting out of cashmere skirts and calico chemises,[67] the payment of workmen, the repair of boots, the milking of the Glasnevin cows and the overall management of the dairy.[68] She had a store of homoeopathic recipes to alleviate every possible affliction, sending detailed instructions on the treatment of ill sisters to Ada, and involving such ingredients as turpentine, castor oil, barley water, cloves of garlic, mustard and 'penny Royal' as well as hot baths ('90 degrees hot enough, the thermometer in the dairy would measure the heat').[69]

The initiation of new candidates into the community was always a concern, with a fairly open admissions policy, and a recognition of how the individuality of each will require some flexibility in formation structures ('Mrs T. will want some consideration and variety with plenty to do').[70] Conferring with John Gowan concerning an unnamed difficult sister ('lacking in simplicity'), he suggests that Margaret 'instruct some one to have a final understanding with her. To tell her that she is welcome to stay and that all will be forgotten provided she give herself entirely to her vocation and give edification, but failing that, that she is welcome to go.'[71] In a note reminiscent of the description in Acts 2: 42–47 of the harmony evident among the first Christians, Margaret claimed in 1869 that 'I have observed in the Community a spirit of charity and obedience, a love of silence, exactitude and punctuality. The works of the Orphanage and Schools and the domestic works are performed by them with great charity and zeal.' Considering Margaret's unfailing directness, it is fair to take this as an honest reading of the climate of the community in the founding decade; if it was otherwise she would simply not have said so.[72]

The first recruit to join Margaret, Ada and Eliza Monahan four months after the release from prison, was a generous and exuberant 16-year-old, Margaret Gaughren (Sr M. Rose), who later spent her final years writing up a history of the congregation (to 1904), and whose brother Anthony Gaughren was to become bishop of Kimberley, South Africa. Miss Aylward, reserved in manner, and diplomatic if stubborn in all her undertakings, found this good natured but tactless and unpolished sixteen-year-old a real trial. She is the only young sister who appears repeatedly in Margaret's letters to Ada, admonished for 'speaking of the instruction given in Confession at

Recreation', followed by opening the tabernacle, apparently to give it a thorough scrub,[73] and then having to be told *again* that there is no necessity for her offering hospitality and *her* hospitality! Bread and butter to the PP'. Living nearby he could not expect it, 'and she is not sufficiently instructed on this point to attempt it'.[74] It is to both Rose's and Margaret's credit that these initial difficulties were overcome, and that Rose recalled her early years with such warmth and pleasure.

Although John Gowan's responsibility for the spiritual formation of the new community relieved Margaret of a major burden, she herself was also intimately involved in determining its future course. Writing in 1869 she explained that as the community was still so new she herself was 'obliged mainly to discharge the duties of Superior, Mistress of Novices, Bursar, Secretary &c., some of the more competent sisters have assisted me and will be soon sufficiently so to warrant us in organizing the community canonically.'[75] An undated memo from John Gowan some years later outlines very simply the procedures to be followed by 'Sister Superior and Council' in the government of the congregation: the superior and each of the councillors will submit 'the business of their office or any propositions they think necessary to make', and decide by simple majority what steps to take. Where 'opinions are divided in any important matter or great difficulty' the 'advice or opinion' of John Gowan might be asked.[76]

Though bound by religious vows, and involved in all the undertakings of the new congregation, whether minor or major, Margaret maintained an independent lifestyle, and had certainly no personal sense of being cloistered, the experience which seems to have most distressed her in her early attempts at religious life. Convalescence was combined with business and pleasure, as she travelled throughout Europe and Ireland, her letters home filled with colourful detail, describing 'all the little children gabbling in French' or the spectacular religious processions held in honour of the Blessed Sacrament and our Lady in France and Germany.[77] Her travels throughout Ireland she does not want to be a topic of discussion in the community, telling Ada that only 'If it be necessary you can say I had to go out of town/to the country/on business, and if it be further necessary you can say to "Waterford", – in the convent *if necessary* you can say will be 2 or 3 days away on business'.[78] She regularly removed herself to friends in Thurstenstown, Beauparc, Co. Meath, where her hostesses 'are most kind and attentive and never even for a moment intrude on my business or solitude' so that she rejoices in being able to write in her room for '6 or 7 hours daily'.[79] However, notes from abroad also include references to being lonely, followed by urgent requests to 'write on receipt of this and tell how all are and how all goes on', 'am longing to get back', and completing a lengthy letter for 'all the good sisters of the noviciate' with the plea to Ada 'now I hope you may think I deserve a long letter in return'.[80] She appears to have found a real warmth in the new community, but at the same time maintained a personal space that only her closest co-workers and long-term friends Ada Allingham and Agnes Vickers, and her sister Jane Fagan (Sr M. Scholastica) shared.[81] Rose Gaughren recalls how, on her return from fundraising trips throughout Ireland she would tell the sisters all about her travels and experiences:

> Sometimes she had very amusing incidents to tell but in some places she met with people who were disagreeable enough, but she was generally received well for she had a very imposing appearance and an attractive and engaging manner. She visited almost all the Archbishops and Bishops of Ireland who afterwards became subscribers to the Orphanage and good friends as long as they lived.[82]

As lay woman and foundress, daughter of St Brigid and first Holy Faith sister, her personal vocational search at least had come gently to rest.

9

Sources of Strength

Tracking the progress of Margaret Aylward's spiritual journey is, by definition, a far greater challenge than following the unfolding of external events which shaped her life and mission. Few letters to her early spiritual directors survive, while the destruction by John Gowan CM after her death of the large number of letters which she had written to him as confessor and spiritual director from the early 1850s is regrettable, although entirely understandable. However, as Margaret's spiritual journey was intimately entwined with the unfolding of her life's work and mission, there remain rich if scattered sources for reconstructing this core aspect of her personhood. Many of John Gowan's replies to letters Margaret wrote are extant, allowing the reconstruction of a small part of this important correspondence, while letters to close friends such as the young Ada Allingham, Dr Kirby in Rome and Dr Cullen in Dublin include reference to her own spiritual life. The published reports of the Ladies' Association of Charity and later St Brigid's Orphanage and Poor Schools include substantial sections on the spiritual foundations for these good works, the earliest of which can be ascribed with certainty to Margaret's pen. There are also a succession of personal and communal 'rules of life' dating from 1852 in her handwriting, and again the earlier editions are her own composition. Her very varied involvement with a significant number of religious orders – Presentation sisters, Irish Christian Brothers, Irish Sisters of Charity, Ursulines, Vincentian Daughters of Charity, Vincentian priests, Oblate priests, Mercy sisters, Jesuit priests – as well as with diocesan clergy throughout Ireland, ensured exposure to a rich range of spiritual traditions and developing spiritualities, further widened by her travels on the continent and fluency in French.

The survival intact of Margaret's personal library is of particular value. Typically, most volumes are marked with her own name and the date of acquisition, from an 1820 edition of *Ancient History from the Earliest Records to the Death of Charlemagne for Use in Schools*, inscribed in a large childish hand, 'Miss Aylward, Feb 16th 1822' (when Margaret was eleven years of age), through to a text by Abbé Fauvre on frequent communion inscribed 'M. Aylward 1881'. This personal library ranges from spiritual classics such as St Augustine's *Confessions* to what could be termed manuals of popular religion, such as Boudon's *The Love of Jesus in the Adorable Sacrament of the Altar* (1834 edition, acquired by Margaret 1846). Several are in French, including Italian works by Alphonsus Ligouri which came to Ireland though France; French originals by authors such as St Francis de Sales and Jean Baptiste de la Salle, and office books and pious handbooks in French. Based on these varied sources, at least some of the threads in Margaret's spirituality can be discerned.

The three central traditions most in evidence in Margaret's spiritual journey are the popular teachings of St Alphonsus Ligouri (1696–1787), the discernment tradition of St Ignatius of Loyola (1491–1556), and the teaching on charity lived by St Vincent de Paul (1581–1660). A fourth but also important 'Celtic' strand can be found in an appreciation of the Irish church heritage, notably its monastic and penal-time traditions and especially fostered by John Gowan CM. It is not surprizing to find these four strands overlapping and intertwining in nineteenth-century Ireland: the Alphonsian tradition was popularized in Ireland by Jesuit and Vincentian missioners, who included Irish as well as French men among their number, while the very practical tradition of Vincentian charity, pioneered in Ireland by lay activists such as Margaret's branch of the Ladies of Charity (1851) and the first branch of the men's association in Ireland (1845) was ideally suited to mid-century urban centres devastated by the continuing post-famine influx of the destitute and diseased.[1] The apparent success of the 1840s and 1850s Protestant evangelical missions provided a sharp spur for Catholic counter-missions,[2] and the Alphonsian tradition, developed purposely for the catechizing of the neglected and uninformed rural poor, could be readily applied to Irish missionary realities. The Alphonsian tradition was taken up in Ireland well in advance of the first Alphonsian foundation (the Redemptorist missioners) in 1851; Waterford city, and in particular the local Ursuline convent, was the earliest and possibly the principal source from which the Italian teaching was to become inculturated into Irish Catholicism.[3] While parish missions were very much a continental practice newly introduced to Ireland, individual missioners such as John Gowan CM used this structure to preach in an avowedly nationalistic way, idealizing Celtic monasticism and its closeness to nature, and emphasizing how Ireland, *semper fidelis*, had persevered through penal days.

The tradition of St Alphonsus Ligouri was the first and most enduring aspect of Margaret Aylward's spirituality. The *Ursuline Manual* (Figure 16), a distillation of Alphonisan teaching, was her first and primary spiritual reader, introduced by her into the boarding school, Glasnevin, with an edition titled *New Ursuline Manual* among the very few precious possessions she disbursed among friends in her will.[4] She took the name 'Alphonsus Ligouri' on reception into the Irish Sisters of Charity; Fr J.P. Cooke, a Jesuit spiritual director and friend, was 'greatly pleased' with the new name, having the

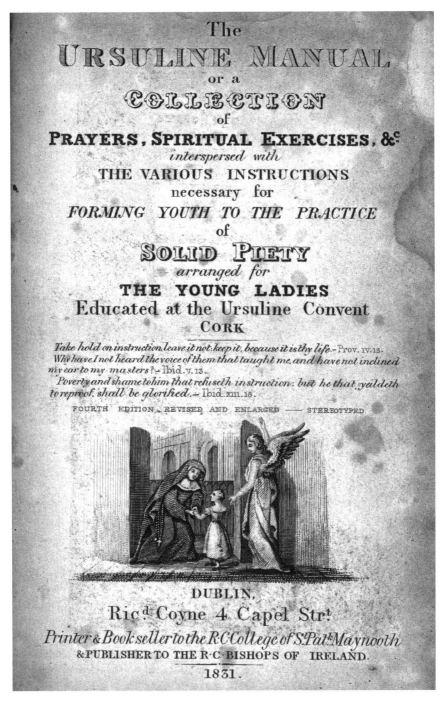

The

URSULINE MANUAL

or a

COLLECTION

of

PRAYERS, SPIRITUAL EXERCISES, &c

interspersed with

THE VARIOUS INSTRUCTIONS

necessary for

FORMING YOUTH TO THE PRACTICE

of

SOLID PIETY

arranged for

THE YOUNG LADIES

Educated at the Ursuline Convent

CORK

Take hold on instruction, leave it not: keep it, because it is thy life.–Prov. iv.13.
*Why have I not heard the voice of them that taught me, and have not inclined
my ear to my masters?*–Ibid. v.13.
*Poverty and shame to him that refuseth instruction: but he that yeildeth
to reproof, shall be glorified.*–Ibid. xiii.18.

FOURTH EDITION, REVISED AND ENLARGED —— STEREOTYPED

DUBLIN,

Ric.d Coyne 4 Capel Str.t

Printer & Bookseller to the R:C.College of S.t Pat.k Maynooth
&PUBLISHER TO THE R·C·BISHOPS OF IRELAND.

1831.

Figure 16: Ursuline manual, 1831

'greatest veneration – I would write affection for the glorious St Alphonsus'; Margaret was 'the first person I heard of who entered on the pursuit of perfection under the auspices of his holy name.'[5] After her brief sojourn there her sister Catherine, who remained in the community, suggested she continue to translate the life of Blessed Alphonsus, ('you know, dearest, the translation would be a great treat to the Lay Sisters'), a noviceship task which she completed in Waterford.[6] While she received the religious name 'Sr M. Agatha' in a lottery conducted by John Gowan CM in 1864, and made triennial vows as a Holy Faith sister under that name, a vow formula written in her own hand in 1875 is made in the name of 'Sr M. Agatha Alphonse'.[7] The Alphonsian tradition to which Margaret was so clearly attached is itself a synthesis of many earlier traditions, drawing together the teachings of the fathers of the church on various central topics and making their teachings acccessible and intelligible to the laity. With its emphasis on the infinite love and mercy of God it stands in contrast to the harsh teaching of Jansenism.[8] In a summary of the central features of the Alphonsian tradition Fr Cooke encourages her to live up to her new namesake's teaching:

> Now indeed we may expect great things from you – great charity, great desire of perfection, great love of labour, great industry in the employment, great humility, great love for your neighbours and zeal for their salvation, great love for Mary, and unbounded confidence in and love for Jesus in the Most Holy Sacrament of His love and charity.[9]

Jesuit influences were also central to her spirituality. She had a succession of Jesuit directors and a wide circle of close Jesuit friends, some of whom she met through family contacts, her brothers having attended Stonyhurst college; her regard for the Society can be seen in her anxiety to establish a Jesuit house in her native Waterford.[10] Perhaps most in evidence is her reliance on the discernment tradition in Jesuit spirituality; her whole life can be viewed as an exercise in ongoing discernment. The 'system of spiritual life' which was 'propounded' in the Constitutions of the Irish Sisters of Charity, with whom she entered 1834–6, was described by her director John St Leger SJ as the system of St Ignatius, 'and as little deserving, in my estimation, of the appellation of *Mystic Theology*, as any thing can possibly be'. He recommended it as 'high perfection and difficult', but at the same time 'totally practical'; 'the soul formed on it will be truly interior, and will have learned that death to self, by which alone it can begin to live to God, and love him'.[11] Margaret's personal experience of the Ignatian tradition, as lived in this religious community, was applied in time to her own community of the Sisters of Faith.

Margaret's intimacy with the Vincentian tradition is well documented: from at least 1841 she was familiar with the constitutions of the 'Ladies of St

Vincent de Paul', making her own translations from the French original.[12] As Kingstown, the first Irish branch, dates from 1843, it appears that Margaret was well informed prior to meeting up with Margaret Kelly, its directress. Reworking the Vincentian teaching for her own Dublin group, as seen in the masterly sections on the philosophy and aims of the association in her published reports, is ample evidence of Margaret Aylward's thorough imbibing of this tradition. She presents its founding vision very simply:

> [St Vincent de Paul] would, therefore, have the members of this Association consider, that in going to visit the sick poor, they are going to visit not them but Jesus Christ in them; that in ministering consolation and relief to the sick poor, they are doing so not to them, but to Jesus Christ in them; and that on retiring from the sick-bed of their poor fellow-creature, they are to treasure the consoling thought, that the charity they have bestowed upon them is already accepted and registered for reward hereafter, as if it were bestowed upon Himself.[13]

In late nineteenth-century nationalist mode, the association of faith and fatherland, and the invocation of an array of Irish saints was yet another strand in Margaret Aylward's spiritual life. Writing of Glasnevin House, which had been secured as headquarters after innumerable difficulties, she likened the peaceful grounds with their 'hermitages, grottoes, waterfalls', to a monastic paradise, bearing the footprints of the local saints, St Canice, St Kieran, St Mobhi and others; 'it is well to touch the sod that bore them'.[14] This theme recurs throughout the orphan and school reports, from the choice of patron and graphic representation (Figure 8, p. 57) through to discussions on the type of education promoted and the rallying calls to subscribers and helpers:

> The [collecting] card is an engraving of St Brigid protecting some orphans. A round tower and an Irish cross are seen on her left arm, the oak of Kildare and the Saint's cell on her right, and the mountains of Ireland form the background. She bears a crosier, showing her authority as Abbess, and her eyes are raised to heaven for protection for her Irish Orphans.[15]

The work of St Brigid's, for Margaret, was in defence of that faith which Ireland 'embraced so generously, defended so courageously, and bled for so profusely' over fifteen hundred years; she saw it as rooted in the 'golden age' of Irish monasticism, a period which can be read in the landscape:

> There is not a glen, nor a lake, nor a hill-side that does not bear some memory of the faith – some ruin, clothed in green, where a thousand years ago, the song of prayer ascended to God; some cross where the wayfarer prayed, or where the funeral procession halted to murmur a last prayer for the departed; some well, used and blessed by saints: and all speak with one voice, this land is the land of faith. The very names of our towns and villages, our kils and cluains and temples, all speak with one voice, this land is the land of faith.[16]

Her letters from abroad are full of striking landscape descriptions, and she evidently found herself very close to God in silent contemplation of these scenes. From Aix-les-Bains, she writes of a magnificent sunset, and of the hills covered in vines, where after a lightning storm, 'a rainbow spanned these mountains and in one start all these hills shone out like gold'.[17] In Glasnevin, the Holy Faith sisters will always associate her with the Palm Walk, overlooking the river Tolka, where oral tradition recalls her spending hours alone, in a wheeled bathchair, in silent reflection.

CENTRAL THEMES

Insights into Margaret Aylward's spiritual life can be built up around several themes: the search for the will of God, personal prayer, the virtue of charity, the practice of self-discipline, communal devotions, faith and trust in providence, and the submission to Church authority.

GOD'S WILL

Margaret Aylward's life can be read as a life-long search, for where the Lord might be leading her. Successive attempts at religious life, and plans to support new foundations in Waterford and Dublin, were the outward expression of the inner struggle to discern her place in God's unfolding (but too often fog-bound) plans. At the crucial time of Margaret's imprisonment, it was a case of joint discernment, with John Gowan writing *en route* to Paris, where he was going to plead the case of St Brigid's and decide on his own Vincentian future:

> We must endeavour now to give ourselves entirely to God. These extraordinary circumstances have arrived unexpectedly, it is therefore our duty to rely firmly on God, to be perfectly calm and not to allow any kind of passion to sway us. We must pray very much. We must above all have recourse to the Mother of God. We must humble ourselves in every way that we possibly can in order that the Almighty God may find the least possible obstacles to His Grace. If you have faith and patience and humility God will accomplish your desires.[18]

An openness and fidelity to spiritual direction is a central plank in Margaret Aylward's story, best exemplified in the Ignatian teaching on spiritual discernment, but central also to the Alphonsian and Vincentian spiritual schools, and found in the *anam chara* tradition of Irish monasticism. Alphonsus Ligouri teaches that 'the summit of perfection', 'the end of our work, of all our desires, of our meditations, of our prayers', is to be the union of our wills with that of God, his favourite prayer 'dispose of me according to your will'.[19]

However, while each individual soul has been called to this union with God, and all walks of life can lead to sainthood, before organising one's life towards this end the Christian must know and choose his/her way. In this fundamental choice only the person can make the decision, the director or confessor warned to stand aside, his role merely to advise.[20] Although John Gowan CM became her principal spiritual director from the early 1850s, and her openness and docility to him in matters of the spirit is remarkable, she had always subjected herself to such guidance. Jesuit priests played this role during her Waterford days and her first stressful experiences in religious life. The call to place herself utterly at God's disposal was encouraged by succeeding directors including St Leger and J. Cooke; despite the difficulties such an ill-defined stance was sure to bring, one could rely utterly on God's assistance. 'Give yourself to God with your whole heart. Have recourse to God in all your difficulties, say frequently "incline unto my aid" and the little prayer "Jesus be with me. Enlighten my mind and touch my heart".'[21] She in her turn acted as spiritual guide to others, most especially the young Ada Allingham: 'Think of God, keep him in view … his will will be your polar star, view it calmly and steadily' and later 'Your path seems as clear as light – shining even so clear does it appear that you are where *He* wishes for you; and *where* His special graces await you.'[22] From the time of imprisonment onwards Margaret becomes increasingly certain of the 'rightness' of St Brigid's work, and more assured in her role as manager; this new-found confidence, after so many years of searching, is discernible in letters to Ada, where minute directions are interspersed with frequent encouragement, 'Keep up your heart, you are very good – be glad to be able to be on the spot now for the work it is most useful.'[23] John Gowan affirms her at every point: 'You must try and do your work cheerfully now that it is put upon you. You know that you are doing God's work – at all events not your own whims, no murmuring any more.'[24]

PERSONAL PRAYER

The touchstone of Margaret's personal life was an abiding reliance or trust in God and his goodness, a certainty of being loved that was nourished in long hours of prayer and takes flesh in very concrete and indeed colourful ways. The Ursuline Convent in Thurles specified 'the spirit of prayer and union with God in the midst of activities' as one of the 'distinctive characteristics' of the Ursulines.[25] Margaret took this teaching to heart in her personal struggle to integrate a very busy life with a deep and sustaining prayer life. In the 'order of day and rule of life' which she drew up for her personal use in 1852, when still a laywoman, her day is punctuated by prayer, including Mass, the recitation of the Office of the Blessed Virgin Mary, angelus, examen, rosary, visit to the Blessed Sacrament and Blessed Virgin, and an hour's meditation.[26] The Mass, described by St Francis de Sales as the 'centre of religion, the heart of devotion, and the soul of piety',[27] was for Margaret 'most profitably heard by meditating on the Passion according to St Francis' direction'.[28] Alphonsian spirituality always returns to the passion of which the Incarnation is the prelude and the Eucharist the memorial: 'I would engage you every day to look at the Passion; because you will find there all the motifs which will make us able to have hope in eternity and to love God. ... If the soul looks and thinks of the passion it is impossible to offend God, and not to love him, and similarly it is not possible to gain sainthood without love.'[29] John Gowan urges Margaret to unite her considerable personal sufferings to Christ's passion, speaking of 'this great consolation', that 'pains and afflictions are a sure sign of God's love for us and a strong guarantee of future glory. "In the Cross is life." Let us then constantly thank our good Saviour for having given us a portion of His Cross.'[30]

While the Mass as a 'holocaust or sacrifice of adoration in which Jesus offers himself to his eternal Father wholly and entirely', most perfectly re-enacts the Passion, the Blessed Sacrament reserved is a continuation of Christ's presence in the Mass, 'the most convincing proof of God's love, and an abundant source of blessings'.[31] The Blessed Sacrament devotion, for which Alphonsus Ligouri is perhaps best known, was central to Margaret's spirituality; a warm and very real presence, she speaks of Christ in the tabernacle as a dear and familiar friend. On getting the Blessed Sacrament reserved in Eccles Street she writes to Ada, 'I am so glad you have our Lord with you – you can't be lonely. Look during the day to the lamp and have it as nice as you can, even a few fresh flowers, geraniums, etc. in long glasses will be more grateful to Him than artificial.'[32] John Gowan affirms her in this devotion, 'Encourage that, indulge in it and by degrees your whole soul will be absorbed by that devotion in such a wonderful manner that there will be no room for those little thorns that at present give you so much pain.'[33] However, frequent reception of the sacraments, as urged by Alphonsus Ligouri, caused problems for Margaret Aylward, and John Gowan as spiritual director expended much energy in trying to dispel her scruples:[34]

> I think you need not at all complain of the week – indeed I was surprised but very glad that you went to Holy Communion so often, what is there to hinder you going as often after each Confession? Have courage, most of these fears have no reality, others are blown into enormous dimensions by your enemy to keep you back from the greatest happiness we can have on earth, that of possessing our most loving Saviour. Tell Almighty God that you can't stay away, that for love of him you will treat these obstacles with the contempt they deserve. You need not have the least fear of going three times after each Confession, always with great confidence and a loving, loving heart.[35]

This intimacy continues in Margaret's devotion to the Sacred Heart, also a feature of Alphonsian spirituality. The Blessed Virgin for Margaret is a close friend to whom one can always turn: 'M. Agnes must only do the best she can, after saying a Hail Mary', the title 'Immaculate Mother of the Child Jesus' being of particular appeal.[36] In this she is affirmed by John Gowan, who advises 'I think your chief devotion ought to be the Rosary because God seems to have given you already an attraction for it.'[37] St Joseph was another stalwart who can always be relied upon. 'Now we must apply to St Joseph to get us a place', declares Margaret when lodged in wretched and expensive hotel rooms in Aix-la-Chapelle, and within one minute of sallying forth under his protection had spied a notice in French offering rooms to let, 'a nice young woman who spoke German, French and some English' showed her excellent apartments, 'and the first room we entered there was *St Joseph's statue* with the Divine Infant in his arms'; not alone had St Joseph directed them to ideal lodgings, but he had placed them under the care of two devout young Catholic women who ensured they were in place for all the devotions of the week.[38]

CHARITY

Margaret's spirituality was essentially apostolic or active: 'I am sorry you had such a poor meeting – everything must grow – we must pray – and work', she writes to Ada from her prison cell. The final end was not abstract contemplation but action, urging her co-workers 'Let all hands be employed in *altering* today against tomorrow'.[39] St Brigid's guildsmen were to be persons 'of good morals and practical faith'.[40] In the teaching of St Vincent de Paul on charity she found the perfect articulation of how to integrate prayer and meditation with service to the poor, and the essential balance between the organization of 'good works' and trust in providence, intelligent activity and trusting surrender.[41] Painstaking translation of the *Rules of the Ladies' Association of Charity*, and the production of her own visiting manuals, were all part of her efforts to apply this model of service to contemporary Dublin, and to form her co-workers in the spirit of St Vincent.[42] She urges 'our dear Associates', to read from time to time the life of our Blessed Founder, 'Abelly's life is certainly, for us, the best; it is more detailed, and contains large extracts of St Vincent's own words. This reading will enkindle the fire of charity in our hearts'.[43] Affirmation that this was indeed the path she was called to was readily forthcoming from those who knew her best: 'What consolation to a soul that values God alone to be thus occupied preparing bed, clothes and food for the Infant Jesus in the person of his dear poor.'[44]

Other formative influences reinforced her resolve 'to sacrifice my time and myself to the dear poor of Jesus Christ.'[45] The fourth vow of the Irish Sisters of Charity was to devote their lives 'to the perpetual service of the Poor'.[46] St Alphonsus Ligouri outlines the foundation upon which the Christian life is built:

> The accent is always placed on these three points: it is our God, he gave himself, he suffered, through love for us and to obtain our love; therefore let us love him, and through love, follow him. It is simple, practical and touching.[47]

Following from this, 'the love of God does not consist in showing tender sentiments but in serving him with courage and humility', in the person of our neighbour, requiring not a tender love but a 'strong love'.[48]

Margaret's own writing on this theme emphasizes the primacy of immediate contact: the 'sick poor' visited by the Association have names and addresses, each with their own unique case-history, and very real and pressing individual requirements. However, visitation is always a two-way process, with the ladies themselves learning 'lessons of resignation, of confidence, and hope', from their poorer neighbours, who so often display 'heroic virtue' in the midst of very real calamity.[49]

There are touching recreations of exchanges in the rooms of the sick and the dying, the simple but profound faith of the poor a constant feature of these reports. In many cases these could be read as treatises on the faith journey of individuals, as they interspersed accounts of their life's hardships with their own understanding of how God was present even now at the hour of greatest need. One woman with agonizing stomach pains which nothing could relieve, on being reminded to offer her sufferings to our Blessed Lord, replies, 'He will not let me forget that; who, dear, will I offer them to if not to my maker and my Blessed Redeemer?'[50] At the bedside of the dying 'we were uniformly consoled with the lively faith, the earnest hope, the patient resignation of these favourites of Heaven', with Margaret urging that others might share in the gratitude the poor expressed, and the abundant benedictions wished upon the visitors.[51] In a typically dramatic rallying call delivered at the annual meeting of 1853, she urges:

> Come, Catholic ladies, come, see the children of sorrow; mingle your tears with theirs; listen to them whilst in patient anguish they relieve their bursting hearts; hear their tales of suffering; see the comfort which even this affords them; the consolation, the peace, the joy.[52]

SELF DISCIPLINE

The successful integration of a life of heavy apostolic commitment with a deep spiritual life demands considerable self-discipline. Margaret's efforts to create a supportive but also flexible structure is evident from her 'rules of life', where from 6 a.m. 'rising punctually, not sooner, not later' in the 1852 edition there are set times for all the activities of the day, including religious exercises, meals, 'business such as visiting the sick, poor, and other works of necessity or utility', recreation ('in the open air if convenient'), spiritual reading, and at 7 p.m. 'supper and some innocent relaxation' before the final period of prayer, retiring at 10 p.m. In a morning prayer written in her own hand she calls in turn on God the Father, the Holy Virgin, 'Glorious' St Joseph, 'St Patrick, St Brigid, St Vincent, St Ignatius, my guardian angel and patron saints', ending each invocation with the refrain 'help me to make it a full day'.[53] In the ten 'Resolutions' which accompany the 1852 rule of life, there is further evidence of her striving towards the fullest possible living out of the offering she has made, resolving to give herself up to God 'by the practice of two virtues – humility and charity. The former is necessary for my own sanctification, the latter for the good of my neighbour'. The Alphonsian tradition outlines how certain dispositions, such as patience, charity and faith, can be cultivated by persevering practice, and similarly how self-discipline can help weed out the contrary vices. Prayer itself is the first discipline, reflection 'the birthing place of holy resolutions'; through prayer 'the heart becomes supple, docile to impressions of grace which one receives more abundantly and strongly'. Without prayer is found 'a spirit distracted by countless matters', and unlikely to persevere. Margaret's private check-lists of resolutions and notes for examen point to this practical approach to fostering spiritual growth:

> In conformity to the holy virtue of humility, I will never speak a word nor perform even the least action for my own praise, nor ever allow my soul to dwell with complacency on anything I do, but refer all generously to the glory of my God. According to charity, I will never drop a word to the dispraise of anyone else unless when my conscience clearly tells me it is necessary. I will also sacrifice my time and myself to the dear poor of Jesus Christ.

The combination of solemn resolution and practical living out is found in innumerable small references: vowing to have at all times 'the most pure intention of pleasing my God and doing his will as the main end of all my actions', structured by proposing this to her soul each morning, and consciously renewing the resolution 'at least three times in the day'. Dealings with co-workers and other contacts are of major spiritual concern; resolutions to refrain from passing rash judgements on others ('and where it is my duty to suspect I will never go farther than the evidence warrants'), and to avoid contributing to the vicious circle of gossip ('I will speak well of all I can, and of those of whom I cannot say anything good I will say nothing') were typically practical responses to the daily challenges her own work created. Frequently at the receiving end of ill-informed and unwarranted criticism herself, she well knew the erosive power of back-biting and slander.

From the surviving letters of direction to the soul in his charge, John Gowan will never be accused of equivocation or loose thinking; in a letter addressed to Margaret during the prison episode he spells out the regime of self-discipline which he recommends in her efforts to 'render yourself perfectly conformable to the designs of God':

> Crush self, work hard in denying yourself. Your own judgement, your own will, your own likings and dislikings, all must be mortified. Pray that God may reign in you. That his will may be your sole rule and guide. Every day deny yourself in something. Even in those things that are good, don't act from impulse but take a little time to put self out of question. Do all for God, all for his glory. Thus all will be well done, thus every tear will hereafter become a pearl and every pain a joy and every sigh an increase of glory.[54]

Patience, predictably, John Gowan regards as a virtue that Margaret has so much need of, 'a virtue that God is determined to teach you at every cost, beating you into His service, as He has been doing all this time by "the staff of his discipline".'[55] John Gowan's urgings under this heading never desist; indeed it appeared to him that she was particularly slow in this department:

> Be patient then in doing what you can do and be patient also in omitting what you cannot conveniently do. In one word, no internal commotion, no external sign of impatience in either doing or refusing. When you are tired after doing too much don't talk about it, but say several times, *Deo Gratias*.[56]

Selflessness is another virtue that John Gowan returns to repeatedly: 'self must be set aside and kept down with constant vigilance and a strong heart' ... 'We must never allow self to stand in the way of God's greater glory';[57] however, in this area he discerned more progress:

> Be patient, labour incessantly, do the work of an apostle; in everything humble yourself. Put yourself below everyone in the house, everyone in the school and every poor thing in the orphanage, be the servant of all, as indeed you are, thanks be to God.[58]

COMMUNAL DEVOTIONS

The colourful public and communal outpourings of Catholic faith traditionally found on the European mainland appealed immensely to Margaret, and notes

from abroad detailing processions and public devotions are annotated repeatedly: 'I will want this again on my return, please to have this note kept
carefully for *me*, MA.'[59] Convalescing in Aix-la-Chapelle in 1867 she provides
minute reconstructions of each stage of the procession, from the decoration
of the houses with statues, flowers, flags and crucifixes, to the dress of the
first communion boys and girls, and each of the groups which follow, with
coloured sashes and wreaths of flowers, ribbons and medals, carrying banners,
brass lamps, thuribles, crucifixes, gilded lilies and statues, the gospel book,
and a chalice, strewing flowers along the way, halting for benediction at
different stages, the routeway lined with crowds and altars. Sodality groups
played an important part; in Aix-la-Chapelle's Blessed Sacrament procession,
St Joseph's sodalities carried banners and branches of white lilies.[60] In the
case of the public veneration of Aix-la-Chapelle's '*great* reliques' held every
seven years, the lengthy procession and final ceremony in the cathedral were
'grand beyond description', with mounted Prussian soldiers, the clergy richly
dressed in the most 'magnificent lace, ancient and most valuable trimming'
and 'every imaginable colour of vestment', the ark of the relics a chest of solid
gold carried shoulder-high amidst a riot of scarlet draperies, accompanied by
'magnificent singing towards the beginning of the procession and near the
reliques the Rosary saying in German by all the people', the final entry
marked by bell-ringing and the firing of cannon.[61]

Margaret's delight in the colour and splendour of these impressive displays
of popular devotion was to very immediate purpose: could not Dublin have
its own processions? Surely the faith of Irish Catholics, tested by centuries
of persecution and derision, could only be enlivened by such public
celebrations, and the pride of a colonial people enkindled? And what honour
would be done to the Blessed Sacrament, to be publicly carried through the
city! The enormous significance of the 'devotional revolution' sweeping
Ireland under Dr Cullen, following on the Synod of Thurles 1850, has been
explored by Emmet Larkin, who sees it as a crucial factor in the moral and
social improvement of the Irish both at home and overseas in the second half
of the nineteenth century. The new devotions introduced 1850–75 were
mainly of Roman origin and included the Rosary, the forty hours perpetual
adoration, novenas, blessed altars, *Via Crucis*, benediction, vespers, devotion
to the Immaculate Conception, jubilees, triduums, pilgrimages, shrines,
processions and retreats, with such devotional exercises designed to
communalize and regularize practice under a spiritual director, through
confraternities and sodalities.[62] Margaret Aylward's detailed memoranda home
were not for tourist purposes, but to assist in planning exactly these type of
'new' devotions for St Brigid's children and parents. From the continent she
notes how poor children are especially included, and the exact way in which
they are regulated: 'The sisters of the Infant Jesus walked with white cloaks

with their poor children about 4 or 6 of them, one occasionally walking in the centre to regulate them', different groups of nuns walking 'with another body of poor children', others with 'little boys in procession'.[63]

From the journal of Crow Street school the earliest Holy Faith Blessed Sacrament and Marian processions, as planned by Margaret Aylward, can be reconstructed.[64] They built upon the school sodalities and their solemn enrolment ceremonies. In Crow Street 'the most grown of the children' on reception into the Children of Mary sodality, each dressed in a white dress, veil and wreath, were 'received by Father Gowan while kneeling around the Blessed Virgin Altar which was decorated with vases of flowers and lighted wax candles'; the processions in Glasnevin gave the sodality children the chance to wear these outfits again, while others were festooned with medals, ribbons and sashes. An undated letter from Flintshire, Scotland refers to the devotions in Holywell and the procurement of a 'pattern frock for processionists'; she had already brought home various 'patterns' from Aix-la-Chapelle.[65] Accounts for Easter 1869 note that the Crow Street children were brought to Glasnevin, remaining some time before the Blessed Sacrament, 'where they recited some prayers in honour of the Blessed Virgin. They afterwards visited St Joseph's Chapel when having received some flowers they went home together'; on 25 July another procession was held, for which tickets were distributed to the children from the city schools, and they were accompanied by their parents. Reports on the Marian processions from 1868 to 1872 (held on 25 July or 15 August) record the route taken: setting out from the Chapel, 'along by St Kevin's Walk and stopped by the cave of Manresa where there was a statue of the Blessed Virgin beautifully decorated with vases of flowers and lighted candles', a shrine titled 'Our Lady of the Waters' in the account for 1872; here Fr Gowan gave a short instruction. The processions then continued to St Joseph's chapel or oratory, where there was another pause for instruction and prayers, before returning to the chapel for benediction. Throughout the procession the Litany of the Blessed Virgin and hymns (including *With all thy Affection*), were sung alternately by the sisters and the children, 'between each division of the children one of the sisters carried a Banner',[66] while glass processional lanterns had been sent directly from Aix-la-Chapelle by Margaret a few weeks earlier.[67] A very modest recreation of the continental model perhaps, but no less stirring and devotional for that.

FAITH AND TRUST IN GOD'S WILL

The theological virtue of faith is recommended to Margaret by John Gowan as the touchstone of all she is about:

> Do all in faith, that is for God and in God. Of ourselves we can do nothing but in God we can do all things. It is astonishing how happy you will feel in your mind if you thus live and work by faith for all your acts and sufferings will be directed to God under the eye of God and, what is the main point, united to the acts and sufferings of our Lord Jesus Christ thro' whom alone they become meritorious of the crown.[68]

In the privacy of communications with Gowan she reveals her fearfulness, vulnerability and feelings of inadequacy, her scrupolosity with regard to observing the Lenten fast and abstinence,[69] morbid anxieties about death, and self criticism that leaves her mind 'clouded and bewildered', so that Gowan urges: 'I wish you had more of that Irish elasticity which amuses itself with its own mishaps and accidents. Don't be so fretful. Laugh it off.'[70] Faith and trust in God's will are the foundation upon which He can build; 'Let us leave all to Him. He knows the road that will bring us to Heaven and if we generously leave ourselves in His hands he will conduct us safely.'[71] In prison she is urged to 'strive and keep yourself very calm, put the most unbounded confidence in God. The Devil is gnashing his teeth, but he nor his can hurt you.'[72] She herself has good reason to trust in God's providence; reflecting on the work of the Ladies of Charity,

> We soon learned a lesson, every day rendered more plain, that those who would do charity, need only to wish it earnestly, and place themselves in the hands of God for the purpose. He 'who opens his hand, and filleth every living thing with benediction' never fails to furnish the necessary supplies.[73]

CHURCH AUTHORITY

Within the context of the 'one only and true Catholic Church', members of which are 'secured from error, and guided in the road that leads to eternal bliss', according to the *Ursuline Manual*, Margaret saw no reason to worry herself with doctrinal debate or questions of church authority.[74] Her starting point was a fundamental loyalty to the Church, and her concern how best to work out one's salvation within that context. That she herself espoused the church's teaching in the fullest manner cannot be doubted:

> The end of *St Patrick's Guild* is to honor God in the protection of Orphans and destitute Children in danger of loss of faith. This end is built upon the eternal and immutable principle that out of the Catholic Church there is no salvation, that the loss of faith is a total shipwreck, that consequently it would be a less evil to the Catholic child for its enemy to dash its brains out than to deprive it of its faith.[75]

Writing in 1866 about the organization of this guild Margaret directed that all the members 'shall ever deem it a primary duty to practise and inculcate a prompt and cheerful obedience to the constituted authorities of the Holy Catholic Church.'[76]

The Dublin diocesan leadership under Cullen advanced the authority and prestige of the Catholic church in a self-conscious way. In a report to Cullen in 1854, Thomas Pope speaks approvingly of the 'ardent piety' of the people towards our Blessed Lady of the Immaculate Conception, who venerate her under that title regardless of the discussions of 'the great dignataries' (*sic*) in Rome. He likens the faithful to 'passengers in the secure and well-built ship of the Church', who 'regard all your discussion as the noise of the chains and cables and tackle on the deck in the midst of storm – they repose securely below, knowing the ship is in hands of experienced mariners, and that their solicitous Father [Cullen] is at the helm'.[77] This was the model of church advanced in mid-nineteenth century Ireland, and to which Margaret readily subscribed; happy to leave the direction of the 'safe ship' of the church to those whose duty it was, she regarded the approbation of proper authority as confirmation that the business in her hands was indeed the will of God. Docility to the church's authority did not however preclude one from ensuring that authority was fully informed on matters of import, and petitioning that authority, repeatedly and insistently as was so often the case.

What can be known of Margaret Aylward's spiritual journey throws much light upon her complex and colourful life story. Immensely fortunate in the quality of her confessors and directors, most notably John Gowan, her honesty in constantly trying to be open to God's will is deserving of particular note. She borrowed freely from a wide variety of spiritual traditions, allowing herself to be enriched, for the purpose of mission, from those schools of thought to which she had access. Ignatian, Vincentian and Alphonsian traditions, as well as a less easily classified Irish monastic and penal days heritage, were all part of this unfinished tapestry. The earnestness and zeal with which she applied herself to Christian service were matched by the seriousness with which she regarded her own spiritual development. While God is indeed the source and end of all, there is much that the soul itself can do to co-operate with grace and grow in love.

10

Keeping Faith

Margaret Aylward had never enjoyed robust health, and in 1869 was seriously ill, with 'a dangerous attack of erysipelas in the head, chest and throat – no hope for my life but in prayer'.[1] In 1872 writing from the spa town of Aix-la-Chapelle, Prussia, she tells Ada who was keeping matters in order at home, that 'you would think I was getting the smallpox from the eruption which came out in the chest and back with the heat – I am told it will take away every interior delicacy – I am much improved, the numbness in the face is gradually going away.' In another undated later to Ada from Beauparc, Co. Meath, she writes that 'a *great* redness shows itself at times in my face' and 'this is the first day since I came that I am free of great pain on both sides'.[2] It was against a backdrop of successive bouts of debilitating illness that Margaret Aylward operated throughout the 1870s. In her later years she was rarely well enough to leave her room in Glasnevin except in a wheelchair, and excursions beyond the grounds were few in number. The last year of her life was spent in bed. John Gowan, though not himself in good health, was still younger and more mobile, and continued to work tirelessly for St Brigid's and the sisters. It is not surprising that some contemporaries credit him alone with the foundation and government of the Aylward ventures, as he was the most visible member of the founding team until his own death in 1897.[3] Though Margaret was out of public circulation in these later years, mentally she was as sharp as ever, and saw to an immense amount of daily correspondence. In 1888, when she was aged seventy-eight her younger sister Ellen tried to advise her, rather sourly: 'it seems to me you ought to try to live quietly from henceforth – the world is not worth *half the trouble* people take about it'.[4]

But ill health, though serious, was the least of Margaret's problems. She outlived most of the churchmen who had been both personal friends and loyal champions of her charities in the 1850s and 1860s, and in Dublin and Ossory, the only dioceses in which she had foundations, her latter years were strained by conflict with ecclesiastical authorities. There was open hostility to her efforts, fuelled in part by jealousy of the protection and privilege she had enjoyed under their predecessors, and her own continuing independence of thought and action. As an institute of pontifical right the Holy Faith communities were subject only to the 'ordinary authority' of the local bishop; most convents of women religious were under diocesan control with the bishop as direct superior. Even where they were constituted under a central authority, the substitution of diocesan control was regarded by local clergy in several instances as a small but essential 'reform'. The Irish sisters of Charity would be most acceptable in Waterford city, Margaret had been assured, once their constitutions were altered to allow diocesan control; 'the alteration of those parts would be a matter of small difficulty'.[5] In Dublin, applications for entry to the diocese by communities of religious from outside Ireland were subjected to rigorous examination on this point.[6] Margaret Aylward and her immediate successor as superior general, Agnes Vickers, were to pay a high price for maintaining the young congregation's pontifical status.

The 'Mullinavat troubles' as they are known within the congregation up to the present day, surfaced in 1883 and continued in a most serious vein until 1892, when the facts of the case were laid open in a painful but ultimately positive manner. In rough notes titled 'ch. IV, to be modified, this only for the Sisters' private information' the biographer Margaret Gibbons claimed that in her preliminary research interviews she found that a surprising amount of the 'mud' which had been 'thrown vigorously' at Margaret Aylward 'sticks in the minds of many priests and people throughout the diocese of Ossory'.[7] Now 'with all the facts and correspondence' from that period before her, she realizes 'how gravely she was wronged' and as biographer regarded it as 'a sacred duty' to place the material before the reader. However, the published text of 1928 omits all reference to the scandal, sufficient testimony to the painful memories which it then still evoked.

Mount St Joseph's, Mullinavat was built at a cost of £1000 by Miss Walsh of Earlsrath, a near relation of Margaret Aylward. The land was donated by Mr John Carroll of Earlsrath, a pious and zealous man, with an oratory in his own home, and a ready letter-writer on matters as varied as the neglect of graveyards and the abuse of drink; John Gowan notes in reference to the offer that Mr Carroll, though certainly devout, 'has been always peculiar'.[8] On the matter of Catholic schools, John Carroll was a particularly energetic and well-informed lobbyist, and a long-standing member of a local Christian Doctrine society.[9] Patrick Moran, nephew to Paul Cullen and formerly vicar general in Dublin and vice-rector of the Irish College in Rome, became bishop of Ossory in 1872, and actively promoted John Carroll's ambitions of bringing Margaret's sisters to staff new schools in Mullinavat.[10] Although he himself initially wanted the sisters for a new foundation in the expanding docklands area of Ferrybank outside Waterford city, he was happy to allow the Mullinavat project to overturn this plan, as if successful it could lead to further useful foundations.[11] In May 1880, although the current parish priest could come no closer to welcoming the new community than to say he was 'neutral', Bishop Moran was delighted with their arrival and brushed aside the coldness of the PP, 'so feeble and so aged', with the assurance that 'he will soon be awaiting his heavenly award and matters can then be arranged in a more satisfactory way'.[12] Though an inauspicious start, Moran himself looked likely to be around as patron and protector of the new community for many more years, and as one of the Mullinavat curates was appointed confessor and chaplain to the community, with faculties granted to John Gowan CM to hear confessions, say Mass and 'to exercise the other duties of the sacred ministry' whenever he would visit, there was no immediate problem.[13] John Gowan's prediction that the project was likely to succeed as 'God usually blesses those religious works that are tried well in the beginning' seemed to be fulfilled.[14] In 1883 Fr James Raftice was appointed as parish priest of Mullinavat; his personal animosity towards Margaret Aylward and the authority she held over the Mullinavat community was to know no bounds. In 1884 the appointment of Bishop Moran to the archbishopric of Sydney deprived Margaret of ecclesiastical support at diocesan level, while relations with his successor, Abraham Brownrigg, were to be tense and unhappy, to say the least. Margaret herself was by now invalided to the extent that she needed to be lifted and 'helplessly assisted' from her bed to a chair or a carriage; she visited Mullinavat in person no more than twice.[15] Agnes Vickers acted as her nurse, attendant and secretary.

The disputes centred around the very different perceptions of the relationship of the parish priest to the community held by respective parties. Fr Raftice claimed that he had received the 'most ample special authority regarding the nuns in his parish that he [the Bishop] could possibly give', in addition to 'the powers every P.P. has from the Canon Law in his own parish'.[16] Although he could not substantiate his claim to 'special powers', it did not in the least hold him back from declaring an absolute right to free communication with individual sisters under the heading of 'spiritual direction'. He stated his position in unequivocal terms:

> The parish priest is the Superior here. He is the common father of the Parish and every one of his spiritual children, be they religious or secular, have a perfect right to approach him with all confidences and without let or hindrance caused by the presence of any one that could be regarded as an obstacle to this free communication either orally or *in Scriptis*.[17]

Regarding himself as the supreme authority in all that pertained to this local community, he bitterly opposed Glasnevin's role, directing his venom against Margaret in the most personal way. He ended weekly Mass in the convent, contrary to the permission granted by Bishop Moran, and created countless difficulties about arrangements for confessions.[18] He vehemently castigated the unfortunate local superior, Sr Brigid Devoy, for sending on to

Dublin a letter he had written 'to be there first scanned, examined and pried into!!! before it was given to the person to whom it was written'.[19] His letter of complaint was duly forwarded to Glasnevin, as he had intended, with the insolent address 'to whomsoever is "in charge" this moment'.[20]

Margaret faced the challenge to her authority in the most direct manner, and kept copies of all correspondence. She warned Fr Raftice 'if you maintain that you can, at your will, set aside the Rules in your intercourse with the Sisters, I submit that you cannot', and in particular warned him against 'taking the superior's place, and making changes in the duties or mode of living of the community or of setting up new regulations; if you were allowed to try you would very soon regret it'.[21] Each of the 'serious charges you have brought against me' was dealt with systematically. Margaret pointed out that while his opposition to the rule of submitting outgoing and incoming letters to the Superior was shared by 'many people of the world', it was universally regarded by religious communities of both men and women as essential, a rule to which 'the most learned priests and the most eminent saints have submitted'. In a cutting reference to his unfamiliarity with the ways of religious congregations, she noted that if he himself had spent some years 'in a well-ordered community' she had no doubt but that 'you would think quite otherwise than you do'. While letters of confession were of course in a different category, she held there was no need for this privilege in the case of Mullinavat where 'penitent and confessor are at no great distance'.[22]

While Fr Raftice's principal grievance was that he was not allowed unqualified jurisdiction over the convent within his parish borders, his complaints ranged over every possible aspect of the foundation. It was his 'unalterable resolve' to refuse the 'miserable pittance hitherto doled out to the clergy of this parish in the shape of dues for the farm of Ballyluskey'; in reply Margaret stated that she had paid 'exactly the dues which Mr John Carroll told me he had been paying to your predecessors', and questioned 'Why did you not tell me quietly long ago that they were not sufficient?' For his information she stated that on the two farms held by the sisters in the Dublin diocese, the parish priests never requested dues; on the contrary, 'they all assisted us more or less with money, and some of them largely, because they saw we were doing an important work of the parish.' He also requested separate payment for the weekly duty of attending to the Blessed Sacrament in the convent chapel, a labour Margaret claimed most priests considered was more than amply rewarded by 'the blessings which accrued to the Parish, Priest and the People, by all the homage paid to our Lord there, and all the prayers laid before His Majesty.' However, he was invited to name his terms, which if found beyond the means of the community would lead them to forego having the Blessed Sacrament reserved, because 'I believe our Lord would not wish us to be involved in debt on His account.'[23] Complaints mounted without pause, including that the sisters kept 'grown boys' of 11, 12 and 13 years in their school contrary to his wishes, and later that the sisters had 'taken' a local farm.[24]

Both Brigid Devoy in Mullinavat and Margaret Aylward in Glasnevin had ample reason to be seriously concerned at the nature and intensity of his involvement with individual sisters. In a letter addressed to the sister-in-charge (presumably Brigid) who had care of an ill sister (Sister Mary Paul) he hopes that she, Brigid, 'will supply my want during the absence of a few days' by insisting that the invalid follow the spiritual exercises he has decided on.[25] These were expounded at length and centred on regarding himself, Fr Raftice, 'in the proper light, *viz.* as the minister of God and the dispenser of the mysteries of Christ', so that any thing he may do for her 'is done by God who uses frequently the poorest and meekest instruments'. The principal task he set the patient was that she might overcome her excessive appreciation of him, for 'it is embarrassing for me to receive profuse gratitude'. Promising to give 'the poor dear creature' more of his time as 'my presence consoles her and makes her happy', his greatest anxiety, repeatedly expressed, was that 'consolation and happiness should be expressed to this proper end, thank God and *not me* for any good she receives at my hands.' It was then Tuesday, and these instructions were to cover his absence until his return on Friday when he would not fail to call by.[26]

There was obviously little point in appealing to reason in these circumstances; difficulties however turned to crisis with the failure of the Ossory authorities to countenance restraining Fr Raftice in any way. Requests from the sisters for a change of confessor were repeatedly forwarded to Dr Brownrigg by Margaret Aylward, with assurances that the community 'will gladly defray the expenses of whatever clergyman your Lordship may be pleased to appoint.' For whatever perverse reason, Brownrigg refused to accede to the requests, and further isolated the community by refusing to undertake the scheduled visitation.[27] Fr Raftice himself actively protected his position, and accused Margaret of applying for a chaplain to replace himself, 'without any intimation whatever to me'; she put the record straight but to little avail. During several months' absence through sickness and convalescence he failed to get a substitute appointed, or even to apprise the authorities that the sisters 'were in this state of spiritual destitution'; after months and months of delay she was obliged to seek to have a confessor (there was no question of a chaplain) *ad interim* appointed.[28] John Gowan restrained Margaret Aylward from complaining, for he feared that 'for her to complain of a parish priest to his bishop would be a very serious matter, and she might come to be looked on as the aggressor' and that the sisters themselves 'would become odious to the priests of the Diocese when reported of having accused the PP to his bishop.'[29] His advice in this instance served only to exacerbate the matter, as he later freely admitted himself, but it had at all times been given in *bona fide*.[30] By late 1888 Margaret was confined entirely to bed, the burning pain of her ulcerated legs making her heavy workload even more difficult; her inability to call personally on the parties in question compounded the problems, and the documentation which had passed between them was of such a complex and dangerous nature that simply sending it on by post to Bishop Brownrigg to resolve as he saw fit could not be countenanced.[31] And the isolation of the convent, set on a hillside about a mile from the village and church of Mullinavat, beyond the main thoroughfares, and with no other Holy Faith house within reach, was particularly intense.

It was directly following the death of Margaret Aylward that the exceptional animosity she faced from this clergyman, whom it appears she had never met in person, and some of the factors which may have contributed to it, becomes painfully evident. The failure of Bishop Brownrigg to intervene also becomes understandable though not excusable. Fr Raftice condemned Margaret's letters as 'notoriously insolent', and considered all communication with Glasnevin as 'unpleasant visiting and useless letter writing' succeeding only in 'perpetuating old sores' and 'widening the breach that unfortunately exists between your foundress and mine'.[32] However, his chief insult centred on her status as foundress and religious sister, claiming that the late superior 'was not a religious or nun in this part of Ireland and the young girls who were educated at Glasnevin always regarded her as a lay woman'. This was intended as the grossest possible insult, for 'it was fortunate she was so regarded, for the epithets so freely and commonly applied to her would ill suit a nun, and would be too profane to mention'. He reported that in an interview with the late Dr Walsh, parish priest of Slieverue, she had stated 'I am not a nun myself' to which Dr Walsh had replied 'Oh! I see that.' According to Raftice another clergyman, who claimed she had threatened to have him suspended, regarded her as 'a pest' and refused to allow her enter his parlour, 'so insolent and aggressive had she become'. Constantly harking back to the initial foundation by Dr Moran, he prophesied gloomily 'I fear the original sin is transmitted and that Convent founded here in direct opposition to the PP will be a source of annoyance for all times to come.'[33]

Also writing on the occasion of her death, Bishop Brownrigg acknowledges that 'Mrs Aylward, whom I had not the pleasure of knowing unless by repute, was, I believe, a woman who deserved well of religion and the Church' through her association 'with some of the most deserving charities of Dublin' and 'her heroism in defence of the faith of the little ones'. He however was severely critical of her relationship with ecclesiastical authority in Ossory:

> Though she had a branch of her community in this Diocese she never thought it worth her while to put herself in communication with the Bishop in reference to it so that for the last five years it has been living its own life and following out its

own devices without any reference to the ecclesiastical authorities – there has been
no visitation – no retreat but one – the srs. come and go seemingly without
reference to any superior and are engaged in working a large farm which was taken
over by them without reference to me.[34]

While his complaint is not entirely fair – it was he who refused to visitate
the convent despite repeated requests,[35] the farm had been donated to the
community, not 'taken', the sisters had made their annual retreats under the
direction of John Gowan, and the invalided Margaret could hardly be blamed
for failing to travel to pay her respects in Kilkenny[36] – nevertheless it exposes
the suspicion that communities of religious women which were not directly
under diocesan control encountered. And Margaret Aylward was a particularly
enigmatic figure to the Ossory clerics, as the gossip surrounding her status
reveals. Should this dangerously spirited woman who had failed so often in
religious life and was now purporting to be superior in a community of her
own making, be considered a nun or a laywoman? And what of this community, founded in distant Dublin and so obviously patronized by the Dublin
hierarchy that there were grounds for suspicion! And how dare the Glasnevin
management appoint and withdraw sisters and generally see to its government
and good order without the daily reference to the diocesan authority that was
surely the mark of a well-regulated convent.

As a postscript to the tensions surrounding Mullinavat from 1883, and
which provided one of the severest trials of Margaret's final years, it should
be noted that an understanding between the community and Dr Brownrigg
was reached in 1892. A new curate Fr P. Downey, appalled at the treatment
of the sisters ('one of the greatest blessings that Almighty God ever sent to
this Parish') wrote in strictest confidence to Fr Gowan in Dublin ('I know
that the Sisters look to you for guidance and that is why I write to you'). He
recommended that the sisters 'show a bold front now', abandon as fruitless
all efforts at compromise with the parish priest, and place the entire matter,
from its start, in the hands of the bishop.[37] Although Brownrigg's initial
response was cool – 'as the archbishop of Dublin is, I believe, the superior of
your Institute perhaps his Grace might more suitably be applied to than I' –
he himself recognized that 'it might be well to put an end to this impasse and
let it be clearly understood where the authority and jurisdiction over your
house here resides', threatening darkly that he will soon 'exercise one
undoubted right which I possess in reference to your house at Mullinavatt'
(*sic*).[38] A crucial and highly-charged meeting was held in Dublin on the
neutral ground of the Loreto Convent, North Great George's Street, between
Srs Agnes Vickers and Rose Gaughren, and Bishop Brownrigg at 10.30 a.m.
on 11 February 1892. He opened with the grossest insults against Margaret
Aylward and her successor, as recorded in Agnes Vickers' notes of the
meeting: that she was entirely unfit to be in charge, 'that there was no person

to direct them what to do, not one was properly instructed in the practise of religious life, that he thought before that we were ladies but that he saw now we did not even know the common usages of decent life.' The tirade increased in intensity on being presented with the file relating to the scandal, the bishop becoming apoplectic that these letters were only now being brought to his attention. The parish priest was entirely in the wrong and the foolishness of the sisters in failing to move earlier had compounded the scandal; the excuse that they acted as advised and 'believed that by suffering patiently God would bless the community' was met with an outraged

> All nonsense! You deserve all you suffered and a great deal more! I don't know how it is to be remedied. I think it must be referred to Rome. Every statement you made, everything you say makes your actions worse and worse.[39]

The storm had broken. This was followed by further exchanges of letters, the bishop considering it 'a matter of duty' to rectify matters if possible, culminating in a formal visitation of the convent in March, while the removal of the parish priest from his role as confessor and chaplain in both convent and school defused the situation greatly.[40] John Gowan acted as adviser and counsellor throughout, drafting letters and memoranda, though not attending the meetings in person; in a letter dated June of that year he warns the sisters not to speak of 'the Bishop's letter', evidence that the secrecy with which the affair had been shrouded from the start was to be maintained.[41] Ironically, in 1909 Bishop Brownrigg was welcomed as Apostolic Visitor of the congregation, appointed by Rome; in this role he wielded considerable authority over the sisters in all the Dublin convents, as well as the single Ossory foundation.[42] Sr Magdalen Maguire (Ellen), described in the register of membership as one of the 'companions of our foundress, Miss Aylward', was among the small circle who knew most intimately the pain and injury the Mullinavat scandal had created for Margaret; it was she who in 1908, during a brief (and also tortuous) period as superior general, initiated research into Margaret's life, with a view to publicising, and vindicating, her memory.[43]

Almost simultaneous with the outbreak of what has been termed the 'Mullinavat troubles' Margaret Aylward had to deal with crises in the Dublin diocese, but here at least she was operating on St Brigid's home ground. One problem related to the Vincentians, who were anxious to regain the full-time services of John Gowan CM, for 'during the season of Missions and Retreats, the Community of St Peter's can, not only, not afford aid, but will require for its homework whatever little help our houses around can spare'. In a letter dated January 1882 the provincial Fr Duff, requires that 'our dear confrere' be therefore relieved of the formal duties of chaplain to St Brigid's, and that the £60 per annum he has been receiving be thus freed to support a replacement (but not from the Vincentian community).[44] Margaret won this round, though again not without a struggle. More serious was a particularly well-documented incident in 1884, which bears testimony again to her unquenchable zeal and fearless honesty. A letter from Dr Donnelly, coadjutor bishop, inflamed Margaret with its half truths, insinuations and ingratitude. The bishop ventured 'in all friendliness' to alert her to a growing 'feeling of indifference if not of hostility to St Brigid's on the part of the Clergy', attributable to 'the great difficulty experienced by the Clergy when critical cases arose of getting the children into St Brigid's without giving a personal guarantee of an annual sum which many of them cannot afford' and a 'decided want of *savoir faire*' on the part of some of the well-meaning officials of the orphanage, interpreted by some clergymen 'as little short of insulting'. He recommended she try to 'regain, if possible, lost popularity amongst the Clergy' by trusting to 'general charity' and quietly enlisting 'the good wishes of the Clergy without appearing to make them pay for their efforts in rescuing the little souls in danger'.[45]

Margaret was outraged by this officious letter, and despite her poor health spared nothing as she dealt systematically with each complaint, over fourteen pages. The ingratitude of certain penny-pinching clergymen who begrudged making any contribution from parochial funds to St Brigid's was slated. The orphanage had worked ceaselessly to support the 1600 children admitted to date, nine-tenths of whom were from the different parishes of the city, at a cost not under £30,000 gathered by tireless fundraising at home and abroad. These children 'lay, so to speak, on the conscience of the Clergy'. Support from the secular priests of the city, who benefited so much from the work of St Brigid's, was disgraceful: of 100 secular priests in the city a mere 12 were currently subscribers. The parish of St Andrew's, Westland Row was singled out for particular attention. From this parish alone over a hundred children had been received, many at the request of 'a priest who had a great name for saving children'. However, this parish had never supported the orphanage financially and the priest who had found St Brigid's so useful 'requited us in the end by withholding his small subscription of ten shillings or a pound, and complaining afterwards at a meeting of the Clergy of the inefficiency of the Orphanage.'[46]

Margaret attacked the unreasonableness of the Dublin priests and their numerous refusals and broken promises which she claimed made a sham of their professed concern for the orphan and destitute child, as they tried 'to impose the whole labour and responsibility upon us'. Her conviction of the inestimable value of the faith of the child contrasts with the lukewarm attitude of the clergy who protest that 'parochial rating' in support of St Brigid's is out of the question:

> But is not the orphan child of the parish local, and when he falls or is about to fall into the hands of heretics is not his salvation before every other demand? Is the seating of a Church or the painting of a Church to be put in comparison? Would

it not be lawful to melt and sell the sacred chalice to save him? Permit me to say
that unless the Clergy have that zeal, that will make great sacrifices, with inimitable
perseverance, they will fail.[47]

Margaret concluded her lengthy reply by noting the uselessness of trying
to 'treat a widespread gangrene with a pennyworth of plaster' and giving
detailed instructions on how the clergy might best tackle proselytism.
Unbowed, she asserts that the orphanage will continue 'to take charge of all
suitable cases from the priests for five pounds per annum each paid in
advance. You will see how much we are doing in this when I tell you that
calculating all expenses they cost us seven pounds ten shillings each.'[48]

Dr Donnelly's reply to this missive is a complete climbdown. He cannot
recall the name and circumstances of the case which was refused 'as it only
indirectly concerned me'. The complaints against the officials he withdraws,
'I am beginning to think that I overstated the case. It was a casual conversation that occurred some three or four years ago where a number of priests
were assembled and some one present said that he had an answer from St
Brigid's that was "little short of impertinent", I think that was the word, not
insulting. At this distance of time I could not recall the facts not even the
name of [the] priest who made the observation.' While not among Margaret's
closest circle of friends, Donnelly certainly knew her both personally and by
repute; her demolition of his case had been prefaced 'with thanks for the
candor and friendliness of your letter and I ask you to allow me to reply in
the same spirit.'[49] The exchanges between Margaret and Bishop Donnelly are
hugely significant for the light they throw on Margaret's indomitable personality, her loyalty to Ada and the other women workers, and her grasp of the
issues involved. While there were obvious contrasts with the simultaneous
difficulties in Ossory, in both instances there were challenges, both real and
perceived, to hierarchical power, while the immense damage that loose gossip,
particularly in clerical circles, can cause, is in evidence. Both cases are also
revealing about the context within which philanthropic Catholic women, whether
religious or lay, operated in late nineteenth century Ireland. Bishop Donnelly
undoubtedly expected his paternalistic advice to be accepted submissively and
acted upon, perhaps even humbly welcomed. It was the assertiveness of the
woman manager of St Brigid's in levying a charge upon the parishes, even
though this followed only after all other efforts to engage the help of the
clergy had failed and 'we saw in the near distance a crash and the total break
up of the orphanage'[50] that led to the hostility of some of the clergy. Clearly
women's contribution to the social mission of the Church was to be welcomed
and extolled but only as long as it was subservient, gratuitous and under
clerical control.

The issue of who controlled the new congregation brought problems in
Dublin as in Ossory. Margaret Aylward's great friend and benefactor Paul

Cullen died on 24 October 1878. Such was his perceived influence on Margaret that contemporaries were quick to involve him as a third party in dealings of minor as well as of major importance, the note 'I know a word from you would be all-powerful with Miss A.' being typical.[51] Cullen's exceptional and very public support of Margaret was matched in full by his immediate successor, Edward McCabe (1879–85). In 1855 Margaret secured his services as vice-president of her Ladies' Assocation; during her time in prison he had made a very public statement of support by taking on the role of secretary to St Bridget's Defence Committee, formed while she was in Grangegorman, to defray her legal expenses. As parish priest of Francis Street he later persuaded her to undertake the care of the Catholic Ragged School in his parish in 1865, and followed that through with continued generous funding. His warm personal regard and support was manifest in small incidents such as immediately investigating the suspension of a school collection for the Coombe, or entrusting to Margaret a large bequest for the orphans of the city, rather than dividing it up among the many orphan charities of the diocese.[52] Glasnevin House was vested in the names of Edward McCabe, Margaret Aylward and Paul Cullen.[53]

However, the appointment of William Walsh (1885–1921) to the see of Dublin was to usher in a very different era; his elevation, coincidentally, was almost simultaneous to that of Dr Brownrigg in Ossory. Dr Walsh was to make Margaret Aylward's final years particularly difficult, with his criticisms of the schools, the 'hidden managers of St Brigid's Orphanage', and her too wide-ranging reports. More seriously he was unhappy with the status of the sisterhood, canonically erected as an institute of pontifical rather than diocesan right; he spoke ominously of 'a strong opinion very generally held that the Institute should be under ecclesiastical control and supervision'.[54] For the first time in almost forty years she found herself deliberately denied ready access to the archbishop, making the criticisms more difficult to refute. However, the esteem and affection with which Margaret had been held by influential churchmen in Dublin, Paris, Armagh and Rome had up to this contributed significantly to her success; her congregation and its ministries were, by the 1880s sufficiently well established to weather this serious clerical opposition. Her own sense of fair play, excellent record-keeping, and unquenchable zeal for what she saw as God's work, ensured that sabre-rattling would be met honestly and openly.

Margaret died 11 October 1889, aged 79, and was buried in the convent cemetery, Glasnevin. While all her personal property had long been made over to the congregation, her will includes one particularly poignant note: 'the Pope's present of the cameo of the Mother of Sorrows to be kept in the Congregation as a remembrance of times gone by'.[55] The prison trial had marked her indelibly. Fifteen of her sisters had predeceased her. Hundreds of Dublin's poor walked out to Glasnevin to the funeral of their 'Lady Aylward', while clergy and close friends travelled from all over Ireland. The Thirty-Third Annual Report, penned by John Gowan, reports on her death:

> We have lost, in this world, the head that planned it, the hand that guided it, and the heart that often throbbed in its various vicissitudes. Margaret Aylward is gone, we hope to a better world. Her disciples will strive to carry on her works; and this will not be the less difficult as she left them not in a fragmentary or disorderly state, but in vigour, order, and supplied with rule and system, that, with God's blessing, will insure a fair amount of success.

Her personal story is one of courage and colour, a woman of great faith taking on the challenge provided by the evangelical missionary movement, and handling it with style and energy. Her impact on the Dublin charity scene from 1851 to 1889 through the three institutions – Ladies of Charity, St Brigid's Orphanage and Poor Schools, and the Sisters of the Holy Faith, was substantial, particularly the pioneering of the out-door system of child rearing, and the network of city schools for the poor. To her persevering efforts the Daughters of Charity owe their North William Street foundation. In Trinidad, Peru, USA, Australia, New Zealand, Samoa and Mexico as well as in the dioceses of Dublin and Ossory, the Sisters of the Holy Faith, their Associates and co-workers have brought something of her heritage. Her youngest sister, Jane Fagan (Sr M. Scholastica), wrote

> My father looked to his son to perpetuate his name, but now – see – it is not his son, but his daughter who will hand it down in honour to posterity.[56]

Notes

1. Waterford Roots

1 Patrick Corish, 'Margaret Aylward – the historical background', lecture, St Patrick's College, Drumcondra, 14 October 1989; see also Kevin Whelan, 'The Regional Impact of Irish Catholicism 1700–1850', in William J. Smyth and Kevin Whelan (eds), *Common Ground. Essays on the Historical Geography of Ireland* (Cork: Cork University Press, 1988), pp 253–77.

2 See Romuald Gibson, *Tomorrow Began Yesterday*, for family tree (Dublin: Holy Faith Sisters, 1982); note complaint from Margaret Gibbons re complexity of the Aylward genealogy, Holy Faith Archives, Glasnevin, Dublin (hereafter GA): GF/D/28a, no. 16a.

3 See files on Aylward property, GA: AP/BR/26, AP/LI/27; also Maurice Mullowney to John Aylward, 13 April 1853, GA: AF/PL/15 no. 8.

4 Julian Walton, 'The Aylward Family' in *Irish Genealogist* 4 (1971), 225; offprint in GA: MA/F/20 no. 29.

5 Will of William Aylward 1840; copy issued on 14 August 1894, GA: AP/BR/26 no. 7.

6 Will of Margaret Murphy, GA: AP/BR/26 no. 13; see also lease of plot of ground by Mary and Margaret Murphy to William Aylward, 20 March 1828, GA: AP/BR/26 no. 2.

7 Account of Estate and Assets of Mary and Margaret Murphy, 2 December 1858, GA: AP/BR/26 nos. 14, 15; Payment to Inland Revenue by Mrs Ellen Aylward, successor, 1858, GA: AP/BR/26 no. 15a.

8 *Saunders' Newsletter*, 24 July 1799.

9 James Wallace to William Aylward, 1831, and reply to same, 31 January 1831, GA: AF/PL/15 nos. 2, 3.

10 William Aylward to James Wallace, 31 January 1831, GA: AF/PL/15 no. 3.

11 Walton (1971), p. 227.

12 Articles of Agreement, 2 September 1834, GA: AP/BR/26 no. 5; the two other sons, Francis and Richard, predeceased their father, and so played no long-term role in the business.

13 Walton (1971), p. 226.

14 Will of William Aylward 1840; copy issued on 14 August 1894, GA: AP/BR/26 no. 7.

15 Margaret Gibbons, *The Life of Margaret Aylward* (Dublin, 1928), p. 20 (hereafter Gibbons, *Life*); there is no record of where the other girls, Mary, Catherine and Ellen, attended school.

16 Notes from Stonyhurst College, GA: AP/BR/26 no. 12a.

17 Myles V. Ronan, *An Apostle of Catholic Dublin, Fr Henry Young* (Dublin: Browne and Nolan, 1944), pp 117–19.

18 Gibbons, *Life* (1928), p. 28.

19 Margaret Aylward to Dr Kirby, May 1862, re new schools, GA: Mc/K/12 no. 27; see also M.C. Normoyle, *A Tree Is Planted. The Life and Times of Edmund Rice* (Christian Brothers, 1976, second ed.).

20 T.J. Nash, *Nano Nagle and the Presentation Sisters*, Monasterevan, Co. Kildare: Presentation Generalate, 1980, first published 1959.

21 Ibid. p. 154.

22 Ibid.

23 Gibbons, *Life* (1928), p. 32; John St Leger (Clongowes Wood) to Margaret Aylward, 26 September 1840, GA: MA/GC/03 no. 36a; includes reference to Mrs Wall, Mrs Knox, Mrs Mulloney, Mrs Kushan.

24 Monsignor Michael Olden, sermon preached in Waterford Cathedral, 8 October 1989, centenary of the death of Margaret Aylward.

25 For example, see John St Leger to Margaret Aylward, 26 September 1840, GA: MA/GC/03 no. 36a.

26 Ellen Bodenham to Margaret Aylward, 1839–1852, GA: MA/GC/03 no. 69.

27 Ellen Aylward to Margaret Aylward, 1858, GA: AF/PL/15A no. 51.

28 Margaret Aylward to Ada Allingham, n.d. but 1859–1860, GA: MA/F/01 no. 31.

29 Margaret Aylward to Dr Kirby, 3 July 1870, GA: Mc/K/12 no. 30.

30 Whelan (1988), p. 269.

31 William Aylward to Margaret Aylward, 30 September 1834, GA: AF/PL/15A no. 48.

32 Sr Rose Gaughren, 'A Little Sketch of the History of the Congregation', handwritten MS, n.d. but written prior to 1923, GA: HC/S/21 nos. 16, 16A (MS and typed copy); also 2, 2A (earlier MS version); hereafter Gaughren, 'History'.

33 'Troubles from Within' in *Life of Mary Aikenhead* (1924), p. 180, quoted in Gibbons, *Life* (1928), pp 35–65.

34 Ellen Bodenham to Margaret Aylward, bundle of letters dated 1839–1842, GA: MA/GC/03 no. 69.

35 John St Leger to Margaret Aylward, 26 September 1840, GA: MA/GC/03 no. 36a.

36 Ellen Aylward to Margaret Aylward: n.d., also 23 and 27 February 1888, 19 March 1888; GA: AF/PL/15a no. 51.

37 See reprints in Gibbons 'Dark days', *Life* (1928), pp 77–88; also GA: JC/C/13.

38 John Curtis to Margaret Aylward, 26 January 1846, GA: JC/C/13 no. 5.

39 Ibid.

40 John Curtis to Margaret Aylward, 17 August 1846, quoted in Gibbons, *Life* (1928), p. 87 (original missing from GA).

41 Same to same, Good Friday, n.d., GA: JC/C/13 no. 2a.

42 John Aylward to Mary Aylward, 1854, GA: AL/PF/15 no. 14; Jane subsequently found refuge with Margaret in Eccles Street, see John Fagan to Jane Fagan, 11 April 1855, AF/PL/15 no. 43.

43 Richard Fitzgerald to Margaret Aylward, n.d., GA: AF/PL/15 no. 22.

44 Ibid.

45 For example, John Fagan to Jane Fagan, 11 October 1854, GA: AF/PL/15 no. 41; also brief note, n.d, no signature, but relating to Fagan's debts, GA: AF/PL/15 no. 27.

46 John Fagan to Jane Fagan, 11 April 1855, GA: AF/PL/15 no. 43.

47 Same to same, 14 June 1857, GA: AF/PL/15 no. 46.

48 Court proceedings and private papers on the matter of Maria Clara *née* White, Petitioner and William Aylward, Respondent, GA: AP/LI/27 nos. 6, 6a, 7, 8.

49 Ibid.

50 Court committal 10 November 1853, discharge, 5 February 1854, general balance sheet, GA: AP/BR/26 no. 17.

51 Bundle of letters from Sr M. Pelagia to Margaret Aylward, 1871–1888, GA: AF/PL/15a no. 61.

2. *Lady of Charity*

1 John Gowan to Miss Aylward, Lent 1853, GA: JG/PL/05 no. 1.

2 See Jacinta Prunty, *Dublin Slums 1800–1925. A Study in Urban Geography* (Dublin: Irish Academic Press, 1998), pp 14, 59–61; chapter 8 of this text deals with the north city parishes including the work of the metropolitan branch of the Ladies of Charity 1851–1900.

3 Ibid., pp 227–31.

4 Ibid., pp 14–15, 23; see also Jacinta Prunty, 'Mobility among women in nineteenth century Dublin', in Siddle, David (ed.), *Migration, Mobility and Modernisation in Europe* (Liverpool: Liverpool University Press, 1998).

5 *First Annual Report of the Ladies' Association of Charity of St Vincent de Paul*, Metropolitan Branch, 1852, pp 7, 32 (hereafter *Ladies of Charity, Reports*); see also GA: O/CD/18 no. 1.

6 *Ladies of Charity, First Report*, 1852, pp 5–6; Matthew 25: 40.

7 *Ladies of Charity, First Report*, 1852, p. 5; *Third Report*, 1854, pp 7–8.

8 *Ladies of Charity, Fourth Report*, 1855, p. 3.

9 James Joyce, *Ulysses*, Bodley Head ed. (1937), pp 410–574; see also John Finegan, *The Story of Monto: An Account of Dublin's Red Light District* (Dublin: Mercier, 1978); Name Book, Dublin City: Notes concerning the City of Dublin compiled during the Progress of the Ordnance Survey in 1837.

10 For a discussion of the workhouse model see Prunty, *Dublin Slums* (1998), pp 213–31.

11 A branch of the male Society of St Vincent de Paul, which visited and relieved the poor in their homes, was established in St Mary's parish in 1848; *Ladies of Charity, Eleventh Report*, 1862, p. 5; *Ladies of Charity, Eighth Report*, 1859, p. 8.

12 *Ladies of Charity, Third Report*, 1854, p. 5; *First Report*, 1852, p. 8.

13 *Ladies of Charity, Third Report*, 1854, p. 4.

14 *Ladies of Charity, Seventh Report*, 1858, p. 10; *Fourth Report*, 1855, p. 4; *Eighth Report*, 1859, pp 5–6.

15 *Ladies of Charity, Second Report*, 1853, p. 4.

16 *Ladies of Charity, Fifth Report*, 1856, p. 7.

17 *Ladies of Charity, First Report*, 1852, p. 16.

18 *Ladies of Charity, Sixth Report*, 1857, pp 6, 11.

19 Rose Gaughren, MS 'History of the Congregation', GA: HC/S/21 no. 16 (hereafter Gaughren, 'History').

20 *Ladies of Charity, Fifth Report*, 1856, p. 7.

21 For example see *Ladies of Charity, Second Report*, 1853, p. 11; *Fourth Report*, 1855, pp 10, 12.

22 *Ladies of Charity, Second Report*, 1853, p. 12.

23 Ibid.

24 *Ladies of Charity, Fourth Report*, 1855, p. 10

25 *Ladies of Charity, Tenth Report*, 1861, pp 6–7

26 For example Margaret Aylward to Fr. O'Neill, 29 October 1857, GA: PC/C/11 no. 3.

27 Fr P. O'Neill to Dr Cullen, 2 May 1861, DDA: file 1 secular clergy, 340/1 no. 70.

28 Ibid.

29 *Ladies of Charity, Tenth Report*, 1861, p. 6; *Fifth Report*, 1856, pp 4–5.

30 *Ladies of Charity, First Report*, 1852, pp 16–17.

31 *Ladies of Charity, Second Report*, 1853, p. 11; *Fourth Report*, 1855, pp 10–11.

32 *Ladies of Charity, Eighth Report*, 1859, pp 5–6.

33 *Ladies of Charity, Seventh Report*, 1858, p. 5; *Second Report*, 1853, p. 7.

34 *Ladies of Charity, Fourth Report*, 1855, pp 11, 20; *Fifth Report*, 1856, p. 6; *Eighth Report*, 1859, p. 6.

35 *Ladies of Charity, Sixth Report*, 1857, p. 6.

36 *Ladies of Charity, Fifth Report*, 1856, pp 6, 8.

37 *Ladies of Charity, Sixth Report*, 1857, p. 5.

38 ARDP Annual Report for 1876, quoted in Kenneth Milne, *A History of the Association for the Relief of Distressed Protestants* (Dublin, 1989), p. 10.

39 *Ladies of Charity, Third Report*, 1854, p. 7; *Eighth Report*, 1859, p. 9.

40 For example, see evidence re rent levels in *Third Report of H.M. Majesty's Commissioners for Inquiring into the Housing of the Working Classes*, Minutes and Evidence, &c., Ireland, 1885, c–4547–I, qs. 22,825–22,829.

41 *Ladies of Charity, Seventh Report*, 1858, p. 6.

42 *Ladies of Charity, Fifth Report*, 1856, p. 7.

43 John Gowan to Miss Aylward, 12 June [1851], GA: JG/CL/06 no. 6

44 *Ladies of Charity, Tenth Report*, 1861, p. 9.

45 *Ladies of Charity, Sixth Report*, 1857, p. 10.

46 *Ladies of Charity, First Report*, 1852, p. 18; Form of Instruction to be given to the Sick, MS copy, n.d. but early 1850s, GA: O/CD/18 no. 2.

47 *Ladies of Charity, Second Report*, 1853, p. 6; *Third Report*, 1854 p. 7; *Seventh Report*, 1858, p. 4.

48 *Ladies of Charity, First Report*, 1852, appendix.

49 Margaret Aylward to Paul Cullen, 20 December 1856, GA: PC/C/11 no. 1.

50 *Ladies of Charity, Fifth Report*, 1856, p. 3.

51 Gaughren, 'History'.

52 Letters from John Gowan to Margaret Aylward from 12 June 1851, in file GA: JG/PL/05; reference made by Margaret Aylward to Dr Kirby, 29 November 1860, GA: Mc/K/12 no. 26b.

53 John Gowan to Margaret Aylward, 12 June 1851, GA: JG/CL/06 no. 6.

54 Same to same, 9 November 1855, GA: JG/CL/06 no. 2.

55 Same to same, 12 June 1851, GA: JG/CL/06 no. 6.

56 Same to same, n.d., GA: JG/PL/05 no. 7.

57 Margaret Aylward to My Lord Archbishop, n.d. but appears to be 1857; GA: PC/C/11 no. 4.

58 *Ladies of Charity, First Report*, 1852, pp 6, 20.

59 *Ladies of Charity, Sixth Report*, 1857, p. 9.

60 *Ladies of Charity, Seventh Report*, 1858, p. 7.

61 *Ladies of Charity, Second Report*, 1853, p. 15.

62 Ibid., p. 26; *Fourth Report*, 1855, p. 5; *Third Report*, 1854, p. 12.

63 *Ladies of Charity, Second Report*, 1853, pp 16–17.

64 Ibid., p. 25.

65 Ibid., pp 15, 25–6.

66 Ibid., p. 25.

67 *Ladies of Charity, Third Report*, 1854, p. 18.

68 Ibid., pp 18–19.

69 *Ladies of Charity, Second Report*, 1853, p. 13; *Seventh Report*, 1858, p. 9; *First Report*, 1852, p. 20.
70 *Ladies of Charity, Second Report*, 1853, pp 6–7.
71 Thomas Kelly to Margaret Aylward, n.d. but probably 1851, GA: MA/GC/03 no. 23.
72 *Ladies of Charity, Second Report*, 1853, p. 6.
73 *Ladies of Charity, Sixth Report*, 1857, p. 6.
74 J.P. O'Hanlon to Margaret Aylward, February 1881, GA: MA/BL/14 nos 74, 74a.
75 *Ladies of Charity, Sixth Report*, 1857, p. 12.

3. Mission Fervour all round

1 Matthew 28: 19.
2 *Them Also. The Story of the Dublin Mission* (London, 1866), p. 2 (hereafter *Them Also*).
3 Joseph Robins, *The Lost Children, A Study of Charity Children in Ireland 1700–1900* (Dublin: Institute of Public Administration, 1987), p. 136.
4 For example, see 'Statistics of Proselytism', in Dublin Diocesan Archives, Walsh papers, 1913 file 384 (hereafter DDA).
5 Minutes of the Irish Church Missions to Roman Catholics, 1 March 1850, no. 223 (hereafter ICM minutes).
6 ICM minutes, 1 March 1850, no. 223.
7 On 16 January 1846 the first mail shot consisting of 20,000 pamphlets titled 'A Voice from Heaven to Ireland' arrived to 'Romanists of the respectable and middle classes' in the 32 counties of Ireland. To ensure the delivery of *all* the letters at *all* the addresses on the same morning took months of secret planning, as did compiling the mailing list to ensure only Catholics were contacted. This is undoubtedly the first instance of large scale unsolicited mailing in Ireland, and was carried out with military efficiency. Alexander Dallas, *The Story of the Irish Church Mission, continued to the year 1869* (hereafter ICM Story)(London, 1875), pp 15–19.
8 Dallas, *ICM Story* (1875), pp 25, 37.
9 *Irish Church Directory and Yearbook*, 1862, p. 141.
10 The agent was Revd Edward Ellis; see ICM minutes, July 23 1857; also 3 June 1858.

11 'The Early History of Mrs Smyly's Homes and Schools', speech by Miss Vivienne Smyly (grandaughter) given 29 May 1976.
12 Dallas, *ICM Story* (1875), p. 208.
13 *Them Also* (1866), p. 272.
14 ICM minutes, permanent arrangement of assistant secretaries, 27 May 1853, no. 61.
15 ICM minutes 11 January 1861, no. 3445.
16 ICM minutes 24 May 1860, nos. 3323, 3324.
17 Alexander Dallas, *A Mission Tour Book in Ireland showing how to visit the Missions in Dublin, Connemara, etc.*, 1862, p. 12; ICM minutes: short history of the ICM to be prepared, 22 July 1858, no. 2894; *Irish Mission Scenes and Adventures*, 23 October 1862, no. 3745; *Good News from Ireland*, 26 February 1863, no. 3793; *How to Expell Rome and Keep Ireland for the Irish*, 28 May 1863 no. 3836; *Handbook of the Romish Controversy*, 17 December 1863, no. 3917; distribution of handbills, 24 November 1864, no. 4051; *Popular Popery*, 27 March 1865, no. 4106; Hymn Book, 28 March, no. 4381; *What are the Irish Church Missions?*, 25 April 1867, no. 4390; see also pamphlets in Margaret Aylward's possession, including GA: O/DB/18A, no. 68, and extended references in annual reports of St Brigid's Orphanage (hereafter *SBO, Reports*).
18 *Them Also* (1866), p. 13.
19 Dallas, *ICM Story* (1875), p. 25.
20 'Report of Honorary Secretary for Missions, with reference to the reduction of missionary expenditure furnished to the Committee according to minutes 2988, 3028, 3029, 3030, 3085'; ICM minutes no. 3087, XXVIII, 9 June 1859 (hereafter 'Report of Honorary Secretary')
21 Alexander Dallas, *A Mission Tour Book in Ireland showing how to visit the Missions in Dublin, Connemara, etc.* (hereafter *Mission Tour Book*), (1862), p. 13.
22 A large cloth-backed map locating the Western mission stations was produced to accompany this illustrated guidebook; no copy of this map however exists in the Croydon headquarters of the ICM, nor in the NLI. The copy held in the ICM, Bachelor's Walk, is lost, feared stolen (October 1992).
23 Dallas, *Mission Tour Book* (1862), Townsend Street, Liberties, Fishamble

Street, Luke Street, Grand Canal Street, pp 8–12; Oriel Street, Montjoy Street, St Michan's, pp 48–50.

24 'Report of Honorary Secretary' (9 June 1859).

25 ICM minutes 25 Nov. 1858, no. 2959.

26 Dallas, *ICM Story* (1875), p. 307; see also *Them Also* (1866), p. 34.

27 *Them Also* (1866), pp 14, 21.

28 Dallas, *ICM Story* (1875), pp 122, 208, 239.

29 Them Also (1866), pp 16–17; p. 20.

30 Dallas, *ICM Story* (1875), pp 239; and *Them Also* (1866), end pages, '*Arrangement of Work*'.

31 Sympathies of the ICM committee extended to Mrs Smyly on the death of her husband Josiah; minutes of ICM, 28 January 1864, no. 3920.

32 ICM minutes, 23 June, 1859, no. 3109.

33 Dallas, *ICM Story* (1875), pp 177–8.

34 *Them Also* (1866), p. 17.

35 Dallas, *ICM Story* (1875), p. 238.

36 ICM minutes, 27 October 1870, no. 4834; 23 March 1871 no. 4890; 25 January 1872 no. 4982.

37 ICM minutes, 24 Nov. 1870, no. 4846.

38 For a detailed study of the Smyly Homes see Margaret H. Preston, 'Mothers' Meetings and Lady's Teas: Lay Women and Philanthropy in Dublin 1860–1880' (unpublished MA history thesis, UCD, 1991).

39 *Dublin Visiting Mission in Connexion with Society for Irish Church Missions, Report for 1869*, published 1870, p. 3; see also *Them Also* (1866), p. 4, which states that Dallas was only involved from February 1850.

40 *Dublin Visiting Mission in Connexion with Society for Irish Church Missions, Report for 1883*, published 1884, p. 3.

41 *Them Also* (1866), p. 271

42 Ibid., p. 75.

43 First Annual Report of the DCM, 1862, pp 10, 16.

44 *Dublin Visiting Mission in Connexion with Society for Irish Church Missions, Report for 1883*, published 1884, p. 3.

45 *Dublin Visiting Mission in Connexion with Society for Irish Church Missions, Report for 1869*, published 1870, p. 11.

46 Dallas, *ICM Story* (1875), 1875, p. 228.

47 *Them Also* (1866), p. 25.

48 ICM minutes, 28 Nov 1867, no. 4473.

49 For example opposition was organized by the ICM to counter Redemptorist retreats in Tinahely (24 November 1859), Garvagh, Londonderry (22 November 1865), and against a Jesuit retreat in Fermoy, (23 May 1861); ICM minutes nos. 3180, 4337, 3520.

50 ICM Minutes, 24 November 1859, no. 3180.

51 ICM minutes, 23 September 1858, no. 2919.

52 *Dublin Visiting Mission in Connexion with Society for Irish Church Missions, Report for 1894*, published 1895, p. 5.

53 For example, ICM minutes, 27 May 1858, no. 2812.

54 ICM minutes, 22 November 1860, no. 3423.

55 Dr Cullen to Margaret Aylward, n.d., GA: PC/C/11 no. 41a; see also reports of Luke Street Work Room and Dormitory, and Lurgan Street Sunday School, Margaret Aylward to Dr Cullen, 8 February 1856, GA: PC/C/11 no. 2; Cullen canvassed other individuals also to provide such data.

56 Dr Cullen to Margaret Aylward, undated, GA: PC/C/11 no. 19.

57 *First Annual Report of the Ladies' Association of Charity*, 1852, p. 23 (hereafter *Ladies of Charity*, Report).

58 Paul Cullen, *Pastoral Letter on the Festival of SS. Peter and Paul*, 1863, pp 9–10.

59 Fanny Taylor, *Irish Homes and Irish Hearts* (London: Longman, Green and Co., 1867).

60 'Irish Birds' Nests' in *The Month*, December 1866, pp 568–9.

61 *Them Also* (1866), pp 42–5; Dallas, *ICM Story* (1875), pp 163, 173, 186–87, 210.

62 Ibid., pp 164, 180.

63 Ibid., p. 242.

64 ICM minutes, 30 July 1860, no. 3383.

65 *Ladies of Charity, Third Report*, 1854, p. 12.

66 *Ladies of Charity, First Report*, 1852, p. 21.

67 Names of Women found attending Weavers' Hall School, The Coombe, on Sunday February 10 1856, GA: ML/VP/16 no. 5.

68 *Ladies of Charity, First Report*, 1852, pp 21, 23 also *Fourth Report*, 1855, p. 8.

69 In 1851 £14, (sick poor fund £126); 1856 £18 (sick poor fund £272); 1858 £5, (sick poor fund £242). From June 1858 this 'accessary work' appears to be subsumed into St Brigid's Orphanage.

70 SBO, Sixth Annual Report, 1862, p. 19.

71 *Ladies of Charity, Fifth Report*, 1856, p. 9.

72 *Ladies of Charity, First Report*, 1852, p. 21.
73 Margaret Aylward to Dr Cullen, 8 February 1856, GA: PC/C/11 no. 2.
74 *Ladies of Charity, Fifth Report*, 1856, p. 9.
75 *Ladies of Charity, First Report*, 1852, p. 22.
76 *Ladies of Charity, Fifth Report*, 1856, p. 9.
77 Ibid., pp 10–11.
78 Ibid., p. 11.
79 *Ladies of Charity, Eighth Report*, 1859, pp 8–9.
80 For example see fundraising leaflet for new Molyneux Church and Blind Asylum (Protestant), DDA: 1860, Cullen papers, file 333/5 no. 177.
81 *SBO, Fourteenth Report*, 1870, p. 5.
82 Margaret Aylward to Dr Kirby, 29 November 1860, GA: Mc/K/12 no. 26b.
83 *SBO, Tenth Report*, 1866, p. 14.
84 *SBO, Second Report*, 1858, pp 17–18.

4. *Shoulders to the Wheel*

1 Margaret Aylward to Monsignor Kirby, 14 September 1860, from Grangegorman prison.
2 John Gowan to Margaret Aylward, 19 June 1861, GA: JG/CL/06 no. 18.
3 For example, see letter from York, 9 November 1855, GA: JG/CL/06 no. 2; from Armagh, n.d., GA: JG/CL/06 no. 5.
4 Margaret Aylward to Dr Kirby, 29 November 1860, GA: Mc/K/12 no. 26b.
5 John Curtis to Margaret Aylward, 22 March 1881, GA: JC/C/13 no. 8a.
6 See drafts of reports for 1886 and 1887, GA: JG/BN/08a no. 11.
7 John Gowan to Margaret Aylward, 29 November 1878, GA: JG/CL/06 no. 28.
8 J.M. Scully, to M. Aylward, 1884, GA: MA/GC/OC no. 45.
9 *Fortieth Annual Report of St Brigid's Orphanage and Schools*, (hereafter *SBO, Reports*), 1897, pp 8–10.
10 *SBO, Twenty-Third Annual Report*, 1880, p. 4; see also Margaret Gibbons, *The Life of Margaret Aylward* (London: Sands, 1928) pp 134–6.
11 Only thirty of these children were entered in the register; it is presumed that the other seven died before the official register entries were made; *SBO Twenty-Third Annual Report*, 1880, p. 4.
12 St Brigid's Orphanage Register (hereafter SBO Register) volume 1, pp 3, 5, 7.

13 Paul Cullen to Canon Pope, 27 August 1859, GA: PC/C/11 no. 43.
14 *SBO, Fifteenth Annual Report*, 1872, p. 10; *Forty-Second Annual Report*, 1899, p. 4; *Fifth Annual Report*, 1861, p. 13.
15 For example see correspondence between Dr Donnelly and Margaret Aylward, GA: MA/CH/02 nos. 64a, 65a, 67a, 10–15 January 1884 (chapter 10).
16 *SBO, Third Annual Report*, 1859, p. 14.
17 *SBO, Twelfth Annual Report*, 1868, p. 3.
18 *SBO, Second Annual Report*, 1858, p. 8; *Fifth Annual Report*, 1861, p. 13.
19 *SBO, Thirteenth Annual Report*, 1869, p. 6.
20 *SBO, Eighth Annual Report*, 1864, p. 31.
21 *SBO, Fourth Annual Report*, 1861, p. 4.
22 *SBO, Third Annual Report*, 1859, p. 11.
23 *SBO, Second Annual Report*, 1858, p. 14; see also the *Thirty-Fifth Annual Report of the Protestant Orphan Society*, 1863, p. 20, where similar limitations are imposed; *SBO, Tenth Annual Report*, 1866, p. 5; *Twenty-First Annual Report*, 1878, p. 8; income figures are only available for the years 1857–79, so it is not possible to correlate income and numbers admitted over the whole period
24 This data is taken from the annual reports of the orphanage, and checked against the register entries. The figures do not correlate exactly, as children were accepted and removed from the care of the orphanage throughout the year, and there were also several re-admissions. The most accurate figure is that of the total number 'on the books' at any one period.
25 *SBO, Twenty Third Annual Report*, 1880, p. 5.
26 W.G. Brooke, 'Report on the Differences in the Law of England and Ireland as Regards the Protection of Women', *Journal of the Statistical and Social Inquiry Society of Ireland* (hereafter *Soc. Stat. Inq. Soc. Ire. Jn.*), 1873, 6 (43), pp 206–7.
27 SBO Register no. 104 (27 November 1858); other examples of children deserted by parents are nos. 912 (5 November 1870); 922 (16 March 1871); 955 (12 September 1871).
28 SBO Register nos. 1087, 1088 (3 May 1873).
29 Among many examples see SBO Register nos. 731–2 (15 May 1868), 757–8 (19 September 1868), 776 (9 January 1869), 785–7 (22 March 1869), 917 (24 December

1870), 925–6 (18 March 1871), 950 (26 August 1871), 1018–20 (31 August 1872).

30 SBO Register no. 832 (29 May 1869).

31 SBO Register no. 171 (October 1859).

32 Including the years 1730, 1737, 1743, 1758, 1760, 1791, 1826, see J. Robins, *The Lost Children: A Study of Charity Children in Ireland 1700–1900* (Dublin, 1980, 1987 reprint), 'The Foundling Hospitals' pp 10–59.

33 For a comparison of the various boarding out systems in England, Scotland and Ireland, see Isabella Todd, 'Boarding out of Pauper Children', *Stat. Soc. Inq. Soc. Ire. Jn.*, 1876, 7 (54), 293–99.

34 W. Neilson Hancock, 'The Mortality of Children in Workhouses in Ireland', *Stat. Soc. Inq. Soc. Ire. Jn.*, 1862, 3 (21), 197.

35 SBO, *Seventh Annual Report*, 1863, p. 6; for an account of the workhouse system as it affected children, see Jacinta Prunty, *Dublin Slums 1800–1925. A Study in Urban Geography* (Dublin: Irish Academic Press, 1998) pp 223–7.

36 SBO, *Seventh Annual Report*, 1863, p. 7

37 On 10 April 1869 St Brigid's Orphan Register numbering jumps from 797 to 828 with the note '32 children recommended by Very Revd Dr Conroy received April 1st 1869 are entered in Special Register previous to the above'. The name, address and nurse of 26 'special register' children are the only details recorded in the general register; the 'special register' itself has not survived.

38 Hancock (1862), p. 197.

39 Helen Burke, *The People and the Poor Law in Nineteenth Century Ireland* (Dublin: Women's Education Bureau, 1987), p. 230; John K. Ingram, 'Additional Facts and Arguments on the Boarding Out of Pauper Children,' *Soc. Stat Soc. Inq. Ire. Jn.*, 6, 49, 1876, p. 522.

40 See also Mrs Morgan John O'Connell, 'Poor Law Administration as it affects Women and Children in Workhouses', and Menella Smedley, 'Comparison between Boarding Out and Pauper Schools', in *Soc. Stat Soc. Inq. Ire. Jn.* 1880, 20–31 and 31–7.

41 For example, Mrs Smyly paid Thomas Elwood and his wife, 17 Crampton Court, at the rate of £6 per annum to care for four year old Joseph Keeffe, until he would be old enough for the Spiddall home (SBO Register, no. 850, 26 June 1869); similarly Mrs Smyly paid for James Crosby to be nursed by Mrs Maher, Mark Street (SBO Register, no. 787, 22 March 1869).

42 Orphan notebook, 1874–5, GA: O/DB/18a no. 70.

43 SBO, *Second Annual Report*, 1858, p. 12.

44 Ibid., p. 14.

45 *Instructions to the Nurses, St Brigid's Orphanage* (Dublin, 1858, reprinted 1899) p. 4.

46 SBO, *Second Annual Report*, 1858, p. 11.

47 SBO Register entry no. 104, 27 November 1858.

48 Orphan notebook, GA: O/DB/18A no. 70, between 11 June and 28 July 1874.

49 Margaret Aylward to Ada Allingham, n.d. but from prison, therefore 1860–1, GA: MA/F/01 no. 14.

50 Margaret Aylward to Ada Allingham, n.d. but from prison, GA: MA/F/01, no. 15.

51 *SBO, First Annual Report*, 1857, p. 5; *Twenty-Seventh Annual Report*, 1884, p. 5.

52 SBO, *Sixth Annual Report*, 1862, p. 14; see also Orphan Register, e.g. vol. II entries nos. 183, 189, 264.

53 SBO, *Second Annual Report*, 1858, p. 14.

54 SBO, *Seventh Annual Report*, 1863, p. 11.

55 John Gowan to Margaret Aylward, 1 January 1879, GA: JG/CL/06 no. 29.

56 Margaret Aylward to William Walsh, 8 January 1886, GA: MA/CH/02 no. 54.

57 Margaret Aylward to Ada Allingham, n.d. but from prison, GA: MA/F/01 no. 20.

58 Orphan notebook, GA: O/DB/18A no. 70.

59 SBO, *Sixth Annual Report*, 1862, p. 11.

60 SBO, *Sixteenth Annual Report*, 1873, p. 10.

61 SBO, *Second Annual Report*, 1858, p. 14.

62 SBO, *Sixth Annual Report*, 1862, p. 11.

63 GA: O/DB/18A nos. 75, 76.

64 William Nolan, 'Society and Settlement in the Valley of Glenasmole,' in F.H.A. Aalen and Kevin Whelan, (eds), *Dublin City and County: From Prehistory to Present* (Dublin: Geography Publications, 1992), pp 181–228.

65 List titled 'Children Ready to Be Placed', 1874, GA: O/DB/18a no. 70.

66 SBO, *Seventh Annual Report*, 1863, p. 14; *Second Annual Report*, 1858, p. 14.

67 *Instructions to the Nurses* (1899 edn.) p. 20.

68 SBO, *Thirty-Ninth Annual Report*, 1896, p. 14.

69 Robins (1987), pp 233–43.

70 *SBO, Thirty-Ninth Annual Report*, 1896, p. 14.

71 *SBO, First Annual Report*, 1857, p. 5; Margaret Aylward to William Walsh, 8 January 1886, GA: MA/CH/02 no. 54; *Sixth Annual Report*, 1862, p. 14.

72 *SBO, Thirty-Eighth Annual Report*, 1895, p. 12.

73 *SBO, Third Annual Report*, 1859, p. 12; *Eighth Annual Report*, 1864, p. 12; *Twelfth Annual Report*, 1868, p. 19; *Tenth Annual Report*, 1866, p. 8.

74 Margaret Aylward to Ada Allingham, n.d. but probably 1863, GA: MA/F/01 no. 2.

75 Same to same, n.d. but from prison, GA: MA/F/01 no. 3.

76 See also SBO Register, e.g. vol. 2, entries nos. 183 (7 January 1860), 189 (23 December 1859), 264 (13 April 1861).

77 See also *SBO, Eighth Annual Report*, 1864, p. 9 where 46 children are changed for this reason.

78 *SBO, Thirty-Ninth Annual Report*, 1896, p. 10.

79 *SBO, Eighth Annual Report*, 1864, p. 10.

80 For example, Mary Anne Brennan was taken on as a servant by Miss Broe, Celbridge, near where she was reared, while Michael Cahill 'is in the waterworks – lives near Mrs Kilbride', his nurse, who had earlier adopted him. Thomas Mills was placed to a trade, but ran back to his nurse, who got him a situation 'in a farming family near her'. SBO Register nos. 1187 (11 April 1874), 1292 (22 May 1875), 879 (7 April 1870).

81 'Applications for Boys and Girls; Children Ready to be Placed, 1874', GA: O/DB/18a no. 70.

82 Account books and relief records, 1879–94: GA: A/LO/36 nos 6, 7.

83 Margaret Aylward, memo re St Patrick's Guild, St Bridget's Orphanage; n.d. but filed with 1866 papers; DDA: Cullen papers, file 327/8 II Laity: July-December 1866, no. 74.

84 Margaret Aylward to Paul Cullen, 29 December 1858, GA: PC/C/11 no. 5.

85 'Irish Birds' Nests' in *The Month*, December 1866, pp 568–9; Paul Cullen, *Pastoral Letter on Mary*, 1864, p. 7.

86 Joseph Dixon to Fr Gowan, 14 March 1863, GA: O/CD/18 no. 8.

87 'Ireland's Teaching' in *The Workman; or Life and Leisure*, no. 16, 22 April 1865,

pp 247–8; Fanny Taylor, *Irish Homes and Irish Hearts*, (London, 1867), p. 56.

88 'Ireland's Teaching' (1865) pp 247–8.

89 Taylor (1867), p. 56.

90 Gaughren, 'History'.

91 Margaret Aylward to Dr Cullen, 10 June 1862, Mc/K/12 no. 27a.

92 Margaret Aylward to Ada Allingham, 31 July 1860, GA: MA/F/01 no. 39, and n.d. GA: MA/F/01 no. 33.

93 Scrapbook, legal notices, GA: SA/SR/37 no. 5.

94 Margaret Aylward to Dr Kirby, 3 July 1870, GA: Mc/K/12 no. 30.

95 File GA: PC/C/11 see Paul Cullen to Margaret Aylward, 30 April 1863 (no. 25); 10 February 1871 (no. 29); Good Friday 1873 (no. 33); 27 December 1873, (no. 35); Margaret Aylward to Paul Cullen, 29 December 1858 (no. 5).

96 Paul Cullen to Canon Pope, 27 August 1859, GA: PC/C/11 no. 43.

97 Margaret Aylward to Dr Cullen, 21 May 1869, DDA: Cullen papers, file 321/2/III nuns.

98 Margaret Aylward, memo re St Patrick's Guild, St Bridget's Orphanage; n.d. but filed with 1866 papers; DDA: Cullen papers, file 327/8 II Laity: July-December 1866, no. 74.

99 See letters in file JS/BC/09 nos 4–7, 10–11.

100 John Joseph Steiner to John Gowan, 21 November 1872, GA: JS/BC/09 no. 4.

101 Same to same, 15 August 1878, GA: JS/BC/09 no. 5.

102 John Gowan to Margaret Aylward, 7 September, probably 1872, JG/CL/06 no. 16.

103 John Joseph Steiner to Sr Mary Gonzaga Landy, 22 July 1914, GA: JS/BC/09 no. 12.

104 John Joseph Steiner to Mother Magdalene [Maguire], 29 November 1908, GA: JS/BC/09 no. 16.

105 For example, see John Joseph Steniner to Sr Mary Agnes [Vickers], 24 January 1897, GA: JS/BC/09 no. 19a.

5. *Troubling Paris*

1 *Ladies of Charity First Report*, 1852, p. 4; note also John Gowan to Miss Aylward, n.d. but early 1850s, urging her 'Don't

grieve for the drudgery of your works of charity but be glad and praise God that He has chosen you for such a glorious life', Holy Faith Archive Glasnevin: JG/CL/06 no. 5 (hereafter GA).

2 Draft notes in Margaret Aylward's hand, n.d. but with statistics as in *Ladies of Charity, Fourth Annual Report*, 1855, GA: MA/GC/03 no. 9.

3 Ibid.

4 Margaret Aylward to Very Reverend Sir [copy of letter sent to Père Etienne, n.d.], GA: MA/CH/03 no. 10a; translations from the French originals have been made by Sr Raymond Ledwidge CHF and are deposited in the Glasnevin archive.

5 Margaret Aylward to Fr Dowley, 17 February 1857, GA: MA/CH/02 no. 33.

6 For example: the Sisters of Charity took over the magdalen asylum, 91 Townsend Street in 1832 and relocated it to Donnybrook in 1837; the Sisters of Our Lady of Charity of Refuge took over a similar asylum in Gloucester Street in 1877; the Sisters of the Holy Faith took over the 'good works' and premises of the men's sodality, Our Lady Queen of Charity, 65 Jervis Street, in 1870.

7 Philip Dowley CM to Margaret Aylward, 15 January 1851, GA: MA/CH/02 no. 40.

8 Margaret Aylward to Père Etienne, n.d. but from content must be 1855, GA:MA/GC/03 no. 10a; Père Etienne to Margaret Aylward, 18 September 1851, original in French, GA: MA/CH/02 no. 50.

9 John Gowan to Margaret Aylward, 4th Sunday in Lent 1853, GA: JG/PL/05 no. 1.

10 *Ladies of Charity, Third Report*, 1854, p. 5.

11 T. MacNamara to Dr Cullen, 4 April 1855, Cullen papers 1855, male religious, file II, 332/7, no. 17

12 Père Etienne to Margaret Aylward, 2 August 1855, GA: MA/CH/02 no. 43.

13 Margaret Aylward to Père Etienne, 19 August 1855, GA: MA/CH/02 no. 56a.

14 Ibid.

15 Ibid.

16 Fr Salvayre to Fr Dowley, 6 November 1856, GA: JG/CL/06 no. 136

17 Margaret Aylward to Sr Josephine Virien, 14 July 1857, GA: MA/GC/03 no. 7a.

18 Margaret Aylward to Père Etienne, 4 October 1856, same to same, 4 November 1856, GA: MA/CH/02 nos. 45a, 47a.

19 Margaret Aylward to Fr Dowley, n. d. but must be February or March 1857; GA: MA/CH/02 no. 32.

20 Margaret Aylward to Fr Dowley, 13 March 1857, GA: O/CD/18 no. 4.

21 Ibid.

22 Fr Dowley to Margaret Aylward, 13 March 1857, GA: MA/CG/03 no. 31; same to same, 16 March 1857, GA: MA/CH/02 no. 41.

23 No name, n.d., but from content Margaret Aylward to Père Etienne, March 1857, GA: MA/CH/02 no. 49a.

24 No name, n.d., but in Margaret Aylward's handwriting, GA: MA/GC/03 no. 10b.

25 Margaret Aylward to Fr Dowley, 13 March 1857, GA: O/CD/18 no. 4.

26 Philip Dowley to Margaret Aylward, 13 March 1857, GA: MA/CG/03 no. 31.

27 Margaret Aylward to Fr Dowley, 13 March 1857, GA: O/CD/18 no. 4.

28 Margaret Aylward to Père Etienne, 8 October 1856; same to same, 4 October 1856, GA: MA/CH/02 nos. 46a, 45a.

29 Same to same, 4 November 1856, GA: MA/CH/02 no. 47a.

30 Fr Dowley to Margaret Aylward, 16 June 1854, GA: MA/CH/02 no. 34.

31 Same to same, 16 March 1857, GA: MA/CH/02 no. 41.

32 For example, see Père Etienne to Margaret Aylward, 18 September 1851, and 21 April 1857, GA: MA/CH/02 nos. 50a and 48.

33 Margaret Aylward to Père Etienne, 4 October 1856, GA: MA/CH/02 no. 45a.

34 Same to same, 8 October 1856, GA: MA/CH/02 No. 46a.

35 The Carmelite community and the orphans in their care removed to Sandymount; Margaret Aylward to Père Etienne, 4 October 1856; GA: MA/CH/02 no. 45a; for dates of Daughters of Charity foundations see Notes on North William Street foundation, box 2, Archives of Daughters of Charity, Provincialite, Blackrock, Co. Dublin (hereafter DC archive).

36 J. Lynch to Margaret Aylward, 28 May 1857, GA: MA/GC/03 no. 28.

37 Ibid.

38 P. Dowley to Margaret Aylward, 13 March 1857, GA: MA/CG/03 no. 31.

39 Thomas MacNamara CM to Dr Cullen 11 July 1865, Cullen papers, DDA: 327/2 file IV male religious.

40 Sr Josephine Virien to Margaret Aylward, 24 June 1857, GA: MA/GC/03 no. 6a.

41 Same to same, 20 June 1857, GA: MA/GC/03 no. 9a.

42 Between 20 and 24 June 1857; see Sr Josephine Virien to Monsignor [Cullen], GA: MA/GC/03 no. 9a.

43 Sr M. Josephine Virien to Margaret Aylward, 24 June 1857, GA: MA/GC/03 no. 6a.

44 Ibid.

45 Sr M. Josephine Virien to Margaret Aylward, 15 June 1857, GA: MA/GC/03 no. 1a.

46 Ibid.

47 Sr M. Josephine Virien to Margaret Aylward, n.d. but between 6–14 July 1857, GA: MA/GC/03 no. 5a.

48 J. Lynch to Margaret Aylward, 30 June 1857, GA: MA/GC/03 no. 28.

49 Sr M. Josephine Virien to Margaret Aylward, 15 June 1857, GA: MA/GC/03 no. 1a; Margaret Aylward to Sr Josephine Virien, 14 July 1857, GA: MA/GC/03 no. 7a.

50 Margaret Aylward to Sr Josephine, 14 July 1857; GA: MA/GC/03 no. 7a.

51 Sr M. Josephine Virien to Margaret Aylward, 20 August 1857, GA: MA/GC/03 no. 4a.

52 *Ladies of Charity, Sixth Report*, 1857, p. 16.

53 Ibid.

54 DC archive, box 2.

55 *Tenth Annual Report of St Vincent's Female Orphanage*, North William Street, 1868, p 5.

56 DC archive, box 2.

57 Ibid.

58 Ibid.

6. Prison Trials

1 Certificate of marriage, GA: MM/CC/17L no.7; certificate of baptism, GA: MM/CC/17L no. 6.

2 Letter from Henry Mathews to James, 8 December [1857], GA: ML/VP/16 no. 18.

3 John Gowan, *Thirty-Third Annual Report of St Brigid's Orphanage and History of Miss Aylward's Trial and Imprisonment*, 1890, p. 28 (hereafter *History of Miss Aylward's Trial and Imprisonment*).

4 E.B.A. Taylor to Henry Mathews, 12 January [1858]; E.B.A. Taylor to Mr Kane, solicitor, 9 September 1858, GA: MM/CC/17L nos. 8,9.

5 E.B.A. Taylor to Henry Mathews, 12 January [1858], GA: MM/CC/17l no. 8.

6 Gowan, *History of Miss Aylward's Trial and Imprisonment*, 1890, p. 28.

7 Mr Brereton, prosecuting, Court of Queen's Bench, reported in *Freeman's Journal*, 6 June 1860.

8 See St Brigid's Register, entry no. 61, 3 April 1858.

9 Mr Sidney, appearing for Miss Aylward, Court of Queen's Bench, reported in *Freeman's Journal*, 18 November 1859.

10 For reference to the struggle to remove Lefroy from power after his ninetieth year see Daire Hogan, 'Vacancies for their friends: judicial appointments in Ireland, 1866–1867', in Daire Hogan and W. N. Osborough (eds) *Brehons, Serjeants and Attorneys, Studies in the History of the Irish Legal Profession* (Dublin: Irish Academic Press, 1990), pp 211–31.

11 *St Brigid's Orphanage, Third Annual Report*, 1859, p. 19.

12 Philip Dowley to Margaret Aylward, June 18 1858, GA: MA/CG/O3 no. 32.

13 Sworn affidavits of Mary Jordan, Essy Quinn, Brigid Byrne, Elizabeth Kenny, Margaret Aylward, John Keegan, GA: MM/CC/17L nos. 11–22; interrogatories and answers of Margaret Aylward, 15 May and 25 May 1860, MM/CC/17L nos. 27, 28.

14 Margaret Aylward to Dr Kirby, 29 November 1860, GA: Mc/K/12 no. 26b.

15 Speech of Canon Roche, delivered at the Fourth General Meeting of St Brigid's Orphanage, 16 January 1861, reported in *Freeman's Journal* 17 January 1861.

16 The case of Edgar Mortara involved a Jewish child of Bologna, baptized secretly by a Catholic servant; Pius lX refused to intervene, and the case achieved notoriety throughout Europe and especially in England. See Margaret Gibbons, *Life of Margaret Aylward* (Dublin, 1928), pp 149–162; *Dublin Review*, 1859–1860; *Irish Times*, 7 November 1861.

17 *Morning News*, 3 December 1860.

18 Ibid.

19 From the scrapbook of Dr Connolly, Physician to the Waterford Lunatic Asylum; kindly provided by Julian Walton, Old Waterford Society.

20 To Margaret Aylward from: Georgina Fullerton, n.d., GA: MA/BL/14 no. 8; John Curtis SJ, n.d. but clearly November 1860, GA: JC/C/13 no. 1; Dr Kirby, GA: Mc/K/12 nos. 1–4; J. Tully, 27 March 1861, GA: MA/BL/14 no. 17.

21 See file GA: MA/BL/14.

22 Dr Dixon to Margaret Aylward, 16 February 1861, GA: MA/CH/02 no. 10.

23 Printed circular, 7 January 1861, GA: MA/CH/02, no. 63.

24 Margaret Aylward to Dr Kirby, 24 January and 24 April, GA: Mc/K/12 nos. 26c, 26d.

25 London *Times*, February 1861.

26 Margaret Aylward to Dr Kirby, 22 January 1861, GA: Mc/K/12 no. 26c.

27 *Freeman's Journal*, 17 January 1861.

28 London *Times*, February 1861.

29 The Trial of Miss Margaret Aylward, GA: C/B1, p. 77.

30 Margaret Aylward to Ada Allingham, n.d. but apparently February 1861, GA: MA/F/01 no. 22.

31 Marian Rawlins to Board of Superintendence, City of Dublin Prisons, 10 November 1860, copy in GA: MM/CC/17L no. 45; Margaret Aylward to Ada Allingham, undated, GA: MA/F/01 no. 13; Gowan, *History of Miss Aylward's Trial and Imprisonment*, 1890, p. 33.

32 Marian Rawlins to Board of Superintendence, City of Dublin Prisons, 10 November 1860, copy in GA: MM/CC/17L no. 45.

33 Ibid.

34 See Robert Cullen, *Life of Thomas L. Synott, Famine Relief Secretary and Dublin Prison Governor*, Maynooth Studies in Local History series, Dublin: Irish Academic Press, 1996.

35 Margaret Aylward to Mrs O'Carroll, 7 March 1861, GA: MA/CH/02, no. 28.

36 Laurence Mooney to Margaret Aylward, 26 November 1860, GA: MA/BL/14 no. 5.

37 John Gowan to Margaret Aylward, n. d. but clearly 1861, probably February, GA: JG/CL/06 no. 10.

38 Margaret Aylward to M. Frances, n.d., GA: MA/F/01 no. 67.

39 Margaret Aylward to Lord Lieutenant, draft notes, n.d. but must be early February 1861, GA: MM/CC/17L no. 39.

40 Margaret Aylward to Lord Lieutenant, 6 February 1861, MM/CC/17L, no. 35; to Lord Chief Justice, 15 February 1861, GA: MM/CC/17L, no. 37.

41 Lord Chief Justice to Governor, Grange Gorman Prison, 19 February 1861, GA: MM/CC/17L, no. 38.

42 Margaret Aylward to Ada Allingham, n.d. but from prison, GA: MA/F/01 no. 3.

43 Printed circular, signed by Margaret Aylward, 3 April 1861, GA: ML/VP/16 no. 9.

44 Margaret Aylward to Ada Allingham, from prison, GA: MA/F/01 nos 9, 24, 30, 8.

45 Same to same, n.d., from prison, GA: MA/F/01 no. 6

46 Same to same, n.d., from prison, GA: MA/F/01 no. 10.

47 Same to same, n.d., from prison, GA: MA/F/01 no. 15.

48 Same to same, n.d., from prison, GA: MA/F/01 nos 16, 21, 30, 27.

49 Margaret Aylward to Dr Cullen, 20 April 1861, GA: PC/C/11 no. 8

50 *Select Committee on Poor Relief (Ireland)*, Minutes of Evidence 1861, published 1864; Evidence of Dr Cullen, May 1861, nos. 3979–3985

51 Margaret Aylward to Dr Kirby, 29 November 1860, GA: Mc/K/12 no. 26b.

52 Ibid.; see also John Gowan to Fr Dowley, 10 October 1860, GA: JG/CL/06 no. 37.

53 Margaret Aylward to Dr Kirby, 29 November 1860, GA: Mc/K/12 no. 26b.

54 Dr Kirby to Margaret Aylward, 12 December 1860, GA: Mc/K/12 no. 4.

55 Margaret Aylward to Paul Cullen, 14 February 1861, GA: PC/C/11 no. 6; to Dr Kirby, 22 January 1861, GA: Mc/K/12 no. 26c.

56 Margaret Aylward to Paul Cullen, 14 February 1861, GA: PC/C/11 no. 6.

57 Père Etienne to Fr Dowley, 5 March 1861 (*en français*), GA: JG/CL/06 no. 139.

58 Margaret Aylward to Dr Kirby, 24 April 1861 GA: Mc/K/12 no. 26d.

59 John Gowan to Margaret Aylward, 12 January 1861, GA: JG/CL/06 no. 12.

60 Margaret Aylward to Dr Kirby, 24 April 1861, GA: Mc/K/12 no. 26d.

61 Gowan, *History of Miss Aylward's Trial and Imprisonment*, 1890, p. 33.

62 Rose Gaughren 'A Little Sketch of the History of the Congregation', MS, written prior to 1923, GA: HC/S/21 no. 2.

63 *Ladies of Charity, Ninth Annual Report,* 1861, p. 4; *Ladies of Charity, Eleventh Annual Report,* 1862, p. 5.

64 Margaret Aylward to Ada Allingham, n.d. but from prison, GA: MA/F/01 nos 13, 16; also *Ladies of Charity, Tenth Annual Report,* 1861, p. 9.

65 Margaret Aylward to Ada Allingham, n.d. but from prison, probably February 1861, GA: MA/F/01 no. 22

66 Obituary, 16 April 1869, Aylward House, Glasnevin.

67 Gaughren, 'History'.

7. Schools of St Brigid

1 *Fifth Report of St Brigid's Orphanage,* 1861, p. 12; reports on the schools were published as appendices to the orphanage reports, and are accordingly named and numbered. The first school report is therefore appendixed to the fifth orphanage report of 1861. The reports are here abbreviated as *SBO Annual Reports.*

2 Margaret Aylward to Dr Kirby, 29 November 1860, GA: Mc/K/12 no. 26b; *SBO, Ninth Annual Report,* 1865, p. 14.

3 *Ladies of Charity, First Annual Report,* 1852, p. 20; *SBO, Seventh Annual Report,* 1863, p. 15.

4 Margaret Aylward to Ada Allingham, n.d. but from the content August 1860 from Cork, GA: MA/F/01 no. 44; John Gowan to Margaret Aylward, n.d. but must be July 1860, JG/PL/05 no. 15.

5 Ibid.; for Cork correspondence see file GA: MA/F/01 nos 37–44.

6 *Ladies of Charity, First Report,* 1852, p. 20.

7 SBO, Twelfth Annual Report, 1868, p. 21.

8 John Coolahan, *Irish Education, History and Structure* (Dublin: Institute of Public Administration, 1981), pp 14–17.

9 See for example T[estis] on Catholic Education, n.d., GA: JB/DN/08b no. 1

10 *SBO, Twenty-Seventh Annual Report,* 1884, pp 11–12.

11 *SBO, Twentieth Annual Report,* 1877, p. 7.

12 *SBO, Twenty-Seventh Annual Report,* 1884, p. 12.

13 *SBO, Thirty-First Annual Report,* 1888, p. 16.

14 *SBO, Twenty-Seventh Annual Report,* 1884, p. 12.

15 *SBO, Thirty-Fourth Annual Report,* 1891, p. 10.

16 *SBO, Twenty-Second Annual Report,* 1879, p. 13.

17 *SBO, Second Annual Report,* 1858, p. 12.

18 *SBO, Twenty-Eighth Annual Report,* 1885, p. 13.

19 *SBO, Ninth Annual Report,* 1865, p. 15.

20 *SBO, Nineteenth Annual Report,* 1876, p. 15.

21 *SBO, Tenth Annual Report,* 1866, p. 8.

22 *SBO, Fifth Annual Report,* 1861, p. 12.

23 *SBO, Twelfth Annual Report,* 1868, p. 22.

24 *SBO, Eleventh Annual Report,* 1867, p. 16.

25 See *Correspondence between the Commissioners of National Education and the Patron of St Peter's National Schools, Phibsborough,* Dublin 1859; GA: GF/ED /28a no. 1

26 *SBO, Fifth Annual Report,* 1861, p. 12.

27 Coolahan (1981), p. 21.

28 T[estis] on Catholic Education, n.d., GA: JB/DN/08b no. 1; see also draft notes in John Gowan's hand, GA: JG/DN/08 (b) no. 4, I–V

29 *SBO, Eleventh Annual Report,* 1867, p. 16.

30 M.C. Normoyle, *A Tree Is Planted. The Life and Times of Edmund Rice* (Christian Brothers, second edition 1976), pp 283–286.

31 Margaret Aylward to Dr Kirby, May 1862, re new schools, GA: Mc/K/12 no. 27.

32 *The Child's First Spelling Book in use at St Brigid's Schools of the Holy Faith,* sixth edition, GA: GF/D/28a no. 7.

33 Sr M.S. Lyons to Lord Cardinal, 29 December 1884, Dublin Diocesan Archive, Clonliffe: McCabe papers, file 360/7/II, nuns (hereafter DDA).

34 SBO, Fifth Report, 1861, pp 11–12.

35 Rose Gaughren, MS 'History of the Congregation', n.d. but written before 1923, GA: HC/S/21 no. 2; *SBO Fifth Report,* 1861, pp 11–12.

36 Query sheet no. 2., n.d. but from contents early 1869, GA: CR/DSC/19 no. 2.

37 *SBO, Twenty-Second Annual Report,* 1879, p. 15.

38 Henry P. Kelly ODC to My Lord Cardinal, 21 January 1869, DDA: Cullen papers, file 321/I/II religious priests, no. 5.

39 *SBO, Thirty-Third Report,* 1890, p. 19.

40 School journal, 'St Brigid's Catholic School, 10 Crow Street', 1861–1 August 1872, GA: C/31/2 no. 1a.

41 Ibid.

42 Gaughren, 'History'.

43 Ibid.

44 Edward Mackready to Miss Aylward, 25 August 1871, GA: O/CD/18 no. 13.

45 John Gowan to Margaret Aylward, 16 September 1864, GA:JG/CL/06 no. 17.

46 For a detailed account of the Coombe schools, formerly the Coombe Catholic Ragged Schools, see Prunty (1998) pp 247–263.

47 West Park Street Journal, 2, 4, 5 December 1901; Gaughren, 'History'.

48 Cecilia Donovan, MS 'History of West Park Street Schools', 1915, GA: C/31/4 nos 3, 3a.

49 *SBO, Thirty-First Annual Report*, 1888, p. 16.

50 Donovan, 'History West Park Street' (1915).

51 Ibid.

52 *SBO, Twenty-First Annual Report*, 1878, p. 11.

53 For example, *SBO, Second Annual Report*, 1858, p. 17.

54 Donovan, 'History West Park Street' (1915).

55 Ibid.

56 Ibid.

57 At the school centenary in 1987, the centrepiece was the formal retracing of the procession from the old site in West Park Street, to the 'New Schools on the Coombe'; children and adults dressed in period costume, and the children played street games, with marbles, hoops and skittles, etc., as their predecessors did.

58 Donovan, 'History West Park Street' (1915).

59 Ibid.

60 *SBO, Thirty-First Annual Report*, 1888, p. 16.

61 William J. Walsh to Fr John Gowan, 4 March 1890, GA: JG/ML/07 no. 18.

62 Margaret Aylward to Dr Kirby, 28 January 1867, GA: Mc/K/12 no. 28e.

63 *SBO, Fifteenth Annual Report*, 1872, pp 15–16.

64 Margaret Aylward to M. Francis, n.d. but 1870s, GA: MA/F/01 no. 67.

65 James Lynch to Dr Cullen, 2 October 1854, DDA Cullen papers, file 325/4

66 Gaughren, 'History'; see also Dr McCabe to Margaret Aylward, 11 September 1877, re taking possession of Celbridge, GA: Mc/K/12 no. 36.

67 Margaret Aylward to Dr Cullen, 31 May 1866, DDA: Cullen papers, file VI nuns, 327/6 no. 16.

68 Query sheet no.1., n.d. but from contents early 1869, GA: CR/DSC/19 no. 2.

69 *SBO, Twenty-Second Report*, 1879, p. 13.

70 Incomplete, but from Mercy sister, 12 August 1871, DDA Cullen papers, 328/7 file V, nuns, nos. 69, 71.

71 Sr M. of St Joseph to Margaret Aylward, 20 February 1873, GA: O/CD/18 no. 14.

72 Pupils also came from Carlingford, Cavan, Kilrush, Parsonstown, Tipperary, Virginia as well as the villages of Roundwood and Lusk; Dublin addresses included South Great Georges Street, Talbot Street, Stafford Street, Gardiner Street, Cabra, Rathgar, Tallaght, Kingstown and Booterstown, while there were also children from Holyhead and London

73 Boarding school account books, 1873–1881, GA: with Aylward library collection.

74 Guest, from *The Leader*, n.d. but probably mid 1890s, GA: GF/ED/28a no. 4a; see also *Uranus*, 1911, GA: MA/F/20 no. 21.

75 Guest, from *The Leader*, n.d. but probably mid 1890s, GA: GF/ED/28a no. 4a.

76 Donegal: Fr P. Kelly to Margaret Aylward, 28 May 1874, GA: MA/BL/14 no. 62; Letterfrack: Margaret Aylward to Dr McEvilly, 5 December 1883–8 May 1884, GA: MA/GC/03 nos 18–21, MA/BL/14 nos 77–77c; Delgany: Sr Ignatius to Margaret Aylward, GA: MA/GC/03 no. 13; Westport: Kate McCormack to Fr Ryan, 8 September 1874, GA: ML/VP/16 no. 19; Headford: Fr Pat Ryan to Margaret Aylward, 27 August–12 September 1874, GA: MA/BL/14 nos 66, 66A, 67.

77 Robins (1987), p. 138; see map of convents in Ireland in Caitríona Clear, *Nuns in Nineteenth Century Ireland*, (Dublin, 1987), p. 38.

78 Margaret Aylward to Dr MacEvilly, 21 February 1884, GA: MA/GC/03 no. 20.

79 Ibid.

80 Same to same, 5 December 1883, GA: MA/GC/03 no. 18.

81 Ibid.

82 Same to same, 21 February 1884, GA: MA/GC/03 no. 20.

83 Dr McEvilly to John Gowan, 3 May 1884, GA: MA/GC/03 no. 22.

84 From Bishop McEvilly, 22 October 1879, DDA: McCabe papers, file I Irish bishops 1879, section 337/4 no. 64.

85 Ibid.

86 Margaret Aylward to Dr MacEvilly, 8 May 1884, GA: MA/GC/03 no. 21.

87 John Curtis SJ to Margaret Aylward, 7 August 1884, GA: JC/C/13 no. 9a.

88 Ibid.

89 *SBO, Thirty-Fourth Annual Report,* 1891, p. 15.

90 DDA: Walsh papers 1913, loose pamphlets, file 384.

91 *SBO, Twenty-Seventh Annual Report,* 1884, p. 10.

8. *Sisters of the Holy Faith*

1 Margaret Aylward to Dr Cullen, 29 December 1858, GA: PC/C/11 no. 5.

2 Margaret Aylward to Dr Kirby, 29 November 1860, GA: Mc/K/12 no. 26b.

3 First public announcement of the congregation including reference to Cullen's patronage, *St Brigid's Orphanage, Tenth Report,* 1866, p. 10 (hereafter *SBO, Reports*).

4 Statement by John Gowan CM, n.d. but c.1863, GA: O/CD/18 no. 5; see also reference by Margaret Aylward to John Gowan as 'our founder' in letter to Francis Allingham, n.d. but c.1863, GA: MA/F/01 no. 71.

5 Madre Maria to Miss Aylward, 24 June 1864, GA: MA/GC/03 no. 63.

6 John Cardinal Simeoni to Reverend Mother [Margaret Aylward], 28 June 1886, original in Italian, GA: CR/DSC/20 no. 3.

7 Margaret Aylward to Dr Kirby, 19 June 1866, GA: Mc/K/12 no. 28d.

8 John St Leger (Clongowes Wood) to Margaret Aylward, 26 September 1840, GA: MA/GC/03 no. 36a.

9 Margaret Aylward to Dr Cullen, 31 May 1866, marked *Copy,* DDA: Cullen papers, file VI nuns 327/6 no. 16.

10 Margaret Aylward to Dr Kirby, May 1862, GA: Mc/K/12 no. 27.

11 Statement by John Gowan CM, n.d. but c.1863, GA: O/CD/18 no. 5.

12 Margaret Aylward to Dr Kirby, 4 September 1869, GA: Mc/K/12 no. 29.

13 Register of Holy Faith Sisters, Aylward House, Glasnevin (hereafter Register of membership).

14 Miss Eliza Monahan, 1859, first entry in Register of membership; see also Holy Faith Obituary, Aylward House, 16 April 1869; Margaret Aylward to Ada Allingham, n.d. from London, GA: MA/F/01 no 31.

15 Query sheets nos 1–5, n.d. but from content 1869, GA: CR/DSC/19 no. 2.

16 Ibid., no. 5.

17 Congregation of St Brigid, draft rule by Fr John Gowan, n.d. but clearly 1858, GA; JG/ML/07 no. 2; order of day 1861, Rose Gaughren, MS 'History of the Congregation', n.d. but written before 1923, GA: HC/S/21 no. 2 (hereafter Gaughren, 'History').

18 Statement by John Gowan CM, n.d. but c.1863, GA: O/CD/18 no. 5.

19 Margaret Aylward to Dr Cullen, 31 May 1866, marked *Copy,* DDA: Cullen papers, file VI nuns 327/6 no. 16.

20 See GA: JG/DN/08, FG/L/22, and FG/L/23.

21 See directives by John Gowan, GA: JG/ML/07 no. 3a.

22 Margaret Aylward to Dr Kirby, 19 June 1866, Mc/K/12 no. 28d.

23 Gaughren, 'History'; see also Register of membership.

24 Ibid.

25 Ibid.

26 Ibid.

27 Margaret Aylward to M. Frances, 3 September 1864, GA: MA/F/01 no. 62 (M. Frances is Ada Allingham's religious name).

28 Same to same, n.d., GA: MA/F/01 no. 77.

29 Same to same, n.d. but presumably 1864, GA: MA/F/01 nos. 77, 69.

30 Margaret Aylward to Ada Allingham, July 1867, Aix la Chapelle, GA: MA/F/01 no. 63.

31 Margaret Aylward to Dr Cullen, 31 May 1866, marked *Copy,* DDA: Cullen papers, file VI nuns 327/6 no. 16.

32 *SBO, Fifteenth Annual Report,* 1872, p. 15.

33 Ibid. p. 14.

34 Margaret Aylward to Dr Cullen, 10 June 1862, Mc/K/12 no. 27a; query sheets no. 5, n.d. but from content 1869, GA: CR/DSC/19 no. 2.

35 For information on the bankruptcy of John Fagan, his flight to Australia leaving

his wife Jane to pay his debts, and his self-pitying correspondence, see GA: AF/PL/15 nos. 26–47, 1854 to 14 June 1857; the term 'dower' is the only term used in Holy Faith records.

36 Caitríona Clear, *Nuns in Nineteenth Century Ireland*, Dublin: Gill and Macmillan, 1987), p. 87.

37 Ibid., pp 91–9.

38 Of the 195 entrants up to 1889 three are recorded as requesting to do the work of 'lay' sisters: in 1866, after the name Ellen Leonard the description (*lay sister*) is entered; in 1877 Kate Roche 'signed a paper saying she came for the Domestic Works'; Margaret Lonergan writes she 'is satisfied if the Superior of the sisters of the holy faith (*sic*) will accept me to do any kind of domestic work. I will try to make myself useful in every way I can', 18 June 1880.

39 Gaughren, 'History'.

40 Margaret Aylward to Ada Allingham, n.d. but prior to 1863, GA: MA/F/01 no. 2.

41 Ibid.; Margaret Aylward to M. Frances, n.d. GA: MA/F/01 no 68.

42 1877 Nannie Geoghegan recommended by Mercy, Clane, Naas; 1878 Rose Finnegan, Poor Clares, Ballyjamesduff; 1885 and 1888 sisters Ellen and Fanny Martin; 1889 Ellie McGrath, Presentation, Mitchelstown; 1880 Mary Tobin, Mercy, Tipperary; 1883 Anne Guinan, Presentation, Rahan; 1879–90 eleven postulants recommended by the Presentation Convent, Carrick on Suir.

43 Rose O'Keeffe, Rathowen Co. Westmeath, entered 6 August 1884 aged 19, appears to be the first postulant from Glasnevin Boarding School; she was sent away 24 September 1885 'having been found unsuitable, partly on account of ill health'. Her dower of £150 was, as always, returned.

44 See voluminous correspondence concerning this foundation dating from 2 August 1876, GA: MA/CH/02 nos. 69–88; MA/C/24; M/LB/25.

45 Mullinavat continued up to the 1960s to provide an exceptionally large number of Holy Faith sisters, relative to its small size, and distance from Glasnevin or other houses of the congregation, (excepting Rosbercon, 1924). The convent was closed 26 July 1992, and the girls school at Mount St Joseph's amalgamated with the boys school in the village to form a co-educational school in a new premises.

46 Clear, *Nuns*, p. 79.

47 Margaret Murphy, entered 8 November 1876, aged 18 years, father took her away June 1877. 'She said she was very sorry to leave the convent'.

48 M. Agnes Vickers to Dr Gentile, 16 September 1903, GA: AV/C/10 no. 82.

49 Dr Gentile to M. Agnes Vickers, 3 April 1907, GA: AV/C/10 no. 83; for an early treatment of the dowry question see the query document (1869).

50 Madame Julia Scully to Dr Cullen, 5 December 1865, DDA: Cullen papers: 327/2 file V nuns, no. 18; also Eileen Coyle RSCJ to Sr Francis, 26 February 1962, GA:GF/D/28a; for acreage see query sheet no. 2 1869, GA:/CR/DSC/19 no. 2.

51 Margaret Aylward to Dr Kirby, 30 October 1864 & 19 June 1866, Mc/K/12 nos. 28, 28d; *SBO, Ninth Annual Report*, 1865, p. 18; *Fifteenth Report*, 1872, pp 15–16.

52 Margaret Aylward to Dr Kirby, 30 October 1864, Mc/K/12 no. 28.

53 Same to same, 19 June 1866, Mc/K/12 no. 28d.

54 Madden A. Reynolds (Solicitor) to Madame Scully (Sacred Heart Convent), 4 December 1865, DDA: Cullen Papers, 327/4, file laity, no. 95; see also memorandum for Madame Scully per W. Roche Esq., n.d. but should be placed with above, Cullen papers, DDA: 327/8 file: laity, July-December 1866, no. 80.

55 Madame Julia Scully to Dr Cullen, 5 December 1865, DDA: Cullen papers, 327/2, file V nuns, no. 18.

56 Ibid.; Margaret Aylward to Dr Cullen, 20 December 1865, Cullen papers DDA: 327/2, file VI nuns, no. 22.

57 Madame Julia Scully to Dr Cullen, 5 December 1865, DDA: Cullen papers 327/2 file V nuns, no. 18.

58 See query sheets nos. 1 & 2 re the quality of the grounds and demesne wall, 1869, GA: CR/DSC/19 no. 2; see also Violet Hill correspondence, GA: GF/D/28a, no. 32.

59 Sarah Atkinson to Margaret Aylward, 24 February 1878, in GA: GF/D/28a, no. 32.

60 Ibid.

61 Margaret Aylward to Dr Cullen, 31 May 1866, marked *Copy*, DDA: Cullen papers, file VI nuns 327/6 no. 16.

62 *SBO, Tenth Annual Report*, 1866, p. 10.
63 Margaret Aylward to Dr Kirby, 19 June 1866, Mc/K/12 no. 28d.
64 John Gowan to M. Agatha, n.d. but c.1865, GA: JG/PL/05 no. 22.
65 Margaret Aylward to M. Frances, n.d. GA: MA/F/01 nos. 68, 76.
66 Same to same, 1869, GA: MA/F/01, no. 75.
67 Same to same, n.d. GA: MA/F/01 nos. 60, 65, 68.
68 Same to same, n.d. GA: MA/F/01 nos. 76, 64, 73.
69 For cures see Margaret Aylward to M. Frances, GA: MA/F/01 nos. 47, 60, 64, 68; re illness of Maggie Vickers see nos. 19, 29, 36.
70 Re Miss Osborne, see Margaret Aylward to M. Frances, 3 September 1864, GA: MA/F/01 no. 62; re Mrs T and 'the Northerner' (Jane Farrell, Sr M. Martha) 23 April 1873, GA: MA/F/01 no. 70; re 'the new sister' and 'Anne' see n.d. GA: MA/F/01 no. 69.
71 John Gowan to M. Agatha, 13 March 1879, GA: JG/CL/06 no. 32.
72 Query sheets no. 5, n.d. but from content 1869, GA: CR/DSC/19 no. 2.
73 Margaret Aylward to M. Frances, n.d. GA: MA/F/01 nos. 59, 76.
74 Same to same, n.d. GA: MA/F/01 no. 71.
75 Query sheets no. 5, n.d. but from content 1869, GA: CR/DSC/19 no. 2.
76 Memo by John Gowan, n.d., GA: JG/ML/07 no. 3.
77 Margaret visited Aix les Bains Saine 1864, Aix-la-Chapelle in 1868, 1872, and Rome in 1864 for the canonization of St Margaret Mary Alacoque.
78 Margaret Aylward to M. Frances, 23 April 1873, GA: MA/F/01 no.70; see also no. 67.
79 Same to same, n.d. GA: MA/F/01 no. 58.
80 Same to same, n.d., GA: MA/F/01 nos. 64, 67, 77.
81 For example see Margaret Aylward to M. Frances, GA: MA/F/01 nos. 65 (16 July 1868), no. 73 (n.d.), no. 28 (20 May 1861).
82 Gaughren, 'History'.

9. Sources of Strength

1 See also T.W.T. Dillon, 'The Society of St Vincent de Paul in Ireland 1845–1945', *Studies*, 1945, 515–21.
2 For example opposition was organized by the ICM to counter Redemptorist retreats in Tinahely (24 November 1859), Garvagh, Londonderry (22 November 1865), and against a Jesuit retreat in Fermoy, (23 May 1861); Irish Church Missions minutes nos. 3180, 4337, 3520.
3 I am indebted to Fr Seamus Enright CSsR for this information.
4 *The Ursuline Manual or a Collection of Prayers, Spiritual Exercises, &c., interspersed with the Various Instructions Necessary for forming Youth to the Practice of Solid Piety, arranged for the Young Ladies educated at the Ursuline Convent, Cork* (Dublin: Richard Coyne, 1831); copy inscribed Margaret L. Aylward, July 1836 in Glasnevin Archive; see also Margaret Aylward to John Gowan, will of 2 April 1874, GA: MA/CH/02 no. 92.
5 J.P. Cooke SJ to Margaret Aylward, n.d., GA: MA/F/20 no. 22.
6 Catherine Aylward to My very dear little Mag, 29 July 1836, GA: AF/PL/15A no. 56.
7 Vow formula, GA: CR/DSC/19 no. 15.
8 *Dictionnaire de Spiritualité Ascetique et Mystique, Doctrine et Histoire*, Marcel Viller, F. Cavallera, J. De Guibert (eds), (Paris: Gabriel Beauchesne et ses Fils, 1937 edn), tome I, hereafter *Dictionnaire de Spiritualité*, p. 358, pp 375–6 (translations by J. Prunty).
9 J.P. Cooke SJ to Margaret Aylward, n.d., GA: MA/F/20 no. 22.
10 John St Leger to Margaret Aylward, 26 September 1840, GA: MA/GC/03 no. 36a.
11 John St Leger SJ to Margaret Aylward, 26 September 1840, GA: MA/GC/03 no. 36a; Margaret entered 2 October 1834 and left 9 July 1836.
12 P. Dowley to Margaret Aylward, 1841, GA: MA/CH/02 no. 37; see handwritten translation, 'Rules of the Ladies' Charitable Association of St Vincent de Paul for the Spiritual and Temporal Relief of the Poor', GA: O/CD/18 no. 1.
13 *Ladies of Charity, First Report*, 1852, p. 6
14 Margaret Aylward to Dr Kirby, 19 June 1866, GA: Mc/K/12 no. 28d.
15 *SBO, Fifth Annual Report*, 1861, p. 9.
16 *SBO, Seventh Annual Report*, 1863, p. 19.
17 Margaret Aylward to M. Frances Allingham, GA: MA/F/01 no. 77.

18 John Gowan to Margaret Aylward, 3 January 1861, GA: JG/CL/06 no. 9.

19 *Dictionnaire de Spiritualité* (1937), p. 379.

20 Ibid., p. 376.

21 John Gowan to Margaret Aylward, 12 January 1861, GA: JG/CL/06 no. 12.

22 Margaret Aylward to Ada Allingham, n.d. but from prison, GA: MA/F/01 nos. 22, 79

23 Same to same, 4 August 1860, GA: MA/F/01 no. 38.

24 John Gowan to Miss Aylward, 9 November 1855, GA: JG/CL/06 no. 2.

25 Sr M. Brendan (Ursulines, Thurles) to Margaret Gibbons, 22 May 1925, GA: MA/F/20 no. 25.

26 Order of Day and rule of life to be observed by Margaret Aylward from the Feast of the Resurrection 1852 to All Saints, GA: MA/F/20 no. 7 [hereafter Order of Day 1852].

27 *Ursuline Manual* (1831) p. 122.

28 Order of Day 1852.

29 *Dictionnaire de Spiritualité* (1937), p. 378.

30 John Gowan to M. Agatha, 8 Februry 1879, GA: JG/CL/06 no. 31.

31 *Ursuline Manual* (1831), pp 75, 320.

32 Margaret Aylward to M. Frances Allingham, n.d. but probably 1865, GA: MA/F/01 no. 76.

33 John Gowan to Miss Aylward, n.d. but early 1850s, GA:JG/CL/06 no. 5.

34 John Gowan to Margaret Aylward, 3 January 1861, GA: JG/CL/06 no. 9.

35 John Gowan to Miss Aylward, 12 June [1851], GA: JG/CL/06 no. 6; see also same to same, n.d. but early 1850s, GA: JG/CL/06 no. 5.

36 Margaret Aylward to Ada Allingham, n.d., Beauparc, Wednesday, GA: MA/F/01; memo from Margaret Aylward re St Patrick's Guild, St Bridget's Orphanage; n.d. but filed with 1866 papers; DDA: Cullen papers, file 327/8 II Laity: July–December 1866, no. 74 (hereafter Memo re St Patrick's Guild).

37 John Gowan to Margaret Aylward, 7 September 1877, GA: JG/CL/06 no. 16.

38 Margaret Aylward to Ada Allingham, Memorandum, n.d. but summer 1867, GA: MA/F/01 no. 81.

39 Same to same, n.d., GA: MA/F/01 nos. 12, 1a.

40 Memo re St Patrick's Guild, 1866.

41 Thomas McKenna, *Praying with St Vincent de Paul* (Winona, Minnesota: St Mary's Press, 1994), p. 14.

42 See handwritten translation, 'Rules of the Ladies' Charitable Association of St Vincent de Paul for the Spiritual and Temporal Relief of the Poor', GA: O/CD/18 no. 1.

43 *Ladies of Charity, Seventh Report*, 1858, p. 11

44 T. Kelly to Margaret Aylward, 22 December 1851, GA: MA/GC/03 no. 25.

45 Order of Day 1852.

46 *The Life and Work of Mary Aikenhead, foundress of the Congregation of Irish Sisters of Charity, 1787–1858* (New York: Longmans, Green and Co., 1924), p 45.

47 *Dictionnaire de Spiritualité* (1937) p. 378.

48 Ibid., p. 380; see also H. Manders, 'Love in the Spirituality of St Alphonsus' in *Readings in Redemptorist Spirituality*, volume II (Rome: Permanent Commission for Redemptorist Spirituality, 1988), pp 21–71.

49 *Ladies of Charity, Second Report*, 1853, p. 11.

50 *Ladies of Charity, Third Report*, 1854, p. 15.

51 *Ladies of Charity, First Report*, 1852, pp 12–13.

52 *Ladies of Charity, Second Report*, 1853, p. 16.

53 Prayer in Margaret Aylward's handwriting, n.d., GA: MA/F/20 no. 9.

54 John Gowan to Margaret Aylward, n.d. but in prison (1861), GA: JG/CL/06 no. 10.

55 John Gowan to Miss Aylward, n.d. but early 1850s, GA: JG/CL/06 no. 5.

56 Same to same, n.d. but early 1850s, GA: JG/CL/06 no. 5; see also same to same, 12 January 1861, GA: JG/CL/06 no. 12; same to same, 13 March 1879, GA: JG/CL/06 no. 32.

57 John Gowan to M. Agatha, 18 January 1878; to Margaret Aylward, 12 January 1861, GA: JG/CL/06 nos 27, 12.

58 John Gowan to Margaret Aylward, n.d., GA: JG/CL/06 no. 06.

59 Margaret Aylward to Ada Allingham, Notes, July 1867 GA: MA/F/01 no. 63a.

60 Margaret Aylward to Ada Allingham, 26 July 1867, GA: MA/F/01 no. 83.

61 Same to same, Notes, July 1867, GA: MA/F/01 no. 63a.

62 Emmet Larkin, *The Historical Dimensions of Irish Catholicism* (Washington: Catholic University of America Press, 1976, 1984) pp 57–89.

63 Margaret Aylward to Ada Allingham, Notes, July 1867, GA: MA/F/01 no. 63a.

64 Journal of St Brigid's Catholic School, 10 Crow Street, 1861–1872, GA:C/31/2 no. 1a

65 Margaret Aylward to M. Francis, n.d., GA: MA/F/01 no. 49; same to same, 16 July 1868, GA: MA/F/01 no. 65.

66 Crow Street Journal.

67 Margaret Aylward to M. Francis, 24 June 1872, GA: MA/F/01 no. 64a.

68 John Gowan to M. Agatha, 18 January 1878, GA: JG/CL/06 no. 27.

69 John Gowan to Margaret Aylward, 28 February; 12 June 1851, GA: JG/CL/06 nos. 3, 6.

70 John Gowan to Margaret Aylward, Fourth Sunday after Easter, GA: JG/CL/06 no. 5.

71 John Gowan to M. Agatha, 29 November 1878, GA: JG/CL/06 no. 28.

72 John Gowan to Margaret Aylward, n.d. but 1860, GA: JC/CL/06 no. 11.

73 *Ladies of Charity, First Report*, 1852, pp 8–9.

74 *Ursuline Manual*, appendix.

75 Memo re St Patrick's Guild, 1866.

76 Ibid.

77 Thomas Pope to Dr Cullen, 5 December 1854, DDA: Cullen papers, file 332/2 no. 197.

10. *Keeping Faith*

1 Margaret Aylward to Dr Kirby, 4 September 1869, GA: Mc/K/12 no. 29.

2 Margaret Aylward to M. Frances, n.d., GA: MA/F/01 nos 78, 53.

3 Bishop Woodlock (Ardagh) to Cardinal Moran (Sydney), 14 January 1897, Sydney Archdiocesan Archives, Moran papers 209, box U23/2/3 no. 20; while Dr Cullen is also mentioned, there is no reference to M. Aylward.

4 Ellen Aylward to Margaret Aylward, n.d. but contents indicate written early 1888, GA: AF/PL/15a no. 51.

5 John St Leger SJ to Margaret Aylward, 26 September 1840, GA: MA/GC/03 no. 36a

6 For example, see application by Petites Sœurs des Pauvres, Sr Henriette Joseph to Monseigneur l'Archeveque, 18 September 1881, DDA: McCabe papers file 346/7/1 religious.

7 Margaret Gibbons, draft notes, 1927, GA: MF/C/24 no. 69.

8 John Gowan CM to M. Agatha, 8 February 1879, GA:JG/CL/06 no. 31; John O'Carroll to Dr Cullen, 16 August 1867, same to same, 18 August 1869, DDA: Cullen papers, file I, laity, 334/7, no. 14; file 321/2 no. 28.

9 John O'Carroll to Dr Cullen, 16 August 1867, DDA: Cullen papers, file I, laity, 334/7, no. 14.

10 See John Carroll's correspondence with Margaret Aylward, letters of 1876–80 (nos. 1–21, 23–28); with Bishop of Ossory (9 August 1879) no. 22; typed copies, no. 28, GA: MF/C/24.

11 Dr Patrick Moran to Monsignor Kirby, 24 August 1876, archive of Irish College Rome, letter no. 247; copy in GA: MF/C/24 no. 48a.

12 Patrick Moran to Margaret Aylward, 8 May 1880, GA: MF/C/24 typed copy, no. 29.

13 Dr Moran to Margaret Aylward, March 1882 GA: MF/C/24 no. 31; see also same to same 16 May & 16 August 1882, GA: MF/C/24 no. 32.

14 John Gowan CM to M. Agatha, 8 February 1879, GA: JG/CL/06 no. 31.

15 Magaret Gibbons states that Margaret Aylward visited Mullinavat only once, around 1883/84; however, draft notes n.d. but from c.1888 in Margaret's handwriting indicate that she had recently visited Mullinavat, GA: MF/C/24 no. 45, while Dr Brownrigg claims she visited at least twice, see Agnes Vickers notes of 11 February 1892, GA: AV/C/10 no. 71.

16 J. Raftice to Sr Brigid, 1 May 1889, MS copy, GA: MF/C/24 no. 42.

17 Ibid.

18 P. Downey to Fr Gowan, 12 May 1890, GA: MF/C/24 no. 55; see also draft notes of John Gowan 1885–1892, GA: MF/C/24 no. 65.

19 J. Raftice to Sr Brigid, 1 May 1889, MS copy, GA: MF/C/24 no. 42.

20 Ibid.

21 Margaret Aylward to Father Raftice, 7 May 1889, GA: MF/C/24 no. 43.

22 J. Raftice to Sr Brigid, 1 May 1889, MS copy, GA: MF/C/24 no. 42; Margaret Aylward to Father Raftice, 7 May 1889, GA: MF/C/24 no. 43.

23 Ibid.

24 Agnes Vickers, notes of 11 February 1892, AV/C/10 no. 71.

25 There is no sister of that name in the membership register; the reference may be

to Sr Mary Paula (Mary McKeogh) who entered in 1865 aged 22 years, and died in 1897 in St Michael's convent, Finglas.

26 J.M. Raftice, to my dear Sister [Brigid Devoy], n.d., GA: MF/C/24 no. 47.

27 Draft notes *c.*1888 in Margaret Aylward's handwriting, GA: MF/C/24 no. 45; in September 1888 the curate in Mullinavat was granted faculties to hear the sisters' confessions, though that did not remove Fr Raftice as confessor, Edward McDonald to Revd Mother, 27 September 1888, GA: MF/C/24 no. 38.

28 Margaret Aylward to Father Raftice, 7 May 1889, GA: MF/C/24 no. 43.

29 John Gowan to Dr Brownrigg, 13 February 1892, GA: MA/CH/02 no. 62.

30 Ibid.

31 Ibid.

32 James Raftice to Sr Agnes Vickers, 18 January 1890, GA: MF/C/24 no. 49.

33 Ibid.

34 Bishop Brownrigg to Sr Agnes Vickers, 17 November 1889, MF C/24 no. 56.

35 Draft notes *c.*1888 in Margaret Aylward's handwriting; Dr Brownrigg to Mrs Vickers, 23 November 1889, GA: MF/C/24 nos. 57, 45.

36 John Gowan to Dr Brownrigg, 13 February 1892, GA: MA/CH/02 no. 62; Agnes Vickers notes of 11 February 1892, GA: AV/C/10 no. 71.

37 P. Downey to John Gowan, 12 May 1890, GA: MF/C/24 no. 55.

38 Dr Brownrigg to Mrs Vickers, 7 January 1892, GA: MF/C/24 no. 58.

39 Agnes Vickers notes of 11 February 1892, GA: AV/C/10 no. 71.

40 Dr Brownrigg to Fr Gowan, 22 February 1892, GA: MF/C/24 no. 62, see also John Gowan to Dr Brownrigg, 13 February 1892, GA: MF/C/24 no. 62.

41 See draft notes of John Gowan 1885–92, GA: MF/C/24 no. 65; also John Gowan to Dr Brownrigg, 13 February 1892 GA:

MF/C/24 no. 62, and Dr Brownrigg to Fr Gowan 22 February 1892, GA: MF/C/24 no. 63; John Gowan to Sister, 10 June 1892, GA: JG/PL/05 no. 67.

42 Dr Brownrigg to Directress, 8 April 1909, GA: CR/DSC/19 no. 18.

43 John Joseph Steiner to Mother Magdalene [Maguire], 29 November 1908, GA: JS/BC/09 no. 16

44 Fr Duff CM to Miss Aylward, 29 January 1882, GA: MA/GC/03 no. 35

45 Dr Donnelly to Margaret Aylward, 10 January 1884, GA: MA/CH/02 no. 64a.

46 Margaret Aylward to Dr Donnelly, 14 January 1884; copy in GA: MA/CH/02 no. 65a, original in DDA: McCabe papers 1884, file 360/7/II.

47 Ibid.

48 Ibid.

49 Dr Donnelly to Margaret Aylward, 15 January 1884, GA: MA/CH/02 no. 67a.

50 Margaret Aylward to Dr Donnelly, 14 January 1884, GA: MA/CH/02 no. 65a.

51 Julia Scully RSCJ to Dr Cullen, 5 December 1865, DDA: Cullen papers, file 327/2/V nuns, no. 18.

52 Edward McCabe to Margaret Aylward, 5 September 1879, 24 September 1881, GA: Mc/K/12 nos 41, 49; see other correspondence in this GA file, also Margaret Aylward to Edward McCabe 3 January 1884, DDA: McCabe papers, file 360/7/II.

53 Query sheet 2, 1869, GA: CR/DSC/19 no. 2.

54 Margaret Aylward to Archbishop Walsh, 10 May 1886, GA: MA/CH/02 no. 55; see also friendly correspondence with John Gowan (after Margaret's death) in GA: JG/ML/07 nos. 11–27, 1 November 1889–19 March 1894.

55 Margaret Aylward to Fr Gowan, 2 April 1874, GA: MA/CH/02 no. 92.

56 Quoted in Romuald Gibson, *Tomorrow Began Yesterday* (Dublin: Holy Faith Sisters, 1982), p. 5.

Bibliography

Barrett, Rose M., *Guide to Dublin Charities*, 1884.

Bowen, Desmond, *Paul Cardinal Cullen and the Shaping of Modern Irish Catholicism*, Dublin: Gill and Macmillan, 1983.

——, *Souperism: Myth or Reality, a Study in Souperism*, Cork: Mercier Press, 1970.

Burke, Helen, *The People and the Poor Law in 19th century Ireland*, Dublin: Women's Education Bureau, 1987.

Camp, Richard L., 'From passive subordination to complementary partnership: the papal conception of a woman's place in Church and Society since 1878', *Catholic Historical Review*, 76, 3, 1990.

Clear, Caitríona, 'The Limits of Female Autonomy: Nuns in Nineteenth-Century Ireland' in Luddy, Maria, and Murphy, Cliona (eds), *Women Surviving: Studies in Irish Women's History in the Nineteenth and Twentieth Centuries*, Dublin: Poolbeg, 1990, pp 15–50.

——, *Nuns in Nineteenth Century Ireland*, Dublin: Gill and Macmillan, 1987.

Coolahan, *John, Irish Education, History and Structure*, Dublin: Institute of Public Administration, 1981.

Corish, Patrick J., *The Irish Catholic Experience. A Historical Survey*, Dublin: Gill and Macmillan, 1985.

Craig, Maurice, *Dublin 1660–1860: A Social and Architectural History*, Dublin: Allen Figgis, 1969.

Crossman, Virgina, *Local Government in Nineteenth Century Ireland*, Belfast: Institute of Irish Studies, QUB, 1994.

Cullen, Bob, *Thomas L. Synnott, The Career of a Dublin Catholic 1830–1870*, Maynooth Studies in Local History no. 14, Dublin: Irish Academic Press, 1997

Cullen, Louis M., 'The growth of Dublin 1600–1900: character and heritage,' in Aalen, F.H.A., and Whelan, Kevin (eds), *Dublin City and County: From Prehistory to Present*, Dublin: Geography Publications, 1992, pp 252–7.

Dallas, Alexander, *The Story of the Irish Church Missions, continued to 1869*, London: Nisbet, 1875.

Daly, Mary E., *Dublin, the Deposed Capital: A Social and Economic History, 1860–1914*. Cork: Cork University Press, 1985.

Donnelly, Nicholas, *Short History of Dublin Parishes*, 17 parts, 4 vols., Dublin: Catholic Truth Society, 1909–20.

Dublin Charities, Association of Charities, 1902.

Finnegan, Frances, *Poverty and Prejudice: a Study of Irish Immigrants in York 1840–75*, Cork: Cork University Press, 1982.

Gardiner's Dublin: A History and Topography of Mountjoy Square and Environs, Dublin: National Council for Educational Awards, 1991.

Gibbons, Margaret, *The Life of Margaret Aylward*, London: Sands, 1928.

Gibson, Romuald, *Tomorrow Began Yesterday: Reflections on Margaret Aylward*, Dublin: Holy Faith Sisters, 1982.

Helferty, Seamus and Refaussé, Raymond, (eds), *Directory of Irish Archives*, Dublin: Irish Academic Press, 2nd edn. 1993.

Hill, Octavia, 'The work of volunteers in the organization of charity', *Macmillan's Magazine*, 26, 1872, pp 441–9.

Keenan, Desmond J., *The Catholic Church in Nineteenth Century Ireland: A Sociological Study*, Dublin: Gill and Macmillan, 1983.

Kerr, Donal A., *A Nation of Beggars? Priests, People and Politics in Famine Ireland 1846–1852*, Oxford: Clarendon Press, 1994.

Lambert, Brooke, 'Charity: its aims and means', *Contemporary Review*, 23, 1874.

Lawton, Richard and Pooley, Colin G., *Britain 1740–1950: An Historical Geography*, London: Edward Arnold, 1992.

Lawton, Richard, 'Peopling the Past', *Transactions of the Institute of British Geographers*, New Series, 112, 3, 1987, pp 259–83.

Lee, Joseph, *The Modernisation of Irish Society, 1848–1918*, vol. 10, Gill History of Ireland, Dublin: Gill and Macmillan, 1973; reprint 1983.

Lerner, Gerda, *The Majority finds its Past: Placing Women in History*, Oxford: Oxford University Press, 1979.

Luddy, Maria, 'Women and charitable organisations in nineteenth century Ireland', in *Women's Studies International Forum*, xi, 4, 1988, 301–5.

Luddy, Maria, and Murphy, Cliona (eds), *Women Surviving: Studies in Irish Women's History in the Nineteenth and Twentieth Centuries*, Dublin: Poolbeg, 1990.

Luddy, Maria, *Women and Philanthropy in Nineteenth-century Ireland*, Cambridge: Cambridge University Press, 1995.

Luttenberger, Gerard H., 'Vincent de Paul's Charism in Today's Church', in *Review for Religious*, Sept/October 1993, 660–83.

Mac Suibhne, Peadar, *Paul Cullen and his Contemporaries 1820–1902*, 5 vols. Naas: Leinster Leader, 1961–77.

MacCurtain, Margaret, and O'Corráin, Donncha, *Women in Irish Society: The Historical Dimension*, Dublin: 1978.

Majerus, Pascal, *The Second Reformation in West Galway: Alexander R. Dallas and the Society for the Irish Church Missions to the Roman Catholics, 1849–1859*; unpublished M.A. history thesis (UCD, 1990).

Maltby, Arthur and Maltby, Jean, *Ireland in the Nineteenth Century: A Breviate of Official Publications*, Guides to Official Publications, vol. 4, Pergamon Press, 1979.

Martin, John H. 'The social geography of mid nineteenth century Dublin city', in Smith, William J. and Whelan, Kevin (eds), *Common Ground: Essays on the Historical Geography of Ireland*, Cork: Cork University Press, 1988, pp 173–88.

McCullough, Niall, *Dublin: An Urban History*, Dublin: Anne Street Press, 1989.

McDowell, Robert B., *The Church of Ireland 1869–1969*, London: Routledge and Kegan Paul, 1975.

McKenna, Thomas, *Praying with St Vincent de Paul*, Winona, Minnesota: St Mary's Press, 1994.

McLoughlin, Dympna, 'Workhouses and Irish Female Paupers, 1840–70,' in Luddy, Maria, and Murphy, Cliona (eds), *Women Surviving: Studies in Irish Women's History in the Nineteenth and Twentieth Centuries*, Dublin: Poolbeg, 1990, pp 117–47.

Milne, Kenneth, *Protestant Aid 1836–1986: A History of the Association for the Relief of Distressed Protestants*, Dublin: Protestant Aid, 1989

Moody, T.W. et al., *The Church of Ireland 1869–1969*, London: Routledge and Kegan Paul, 1975.

Mulligan, Cáit (ed.) *Fr. John Gowan CM, co-founder of the Sisters of the Holy Faith*, Dublin: Holy Faith Sisters, 1997.

Murnane, Brian, 'The recreation of the urban historical landscape: Mountjoy Ward, Dublin *c*. 1901', in Smith, William J. and Whelan, Kevin (eds), *Common Ground: Essays on the Historical Geography of Ireland*, Cork: Cork University Press, 1988, pp 189–207.

Ní Chearbhaill, Maire, *Margaret Aylward, Foundress of the Sisters of the Holy Faith*, Dublin: Holy Faith Sisters, 1989.

Ní Chumhaill, An tSiúr Áine, *O Gheamhar Go Cruithneacht, Beatha Mhaighréad Aighleart* – Margaret Aylward, Baile Átha Cliath: Foilseacháin Ábhair Spioradálta, 1990.

O'Brien, Joseph V., *Dear Dirty Dublin: A City in Distress, 1899–1916*, Berkeley and Los Angeles: University of California Press, 1982.

O'Donnell, E.E., *The Annals of Dublin, Fair City*, Dublin: Wolfhound, 1987.

Preston, Margaret H., 'Lay Women and Philanthropy in Dublin, 1860–1880', *Eire-Ireland*, Winter 1993, 74–85.

Preston, Margaret H., 'Mothers' Meeting and Lady's Teas: Lay Women and Philanthropy in Dublin 1860–1880', unpublished MA history thesis, UCD, 1991.

Prochaska, F.K., *Women and Philanthropy in Nineteenth Century England*, Oxford: Clarendon Press, 1980.

Prunty, Jacinta, 'The Textile Industry in Nineteenth Century Dublin: Its Geography, Structure and Demise' in Diederiks, Herman and Balkenstein, Marjan (eds), *Occupational Titles and Their Classification: the Case of the Textile Trade in Past Times*, Göttingen: Max-Planck Institut für Geschichte, 1995, pp 193–216.

——, 'From City Slums to City Sprawl: Dublin in the Nineteenth and Twentieth Centuries', in Clarke, Howard (ed.), *Irish Cities*, Thomas Davis Lecture Series, first broadcast April–June 1995, Cork: Mercier Press/Radio Telifis Eireann, 1995, pp 109–22.

——, 'Margaret Louisa Aylward, 1810–1889' in Luddy, Maria and Cullen, Mary (eds), *Women, Consciousness and Power in Nineteenth Century Ireland*, Dublin: Attic Press, 1995, pp 55–88.

——, 'Mobility among Women in Nineteenth Century Dublin' in Siddle, David (ed.), *Migration, Mobility and Modernisation in Europe*, Liverpool: Liverpool University Press, 1998.

——, *Dublin Slums 1800–1925, a Study in Urban Geography*, Dublin: Irish Academic Press, 1998.

Readings in Redemptorist Spirituality, vol. II, Rome: Permanent Commission for Redemptorist Spirituality, 1988.

Revington, Carol, 'The Kildare Place Society: Its Principles and Policies', unpublished MEd thesis, TCD, 1981.

Robins, Joseph, *The Lost Children. A Study of Charity Children in Ireland, 1700–1900*, Dublin: Institute of Public Administration, 1987.

Taylor, Fanny, *Irish Homes and Irish Hearts*, London: Longman, Green and Co., 1867.

'Them Also.' The Story of the Dublin Mission, 2nd ed., London: Nisbet, 1866.

Young, Arhlene, *Praying with Margaret Aylward*, Port of Spain: Holy Faith Sisters, 1997.

Ward, Margaret, *The Missing Sex: Putting Women into Irish History*, Dublin: Attic Press, 1991.

Index

Aikenhead, Mary, 16

Aix-la-Chapelle (Aachen), 127, 146, 150–151, 154

Aix-les-Bains, 126, 143

Allingham, Ada, 57, 59, 65–66, 71–77, 97, 99–101, 108, 122, 126–127, 135–137, 144, 145, 146, 163

Alphonsian spirituality, 139–147, 153

America, 22

Anne Street (St Michan's parish), 23–24, 27, 34, 37, 48, 101

Arran Quay, 38

Atkinson, Sarah, 134

Australia, 18, 22, 36, 40

Aylward family, 13–21, 141, 154

Ballinasloe, 50

Bazaars, *see* fundraising

Beauparc, 136, 154

Bellingham, Fanny, 48

Benedictines, 14

Berkeley Street, 24

Bible readers, 48, 52, *see also* ICM

Bird's Nest, *see* ICM, Ellen Smyly

Bodenham, Ellen Augustine, 16

Bow Street, 48

Britain, 14, 22, 42, 56, 60

Brownrigg, Abraham, 156, 158–161, 164

Cabra, 59, 83, 86–87, *see also* Dominican sisters

Cape Clear, 37–38

Carrick on Suir, 18

Carroll, John, 155, 157

Carroll, Margaret (Sr M. Camillus) 130

Catechesis, 23, 37, 103, *see also* education

Catholic Cemeteries Committee, 132–134

Celbridge, 115

Celtic monasticism, 132, 139, 142–143, 153

Charity, sisters of (Irish), 14, 16–17, 19, 107, 122, 138–139, 141, 147, 155

Christian Brothers, 14–15, 106–107, 120, 138

Church authority, 152–153

Clarendon Street, 108–110, 116, 119, 127

Clontarf, 20, 39

Colclough, Catherine (Sr M. Lucy), p. 130

Collier, Fr, 16

Confraternities, 59, 74–77 *see also* guildsmen

Cooke, J.P., 139, 141, 144

Coombe, 47, 52–54, 103–104, 108, 111–114, 119–120

Cork, 38, 39, 74, 77, 101

Coughlan, Brigid (Sr M. Gabriel), 130

Coughlan, Maggie (Sr M. Bonaventure), 130

Cross and Passion sisters, 115

Crow Street, 101, 107–110, 119, 121, 151

Cullen, Paul, 32, 34, 50–52, 58–59, 73–75, 77, 80, 88, 95, 98–99, 102, 107, 109, 115–116, 121–124, 126, 132, 134, 138, 150, 153, 164

Curtis, John, 17–18, 32, 56, 94, 118–119

Daily Express, 96

Dallas, Alexander, 41–42; 49–50

Daniel, Canon, 113

Daughters of Charity, 59, 79–90, 138

Daughters of St Brigid, 99, 122

Devoy, Brigid, 156–158

Dixon, James, 89

Dixon, Joseph, 73, 94, 99

Dominican priests, 50

Dominican sisters, 31, *see also* Cabra

Donnelly, Dr. 162–163

Donovan, Julia (Sr M. Cecilia) 109–112
Donovan, Emma, 89
Dorset Street, 23, 35
Dowley, Philip, 15, 80, 83, 85–86, 93, 98–99
Dowling, Mary Jane (Sr M. Peter) 130
Dublin Visiting Mission, 48
Duff, Fr, 161

Eccles Street, 24, 31, 72, 81, 97, 99–100, 124, 127
Education, 15, 23, 34, 40; *see also* St Brigid's schools; national education
Emigration, *see* migration
Employment, 22, 27–28, 35–37
Etienne, Père, 80–86, 98–99
Evangelical missions, 40–55, 101, 120, 139; *see also* ICM

Fagan, Jane, 13, 17, 18, 110, 126–127, 137
Faith, 55, 56, 102–103, 134, 142, 147, 151–152, 162–163, 165
Famine, 21
Fee-paying schools, 115–117
Fellowes, Emily, 17
Ferrybank, 155
Fitzgerald, Richard, 18
Fitzgibbon Street, 31
Foran, Nicholas, 15
Foundlings, 58–59, 62,
Francis Street, 85–86
Freeman's Journal, 52, 93, 95
Fullerton, Georgina, 94
Fundraising, 16, 31–32, 35, 54, 73–77, 97–98, 107

Gardiner Street, 20–21, 24, 37, 80, 101, 107
Gaughren, Margaret (Sr M. Rose), 32, 74, 109, 115, 125–126, 129, 135–136, 160
Georges Street, North Great, 18, 160
Gibbons, Margaret, 155
Glasnevin, 109, 116, 124, 126, 129, 132–134, 142–143, 151, 154, 159, 164–165

Gowan, John, 32–34; 56–57, 59, 80, 88, 96–99, 101–102, 106, 108, 110, 112, 118, 121–126, 134–136, 138–146, 149, 151–156, 158–161, 165
Grangegorman prison, 93–98, 121
Greek Street, 28
de Gud, Robert, 63
Guildsmen, 74, 146, 152–153
Guinness, Arthur, 48

Hastings, 17
Headford, 117
Health, 16, 20, 27–28, 99, 154, 159
Henrietta Place, 21
Holy Faith Sisters, 121–137; congregational status/government, 115, 122, 134, 154–155, 159–160, 164; constitutions 122, 124–125, 131; religious names, 125; religious dress, 125–126; dowers 127–131; title 124, 134; recruitment/vocations 101, 114, 123, 127–131, 135
Home rule, 13–14

Illegitimacy, see foundlings
Illness, see health
Industrial schools, 104, 119
Irish Church Missions 41–55, 101, 120
Irish Times, 93–94

Jervis Street, 108, 119, 127
Jesuit spirituality, 139, 141–142, 144, 153
Jesuits, 14, 17, 24, 50, 138, 148, *see also* Cooke, Curtis, St Leger

Kelly, Henry, 108–109
Kelly, Margaret, 22, 23, 142
Kennedy, Ignatius, 95, 108
Kilcullen, 114–115
Kingstown, 22, 32, 38–39, 42, 52
Kirby, Tobias, 15, 94, 98, 122, 138

Ladies of Charity, 16, 22–39; 52–53, 55–57, 72, 79, 83–84, 97, 99–101, 119, 121, 124, 142, 146
Larkin, Emmet, 150

Leader, Henry, 38
Lefroy, Judge, 91, 93
Lenehan, Teresa (Sr M. Benedict) 130
Letterfrack, 117–118
Libraries, 104–105
Ligouri, Alphonsus, 16, 139, *see also* Alphonsian spirituality
Loreto sisters, 18, 160
Lynch, James, 115
Lynch, John, 83, 86, 88

Mabbot Street, 62
Maguire, Ellen (Sr M. Magdalen), 111, 126, 161
Maloney, Rose (Sr M. Borgia), 130
Marlborough Street (St Mary's parish), 22–24, 32, 103
Mathews, Mary *see* trial and imprisonment
McCabe, Edward, 32, 58, 83, 85, 88, 94, 97–98, 113, 118, 164
McCarthy, C.F., 48, 53
McEvilly, John, 117–118
McNamara, J. 38, 80, 83
Meagher, Thomas Francis, 14
Mercy sisters, 115–116, 129, 138
Migration, 21–22, 28, 56, 60, 70
Monahan, Eliza, 100, 122, 124, 135
Mont de Piété, 15
Mooney, Laurence, 96
Moran, Patrick, 155–156, 159
Morning News, 94, 96
Mullinavat, 114, 115, 119, 130, 155–161
Mullowney, John & Teresa, 15
Mullowney, Maurice, 13
Murphy, Patrick Joseph, 15
Murray, Daniel, 22, 102
Murray, Frances, 31, 57, 99
Myers, Mr, 113

National education, 15, 89, 102–107, 117–118
New Zealand, 44

O'Carroll, Mary, 96
O'Connell, Daniel, 14

O'Neill, Fr. 27
Oblates, 107, 138
Ossory, *see* Mullinavat

Parental support, 60, 65–66, 72, 104–105
Pastorals, 50, 73–74
de Paul, Vincent *see* Vincentian spirituality,
Phelan, Josephine (Sr M. Regis), 129–130
Phibsboro (St Peter's parish), 23, 32, 81
Pius IX, 94
Poor Law, 24, 55, 58, 62, 64–65, 98
Pope, Thomas, 153
Portadown, 39
Prayer, 125, 127, 144, 148
Presbyterian Orphan Society, 65
Pre-school education, 36
Presentation sisters, 15, 101, 127, 129, 138
Prison, *see* trial
Processions, *see* sodalities
Proselytizing, 39–55, 62–63, 89, 95, 101, 103, 105, 111, 117–118, 120
Protestant Orphan Society, 65
Protestant Orphan Union, 60
Public meetings, 24, 26, 88–89, 95, 147

Raftice, James, 156–161
Rathmines, 39
Rawlins, Marian, 96–97
Redemptorists, 50, 139, *see also* Ligouri; Alphonsian spirituality
Relief distribution, 28–30,38, 111–112
Reports, annual, 26, 40, 56–57, 79, 88–89, 95, 102, 138, 142, 147, 165
Rice, Edmund, 15, *see also* CBs
'rules of life', 124–125, 138, 144–145, 148
rural schools, 114–115

Sacred Heart sisters, 132
Schools, *see* education
Scully, Agnes Mary, 31, 57
Scully, Julia, 132
Seaver, Miss, 99
Skerries, 115
Smyly family, 92

Smyly schools 41–47, 50–55
Smyly, Ellen, 42, 47, 62–63
Sodalities, 109, 136, 149–151
Sœurs de Charité see DCs
Soldiers, 22
St Brigid's Defence Committee, 94–95, 164
St Brigid's Orphanage: 31, 52, 56–78, 97–100, 121, 142; foundation 56–59; admissions 59–64; boarding-out, 64–70; supervision 70; final placement 71; funding, 73–77, 162–163
St Brigid's Schools, 72, 101–120; rural schools, 114–115; fee-paying schools, 115–117
St Brigid's Society, *see* Daughters of St Brigid
St Leger, John, 15, 141, 144
St Mary's Industrial Institute, 34–37
St Vincent de Paul Society, 35, 52, 139
Steiner, John Joseph, 75–77
Strand Street Great, 108, 119
Synnott, Thomas, 96

Taylor, Fanny, 51, 73
The Leader, 116–117
The Month, 51, 73
The Workman, 73
Thurles, 14
Times, 93, 95
Tinahely, 50
Townsend Street, 46–47, 52–54

Tramore, 18
Trial and imprisonment, 91–100, 121, 143, 149, 152, 164–165
Tully, Fr, 94

Ursulines, 14–15, 17, 138–140, 144

Vickers, Margaret (Sr M. Agnes), 113, 126, 131, 137, 146, 155–156, 161
Vincentian priests, 50, 138, 161, *see also* Dowley, Duff, Etienne, Gowan, Lynch, McNamara
Vincentian spirituality, 22–24, 37–38, 59, 62, 79, 139, 141–143, 146, 153
Virien, Josephine, *see* DCs

Walsh, William, 114, 164
Waterford, 13–19, 22, 94, 101, 122, 141, 155
West Indies, 40, 91–93
West Park Street, *see* Coombe
Westland Row (St Andrew's parish), 39, 109, 162
Whately, Archbishop & family, 42, 46–47, 53, 105–6,
William Street, North, 62, 81, 83, 85–86
Wiseman, Cardinal, 50
Women, 16, 22, 27–28, 35–37
Workhouse 16, 98 *see also* poor law

Yore, Dr, 39
Young, Ursula, 14